The Fusion of Accounting and Accountability

Valentina Minutiello

The Fusion of Accounting and Accountability

A Review of the Evolution of the Main Non-Financial Reporting Tools

palgrave
macmillan

Valentina Minutiello
Carlo Cattaneo University, LIUC
Castellanza, Italy

ISBN 978-3-031-81384-9 ISBN 978-3-031-81385-6 (eBook)
https://doi.org/10.1007/978-3-031-81385-6

This Palgrave Macmillan imprint is published by the registered company Springer Nature Switzerland AG
The registered company address is: Gewerbestrasse 11, 6330 Cham, Switzerland

To my son
I wish for you to always approach life with curiosity and a sense of lightness.

Foreword

The landscape of corporate reporting has undergone a significant transformation in recent decades, driven by growing awareness of the broader impact of business activities on society and the environment. Traditional financial reporting, once the sole focus of corporate disclosure, is increasingly being supplemented—or in some cases, supplanted—by non-financial reporting. This evolution reflects a paradigm shift in the way organizations understand and communicate their role in the world, moving beyond mere profit to encompass sustainability, social responsibility and long-term value creation.

This book seeks to explore this critical evolution in corporate reporting practices. It is designed for scholars, practitioners and students interested in understanding the development, implementation and implications of non-financial reporting within the broader context of corporate governance and sustainability. By examining the key components and emerging trends in this field, the book aims to provide a comprehensive overview of the current state and future directions of non-financial reporting.

Chapter 1 sets the stage by tracing the historical roots and legal foundations of non-financial reporting. This chapter examines the antecedents that have led to the rise of non-financial disclosures, as well as the legislative frameworks that have shaped and standardized reporting practices globally.

Chapter 2 delves into the specific practice of sustainability reporting, a key component of non-financial reporting. This chapter outlines the various standards and frameworks that guide organizations in disclosing their environmental, social and governance (ESG) impacts. It also discusses the motivations behind sustainability reporting and the challenges faced by companies in providing transparent and meaningful disclosures.

Chapter 3 explores the concept of integrated reporting, which combines financial and non-financial information into a single, coherent narrative. This chapter highlights how integrated reporting reflects the growing recognition of the interconnectedness of financial performance and sustainability, by discussing the benefits and challenges of adopting an integrated approach to corporate reporting.

Chapter 4 addresses the critical issue of assurance in non-financial reporting. As stakeholders increasingly rely on non-financial information to make informed decisions, the credibility and reliability of these disclosures become paramount. This chapter examines the role of third-party assurance providers, the methodologies they employ, and the evolving standards for ensuring the accuracy and completeness of non-financial reports.

Chapter 5 contains case studies on the adoption of non-financial reporting; it presents a series of real-world examples of organizations that have adopted non-financial reporting practices. Through these case studies, readers can gain insights into the practical challenges and benefits of implementing non-financial reporting in diverse organizational contexts, as well as the impact of such reporting on corporate strategy and stakeholder engagement.

In sum, this book provides a comprehensive exploration of the evolution and current state of non-financial reporting. By understanding the principles, practices and challenges associated with non-financial disclosures, readers will be better equipped to navigate the increasingly complex world of corporate reporting and contribute to the ongoing dialogue about the role of business in society.

The work of Valentina Minutiello is the result of several years of research, which began during the writing of her thesis at the Faculty of Economics of the University of Eastern Piedmont. Her research on ESG and Integrated Reporting was the focus of her Ph.D studies at Cattaneo University—LIUC in Castellanza, where she now continues her academic journey as a Researcher.

We have both had the pleasure of mentoring Valentina over the years, fostering a fruitful collaboration between our Universities.

August 2024
Milan, Italy

Maurizio Comoli
Full Professor of Business Economics
University of Eastern Piedmont

Patrizia Tettamanzi
Full Professor of Financial Accounting and Sustainability Management
Cattaneo University (LIUC)

Acknowledgments

I want to express my gratitude to everyone who sincerely supports my daily work.

I would like to thank Prof. Comoli for initiating the most beautiful journey of my professional life.

I am especially grateful to my mentor and supervisor, Prof. Patrizia Tettamanzi, for her unwavering support during my growth from a Ph.D. student to a researcher. She has been not only a professional guide but also a friend and a valuable advisor during challenging times.

I appreciate my entire scientific community for the stimulating daily interactions that have allowed me to learn everything I know, while continually reminding me that there is always more to discover.

I'd also like to thank my lifelong friends for witnessing my growth and maturity each day.

Lastly, I am deeply thankful to my family and my partner, because without their support, I would not be the woman I am today.

Introduction

This book focuses on Non-financial Disclosure, exploring the intersection of Accounting and Accountability with an emphasis on Sustainability and Integrated Reporting.

Interest in environmental issues has grown significantly due to the effects of climate change, including global warming, deforestation and species extinction. In response to these urgent challenges, a series of environmental treaties have emerged, reflecting a global commitment from leaders to foster a fundamental shift in mindset. This change is essential to mitigate the ongoing destruction of our planet.

In addition to environmental concerns, there has been an increasing focus on social issues, driven by the need to uphold human rights and promote a fair and inclusive society that respects diversity.

In recent decades, there has been a growing awareness of the important role that companies play in society. Many firms have emerged as advocates for both economic and technological progress while also being mindful of environmental and social issues, such as pollution, waste creation and disposal, resource depletion, labor safety and security and respect for human rights. This increased awareness has led to a perception that companies should be accountable not only to their shareholders but also to the broader society in which they operate.

Additionally, we cannot overlook the significant impact of mass media, which can harm a company's reputation and erode the trust of its stakeholders. It is important to recognize that fostering a climate of trust is essential for the survival of a business.

This new way of thinking is a crucial first step towards creating a sustainable world.

To address the needs mentioned above and the public's demand for greater social and environmental responsibility from companies, it has become necessary to adopt an evolutionary approach. This approach encourages businesses to pay closer attention to the creation and distribution of value, enabling them to tackle the challenges presented by a constantly changing environment.

This process of change also requires improved corporate disclosure: many businesses, in fact, have begun to incorporate environmental and social issues in their reports and new certifications were born (consider ISO 14001 global certification). In response to a request from the stakeholders for greater clarity and transparency of corporate disclosure, a debate has arisen on the forms of disclosure deemed most appropriate to meet their expectations.

From a regulatory perspective, numerous international regulations have been issued to promote and regulate the dissemination of non-financial information. The primary goal is to keep the community informed about the activities conducted by companies while also encouraging comparisons between different organizations. This helps to prevent opportunistic practices that might reduce non-financial reporting to merely a tool for maintaining a positive market reputation.

The legislation seeks to increase clarity in a context that provides for different forms of non-financial reporting. Among these, the main and most widespread to date are undoubtedly Sustainability Reporting (SR) and Integrated Reporting (IR). The first was created with the aim of providing a representation exclusively of non-financial performance but has been subject to continuous evolution over the years. Companies can adopt various frameworks for drafting this report, which means that the format is not standardized and the information presented may differ significantly. Integrated Reporting was introduced as a tool designed to meet the diverse needs of stakeholders by consolidating three corporate dimensions—economic-financial, social and environmental—into a single document.

These elements explain the current focus of academic research on the issue of sustainability and all its related aspects, such as the importance of a circular economy. Essentially, companies are called to commit themselves to sustainability. A tool that can help businesses achieve this task is corporate disclosure (and, typically, non-financial disclosure).

Given this context, there is a clear need for a comprehensive volume that addresses how companies utilize non-financial disclosure. Despite the growing recognition of its importance, there remains a considerable confusion regarding the various types of non-financial reporting, how to properly introduce and draft them and their potential impacts on organizations. Furthermore, Integrated Reporting still appears to be an imperfect tool that requires further refinement and adjustments.

The objectives of this work are threefold: 1) to provide a systematic discussion of the evolution of non-financial reporting from its birth to today; 2) to compare the two primary non-financial reporting tools (Sustainability Reporting vs. Integrated Reporting); and 3) to assist companies in identifying the necessary steps for the proper implementation of non-financial reporting.

The volume will be structured as follows. It will initially include an introduction to important concepts related to non-financial reporting, such as Sustainability, Corporate Social Responsibility and ESG criteria. Following this introduction, the evolution of non-financial reporting in terms of regulatory frameworks will be presented. The next two chapters will focus on the two main non-financial reporting tools: Sustainability Reporting and Integrated Reporting. Each chapter will describe the main characteristics, as well as the advantages and disadvantages of each tool. The Integrated Reporting (IR) chapter will also include an in-depth analysis of Intellectual Capital Disclosure. The IR Framework explicitly includes intellectual capital as a resource that companies utilize to create value. This section will complement the theoretical discussions presented throughout the volume with an empirical analysis that employs statistical methodologies. The final theoretical chapter will address the assurance of non-financial reporting, a relatively new discipline that emerged alongside the proliferation of such reports, aimed at enhancing their credibility. This chapter will include a systematic literature review of key academic contributions on the topic to identify characteristics, challenges and future improvement suggestions. Finally, three case studies of companies that have implemented non-financial communication will be presented. These case studies will provide detailed insights into the reporting processes, as well as the structure and key features of the reports. Additionally, they will serve as a valuable resource for comparing different types of non-financial reports. In conclusion, the final remarks will discuss potential future developments in the field.

Contents

About the Author

Valentina Minutiello (Ph.D.) is Research Fellow in Accounting at Cattaneo University (LIUC) and Certified Chartered Accountant. She serves as Assistant Professor at the same University, teaching courses in Management and Principles of Accounting, Accountability and Sustainable Accounting, Accounting and Financial Reporting, International Financial Reporting, as well as Impact Accounting and ESG Reporting. Since beginning her academic career as a Ph.D. student in Management, Finance and Accounting, she has developed a keen interest in several research topics. These include the adoption of Sustainability Reporting and Integrated Reporting, as well as identifying factors that can enhance their quality. Additionally, she explores the evolution of Accounting Education, corporate governance issues and their implications for corporate reporting, the unique characteristics of family businesses and SMEs in relation to sustainability, Intellectual Capital Disclosure and the practices surrounding Diversity, Equity and Inclusion. Her commitment to these areas is demonstrated by her numerous scientific articles and books published in both national and international contexts and journals.

Abbreviations

A4S	Accounting for Sustainability
ACCA	Association of Chartered Certified Accountants
BoD	Board of Directors
BSC	Balanced Scorecard
CA	Combined Assurance
CDP	Carbon Disclosure Project
CEO	Chief Executive Officer
CEPAA	Council of Economic Priorities Accreditation Agency
CERES	Coalition for Environmentally Responsible Economies
CFO	Chief Financial Officer
CNA	Citation Network Analysis
CoE	Communication on Engagement
CoP	Communication on Progress
CSO	Chief Sustainability Officer
CSR	Corporate Social Responsibility
CSRD	Corporate Sustainability Reporting Directive
DNF	Non-Financial Declaration
EFRAG	European Financial Reporting Advisory Group
ESG	Environmental Social Governance
ESGSTE	ESG and Energy Transition Scenarios Committee

ESRS	European Sustainability Reporting Standards
FSC	Forest Stewardship Council
GRI	Global Reporting Initiative
IAASB	International Auditing and Assurance Standards Board
IAS	International Accounting Standards
IASB	International Accounting Standards Board
IC	Intellectual Capital
ICD	Intellectual Capital Disclosure
IFC	International Finance Corporation
IFRS	International Financial Reporting Standards
IIRC	International Integrated Reporting Council
IIRF	International Integrated Reporting Framework
IR	Integrated Reporting
ISA	International Standards Principles
ISEA	Institute of Social and Ethical Accountability
ISO	International Organization for Standardization
JSE	Johannesburg Stock Exchange
KPIs	Key Performance Indicators
MCSs	Management Control Systems
NFRD	Non-Financial Reporting Directive
NFS	Non-Financial Statement
NGOs	Non-Governmental Organizations
OECD	Organization for Economic Cooperation and Development
PEFC	Programme for the Endorsement of Forest Certification
PRI	Principles for Responsible Investment
ROA	Return on Assets
ROE	Return on Equity
SAC	Sustainable Apparel Coalition
SASB	Sustainability Accounting Standard Board
SBSC	Sustainable Balanced Scorecard
SBTN	Science-Based Target for Nature
SDGs	Sustainable Development Goals
SFDR	Sustainable Finance Disclosure Regulation
SLNA	Systematic Literature Network Analysis
SLR	Systematic Literature Review
SR	Sustainability Reporting
SSEI	Sustainable Stock Exchange Initiative
TBL	Triple Bottom Line
UN	United Nations

UNCED	United Nations Conference on Environment and Development
UNEP	United Nations Environment Program
UNEP FI	United Nations Environment Program Finance Initiative
UNFCCC	United Nations Framework Convention on Climate Change
VRF	Value Reporting Foundation

List of Figures

List of Tables

1

The Evolution of Non-financial Reporting: Antecedents and Reference Legislation

This chapter provides an overview of the concept of sustainability by carefully defining what sustainable development is and by describing how sustainability relates to the Triple Bottom Line (TBL), Corporate Social Responsibility (CSR), Environmental, Social and Governance (ESG), and sustainable finance, with specific reference to the Principles for Responsible Investments (PRI). Moreover, the main initiatives launched globally to manage sustainability issues and the regulatory evolution on the topic are described, as well as the role played, and pressure brought by stakeholders. The chapter will end with an introduction to the most widespread types of non-financial reporting (Sustainability Reporting and Integrated Reporting), which will be explored in greater depth in subsequent chapters.

V. Minutiello, *The Fusion of Accounting and Accountability*, https://doi.org/10.1007/978-3-031-81385-6_1

1.1 The Concept of Sustainability

The word sustainability comes from the Latin word "***sustinere***", which has different meanings. It primarily means to support and to maintain, but also to defend and to give proof of endurance.[1]

The first use of this concept as it is currently known can be traced back to **the United Nations Conference on the Environment** held in Stockholm in 1972, in which more than 100 States took part. Here, for the first time, it was recognized that environmental issues can influence people's standard of living. At the end of the Conference, 109 recommendations and 26 principles were drawn up with useful suggestions for safeguarding natural resources (United Nations, 1972). This also resulted in the birth of the United Nations Environment Program (UNEP), a body based in Nairobi with a role of coordination and orientation of environmental policy.

This concept is again found in the report "*Our Common Future*" (also known as "***Brundtland Report***"), by the UN's World Commission for Environment and Development in 1987. The report is divided into three sections: the first dedicated to common concerns, the second relating to collective challenges and the third dedicated to the common efforts to be undertaken. The three sections describe humanity's main challenges in developing the economy following a principle of sustainability. On this occasion the definition of sustainability was associated with that of sustainable development. In fact, the report introduced the concept of **sustainable development** defined as follows: "*an economic-development activity that meets the needs of the present without compromising the ability of future generations to meet their needs*" (The World Commission on Environment and Development, 1987). In essence, sustainable development can be defined as a continuously evolving process in which the use of resources, technological development, investments and institutional changes are managed in a balanced way to preserve and promote present and future well-being. This definition focuses on the importance of achieving intergenerational equity. The main objectives of this approach are the following:

[1] Treccani Dictionary.

- an equitable distribution of resources, to ensure that all people in the world enjoy an acceptable standard of living;
- the transition from a "*disposable*" to a "*cradle to grave*" approach, promoting the production and use of durable and recyclable goods;
- the gradual transition from non-renewable to renewable energy sources;
- research and development of technologies that allow increasingly efficient use of energy;
- the transfer of technological and financial resources to developing countries.

Finally, the document introduces for the first time the "*polluter pays*" principle, which invites companies and institutions to take on the costs of cleaning up, restoring contaminated places and the health and social costs resulting from the damage caused.

Sustainability derives from the intersection of three areas (**environmental, economic and social**) which must be equally pursued: it is therefore necessary to protect the environment, promote economic growth and support equity. There must be harmony in the coexistence of these areas to promote economically sustainable growth that does not damage the environment and, most importantly, future generations.

It is immediately evident that businesses represent fundamental actors in the process of achieving sustainable development, due to their impacts (positive and/or negative) on the environment and society. The definition of sustainability can and must be interpreted by companies as meeting the needs of all stakeholders without compromising the possibility of satisfying the needs of future stakeholders (Dyllick & Hockerts, 2002). This implies a long-term perspective on three different dimensions:

- **Economic sustainability** refers to the management of economic capital so as to achieve economic efficiency by maximizing the economic value for stakeholders (Ikerd, 2012). Economic capital can be financial (debt and equity instruments), tangible (tangible assets) and intangible (intellectual property, goodwill, brand reputation, etc.);

- **Environmental sustainability** concerns the management of natural resources in terms of consumption and is aimed at improving management efficiency and minimizing waste;
- **Social sustainability** is achieved in the presence of legitimacy to operate on the part of stakeholders and society in general. It is achieved by requesting approval of one's actions from stakeholders and by establishing solid and lasting relationships with them based on trust (Moffat et al., 2015).

To achieve corporate sustainability, businesses should minimize their negative environmental and social impacts and maximize their positive impacts, while maintaining economic stability. As will be recalled later, it necessarily requires an adjustment at a strategic and operational level, which also involves the definition of new objectives and performance measurement tools, as well as an adequate reporting process towards its stakeholders.

A further definition of sustainability for companies is provided by the **Dow Jones Sustainability Index**: "*Sustainability is a company's ability to thrive in a hyper competitive and changing global business environment. Companies that anticipate and manage current and future economic, environmental, and social opportunities and risks by focusing on quality, innovation and productivity will emerge as leaders that are more likely to create a competitive advantage and long-term stakeholder value*" (S&P).[2]

Sustainability, therefore, implies a win–win condition for businesses and society as it produces a series of social, environmental and economic benefits and leads to the creation of shared value. The creation and sharing of value precisely represent the key to achieving a competitive advantage for companies (Porter & Kramer, 2011). This result can be achieved by redefining the concepts of quality, innovation and productivity throughout the supply chain, while at the same time taking into consideration the needs expressed by stakeholders and society more generally. Their involvement is essential to achieve sustainable development.

[2] https://www.spglobal.com/spdji/en/indices/esg/dow-jones-sustainability-world-index/#overview.

Concerning businesses, sustainability can bring a series of **advantages** from a financial and non-financial point of view. A good sustainability performance can lead to cost savings, thanks to an improvement in the management of resources and the minimization of waste. Furthermore, taxes and litigation costs are reduced. Companies attentive to sustainability demonstrate a greater propensity towards innovation, both at the product and production process level. Some studies have also shown how more sustainable companies present better results than their competitors in terms of return on assets (ROA), return on equity (ROE) and stock market returns and record lower stock volatility (Eccles et al., 2012). Other advantages concern the improvement of brand reputation and customer satisfaction and the discovery of new market opportunities. Customers today are increasingly inclined to purchase socially responsible and environmentally friendly goods and services from highly sustainable brands. It also increases employee satisfaction and stakeholder involvement, with greater exploitation of possible opportunities and greater mitigation of risks (Epstein et al., 2014).

Connected to the idea of sustainability, other concepts that were introduced subsequently are discussed below.

1.1.1 The Evolution of Corporate Social Responsibility (CSR) over Time

The concept of **Corporate Social Responsibility** (CSR) is strictly related to sustainability, and can be defined as the responsibility, namely legal, economic and social, that corporations have towards society. This paragraph aims to report the main contributions in the literature on the topic of Corporate Social Responsibility (CSR) with the aim of summarizing how academics and economists have interpreted this concept over the years.

The origins of the term date back to the eighteenth and nineteenth centuries in Europe and the United States, thanks to various social reforms introduced to address problems linked above all to issues of poverty and female and child labor. Attention to working conditions increased further during the twentieth century, following increasing urbanization and industrialization and the spread of large-scale production. Companies were, therefore, no longer able to pay attention only to profit maximization, but also and above all to improving the living conditions of workers.

However, it is only from the 1950s on that the first significant contributions can be identified in the literature. The appearance of the concept of Corporate Social Responsibility is traced back to **Howard R. Bowen** in 1953. The author is therefore known as the "*Father of Corporate Social Responsibility*". In his book "*Social Responsibilities of the Businessman*" he focused on the effects of businessmen's decisions on the entire community. The author stated that a businessman's decisions greatly influence shareholders, employees, customers and society as a whole. This implies that each action pursued by companies—such as, for example, marketing a new product or service, maintaining a factory or closing it, outsourcing processes or keeping them internally and so on—produces impacts on society. Bowen for the first time expresses the need to become aware of this aspect. According to Bowen, social responsibility "*refers to the obligation of businessmen to pursue those policies, to make those decisions, or to follow those courses of action which are desirable in terms of the objectives and values of our society*" (Bowen, 1953). Businesses, consequently, must take into consideration the effects of their decisions on the well-being of the community, since, considered as a whole, they are able to determine the prosperity or otherwise of a country (Bowen et al., 2013). Furthermore, it is essential that businessmen do not put personal desires before those linked to the common good. Bowen, therefore, provided a first definition of a company's social responsibility which is defined as the obligation to pursue activities which are in harmony with societal beliefs. He began to notice how in the US, starting from the twentieth century, the view of many businessmen had begun to change and the attention towards social issues (e.g., justice, equity, freedom, human rights, etc.) had increased, even if not everyone was sincerely interested in these issues, but rather in improving their corporate reputation and promoting a certain image of their company. This new way of conceiving business has justified the development of numerous policies at an international level to encourage sustainability-oriented initiatives (Bowen et al., 2013).[3]

Over the years, other authors further explored the concept of CSR, essentially due to their concerns with corporate behavior and the rising awareness of social and environmental issues.

A subsequent contribution is that of **Keith Davis**, professor at the University of Arizona, who provided several definitions of CSR. In an article published in the California Management Review magazine, he highlighted how the decisions made by businessmen must go beyond the economic interests of the company, as socially responsible conduct leads, in the long term, to a growth in economic returns (Davis, 1960). He stated that the social responsibility of businessmen refers to any decision or action "*taken for reasons at least partially beyond the firm's direct economic or technical interest*" (Davis, 1960). He identified two different types of social responsibility: the first, more "*economic*" one, refers to the fact that businessmen have the duty to respect the economic development of the context in which they operate and, consequently, the welfare of citizens (in terms of level of employment, inflation rate, etc.); the second type is more connected to human aspects and refers to the duty to develop fair human values. These two perspectives are not independent but connected to each other and the social responsibility of companies should take them both into consideration, seeking a balance. Davis defines the impact of businessmen on society as "*social power*". The higher the social power of a businessman, the higher the social responsibility of companies should be and vice versa. Firms must cope with their social responsibilities arising from social, economic and political pressure because in the long-term social responsibility may give rise to economic returns. Subsequently, in 1973 Davis provided a further definition of CSR: "*CSR begins when the law ends and a company cannot limit itself to carrying out minimum social responsibility actions required by law, because this would be what any good citizen would do*" (Davis, 1973). It is possible to deduce, therefore, that a company cannot consider itself socially responsible if it merely complies with what is required by law, but it must be responsible towards the economic context and citizens.

[3] For further information on regulatory evolution, please refer to the paragraph 1.4.

Another important contribution in the literature is that of **Milton Friedman**, Nobel Prize winner for economics in 1976, who argued that companies should not take into consideration social responsibilities other than those imposed by local laws or shared ethical values (Zimmerli et al., 2007). Businessmen should only pay attention to profit maximization; social responsibility measures should only take into consideration the financial aspects of the business. CSR activities were thus completely irrelevant and inappropriate and represented a waste of the company's resources. In his work "*Capitalism and Freedom*" Friedman argues that the ideas deriving from CSR are in contrast with the ideologies of capitalism according to which the only objective for the company to pursue is "*to make as much money as possible for shareholders*" (Friedman, 1912). He places **stakeholder theory** at the center of his studies and in 1984 published his book "*Strategic management: a stakeholder approach*". According to this theory, the activity of a company is the result of a set of relationships between groups that have an interest in its activity. Therefore, it becomes critical to understand and properly manage such relationships over time. These relationships represent an opportunity for growth for companies, as well as representing a moral and ethical obligation.

In the 1970s, the first empirical research began on how companies were approaching the topic of Corporate Social Responsibility. In 1979, **Archie B. Carroll**, a professor at the University of Georgia, proposed a systematic approach to CSR (Carroll, 1979). In 1991 he defined the "***Pyramid of Corporate Social Responsibility***", identifying four main areas of social responsibility for each organization: economic responsibility, legal responsibility, ethical responsibility and lastly philanthropic responsibility. The economic is the most important since each company is a unit of an ecosystem and without companies no need can be satisfied (indeed, the condition could even be reached in which no product or service is marketed and the level of employment is significantly low). It refers to the primary function of businesses, namely producing and selling goods and/or services. Legal responsibility is understood as compliance with current legislation. Ethical responsibility, on the other hand, refers to the actions that companies decide to implement without an obligation deriving from the law, but because they are requested by society. Philanthropic/discretionary responsibility concerns any other type of voluntary activity that companies may decide to adopt; in this case, therefore, there is no imposition by law nor are there expectations on the part of society towards companies, which decide to undertake certain measures exclusively based on their own assessments. Furthermore, he tried to identify the issues that should be included in social responsibility, which involves identifying in which areas companies have influence. In this case the main problem lies in the different characteristics of the companies (there are, in fact, companies that produce much higher impacts on the environment than others, such as manufacturing ones). Moreover, the problems that the companies find themselves facing can change; consequently, there are no social responsibilities that remain unchanged over time. Finally, the author defined what he called "*social responsiveness*", which consists of the strategy that the management of a company decides to adopt in terms of socially responsible actions (e.g., proactive or reactive).

In the 90s the concept of CSR gained international appeal as organizations became fully aware that in order to adequately balance challenges and opportunities, to succeed in an increasingly competitive market and to achieve an outstanding performance, they had to be socially responsible. Furthermore, numerous international conferences and regulations have further increased attention towards this topic. In 1994, **John Elkington** introduced the concept of Triple Bottom Line (TBL) and numerous initiatives were promoted with reference to CSR. TBL refers to the inclusion of not only the economic dimension, but also the social and environmental one, in corporate management and reporting. This model subsequently significantly influenced financial and non-financial performance measurement models. It can be defined as a framework used to examine three types of sustainability, namely social, environmental and economic, which are the basis for the establishment of a competitive advantage in the market and for the integration of sustainability in corporate strategies:

- **the Social dimension** has to do with social, ethical and cultural issues and with corporate social responsibility and is key to achieving progress in the environmental area; it refers to the impact on society's wealth and on stakeholder welfare, such as employees, consumers and the local community;

- **the Environmental dimension** is related to environmental risks and to organizational attempts to minimize their environmental impact. As highlighted by Elkington, it is necessary to account for any impact on natural capital and on the ecological bottom line since environmental concerns are of prime importance;
- **the Economic dimension** focuses on the value created by firms and on their economic stability (Correia Salome, 2019). Among the most relevant issues related to the economic bottom line, it is worth pointing out the need to use any form of capital, namely physical, financial, social, natural, human, or intellectual, to measure whether firm operations are economically sustainable and the necessity of boosting accountability at board level.

The main idea behind the TBL is that companies have the possibility of "*doing well by doing good*" (Miller, 2020). The TBL was thought of as an accounting tool available not for just for-profit firms, but for whichever institution wanted to adopt it, so including non-profit and government organizations. However, there was—and still is—a significant gap between the assessment of the financial measures and the social and environmental ones. As far as the former is concerned, there are consolidated accounting principles to be applied at both national and international levels, together with established reporting formats required by authorities and well-defined methods and procedures used for the auditing made by independent professionals or companies. On the other hand, there are no universal techniques for accounting, reporting and auditing social and environmental measures. The main risk is that each firm can have a different interpretation on the performances to take into consideration and the output of the measures they concretely implement, with the resulting difficulty of comparing reports (Venkatraman & Nayak, 2015). Differences in the approach adopted for the TBL and the performances assessed may also arise due to the distinct geographical locations of organizations and their scope. It would therefore be important to reduce to a minimum the dissimilarities that exist between firms of different industries—some industries undoubtedly deal with social and environmental variables more often compared to others that have little or no impact on those variables—and different regions and countries.

As we can see, the TBL does not require the adoption of well-defined performance indicators, and so it represents a flexible framework which, in the end, depends on the specific characteristics of each organization that decides to embrace it and on the requirements of the stakeholders.

In line with the Triple Bottom Line, in 1995 the **3P model**, namely "*people, planet and profit*" was developed. According to Elkington, the only way to achieve an outstanding sustainable performance is by measuring not only economic profit or loss (profit), but also the well-being of the society (people) and the health of the planet (planet) (Elkington, 2018).

Starting from the 2000s the concept of CSR began evolving towards corporate and global citizenship in which stakeholder engagement and sustainability play a central role. However, these are also the years of important corporate scandals, which brought to light the problems related to so-called greenwashing. This suggested that some companies had adopted CSR only superficially, making opportunistic use of it. To overcome this problem, two professors from Harvard University, **Porter and Kramer**, proposed a strategic approach to CSR in organizations. They forced companies to rethink their business model, since the adoption of CSR involves the redefinition of corporate mission and vision in order to integrate environmental and social aspects and effectively contribute to the construction of a competitive advantage. The studies of the two authors led to the definition of the concept of "*shared value*" in an article published in 2011 in the Harvard Business Review entitled "*Creating Shared Value*" (Porter & Kramer, 2006). By "***shared value***" we mean the dual need of companies to generate profits while also producing social benefits. This concept has become fundamental in trying to solve some global problems such as climate change and to prevent companies from continuing to prosper to the detriment of the entire community.

1.1.2 The Definition of ESG (Environmental, Social and Governance)

The birth of the acronym **ESG**, acronym for Environmental, Social and Governance, is much more recent than that of CSR. The first mention dates back to 1998 in the book "*Cannibal with Forks: The Triple Bottom Line of 21st Century Business*" (Elikington, 1998). The author, in fact, highlights the need for companies to consider not only the economic-financial aspects, but also the social and environmental ones.

In reality, the true use of ESG criteria can only be identified in the early 2000s.

In 2003, the Secretary General of the United Nations, Kofi Anan, began the reform of the UN and at the beginning of 2004 he invited more than fifty CEOs of internationally active companies to participate in the International Finance Corporation (IFC). The objectives introduced by the IFC in 2005 are the following: expand access to finance, increase private participation in strategic sectors (e.g., education and health care), help successful businesses grow, focus on the places where there is greatest need and ensure sustainability (IFC, 2005).

The document underlying the ESG criteria, known as "***Who Cares Wins***" (United Nation, 2004), was published. It has the strategic intent of directing the attention of the markets, especially financial ones, to the ongoing change, supporting the integration of environmental, social and governance aspects into asset and investment management strategies. It is based on the voluntary initiative of companies such as banks and investment funds and contains guidelines and recommendations on the management of environmental, social and governance issues. Organizations that perform best on these issues are able to increase their shareholder value and improve their corporate reputation. Adopting an ESG strategy means investing in a company with a good score (or ESG rating) in the social and environmental responsibility assessment scales.[4]

---

[4] The Global Compact, 2005: "Who cares Wins, Connecting Financial Markets to a Changing World", https://www.unepfi.org/fileadmin/events/2004/stocks/who_cares_wins_global_compact_2004.pdf.

In 2005, the **Freshfield Report** was published by the United Nations Environment Program Finance Initiative (UNEP FI) (United Nations, 2005). The document contains a legal framework for integrating social, environmental and governance issues into institutional investments. It is connected to the legislation on ESG factors present in the various countries.

Both of these publications were the starting point for the development of the **Principles for Responsible Investment (PRI)** in 2006 by the New York Stock Exchange. These principles are intended to guide new investments and represent a starting point for the implementation of ESG standards.

In the history of the acronym ESG, we can next identify the **Sustainable Stock Exchange Initiative** (SSEI), launched in New York in 2009 by the Secretary General of the United Nations, Ban Ki-Moon. The mission was to promote the sustainability performance of financial market issuers and encourage stakeholders to improve communication relating to ESG factors.

The acronym ESG, therefore, refers to the factors used to analyze company performance from an economic, social and environmental perspective and represent parameters increasingly used for the evaluation of investments made. They are divided as follows:

- ***E ("Environmental")***, which refers to the corporate impacts regarding the environment (e.g., the reduction of greenhouse gas emissions, reduced use of water resources and waste management) and includes all the actions implemented to limit the impacts on the environment and on the territory in which the company operates;
- **S ("*Social*")**, which includes companies' relationships with all stakeholders (e.g., local communities, investors, employees and so on) and refers to all company initiatives and decisions that have a social impact regarding rights human health, worker health and safety, diversity and inclusion and so on;
- **G ("*Governance*")**, which concerns the corporate structure and the responsibility of companies and involves aspects such as the fight against corruption and respect for the principles of meritocracy and transparency in corporate management. It refers to the quality

and transparency of company management, control systems and the composition of the main corporate governance bodies.

Some examples of methodologies and frameworks used to evaluate the ESG impact of a company are:

- The **Dow Jones Sustainability World Index**, which represents the top 10% of the 2500 largest companies in the S&P Global Broad Market Index based on long-term environmental, social and governance criteria;
- The **Dow Jones Sustainability Europe Index**, which refers exclusively to European companies;
- The **Global Reporting Initiative**, an international body that defines standards for ESG performance reporting;
- The **Carbon Disclosure**, a non-profit organization that provides an environmental measurement and reporting tool.

In conclusion, ESG factors can be used to evaluate a company's ability to pursue positive performance not only from an economic, but also a social, environmental and governance point of view.

1.2 International Initiatives on Sustainability

The main theoretical frameworks dedicated to the definition and different interpretations of CSR have previously been illustrated. At the same time, starting from the second half of the nineteenth century, various alternatives were proposed by public and international organizations to implement this concept and consequently increase attention towards social and environmental issues.

Some of the most significant events are the United Nations summits and, in particular, the **United Nations Conference on Human Environment** that took place in Stockholm in 1972. It represents the first world meeting dedicated to environmental issues. Its main output is the Stockholm Declaration and Action Plan for the Human Environment. The Declaration contains 26 principles to increase international attention on environmental issues and represents a starting point for the establishment of international collaboration between countries on issues such as economic growth, citizens' well-being and environmental pollution. The Action Plan coherently proposes three pillars:

1. The Global Environmental Assessment Programme;
2. The Environmental Management Activities;
3. The International Measures useful in order to support, both at the national and international level, the management activities.

Those three pillars were then divided up into a hundred and nine recommendations (United Nations, 1972).

One important consequence of the UN Conference of 1972 was the appointment of the **United Nations Environment Programme** (UNEP), aimed at solving problems related to the environment. It established the global environmental agenda and promoted the adoption of measures to achieve sustainable development.

Subsequently, in 1983, the General Assembly of the United Nations decided to create the **World Commission on Environment and Development** (also known as the "*Brundtland Commission*"), with the aim of formulating a global agenda on the main challenges facing world countries and the possible solutions to adopt regarding sustainability. The Commission is responsible for defining long-term environmental strategies to achieve and maintain sustainable development, encouraging cooperation between socially and economically different countries (i.e., industrialized countries vs developing countries). In particular, it should aim to achieve environmental objectives regarding people, resources and development, to propose methods that can improve the international cooperation of nations on environmental issues and promote the increase of a general sense of duty towards environmental issues among communities around the world, emphasizing the importance of achieving long-term sustainable development. As previously mentioned, this Commission introduced a definition of the concept of sustainability within the Brundtland Report.

Another crucial event was the 1992 **United Nations Conference on Environment and Development** (UNCED), held in Rio de Janeiro (also known as the "*Earth Summit*"). It was attended by politicians, diplomats and non-governmental organizations (NGOs) from 179 different countries. This occasion demonstrated how the economic, social and environmental aspects are closely linked to each other and how it is thus necessary to promote improvement in all three areas. The main objective of the Conference was to create an agenda to support countries to achieve objectives related to the environment, increase their cooperation, identify new policies to apply and, finally, increase citizens' awareness on these issues. In this case, in fact, the focus was not solely on the companies, but on each individual. Five treaties were signed here, three of which are legally non-binding while two are legally binding conventions.

1. The **Rio Declaration on Environment and Development** defines 27 principles, rights and responsibilities of nations to pursue sustainable development. In particular, it was highlighted that "*Human beings are at the center of concerns relating to sustainable development*" (Principle 1), "(…) *States have the sovereign right to exploit their resources according to their environmental and development policies, and have the duty to ensure that activities under their jurisdiction or control do not cause damage to the environment* (…)" (Principle 2), "*All States and all peoples will cooperate in the essential task of eliminating poverty, as a requirement indispensable for sustainable development, in order to reduce disparities* (…)" (Principle 5), "(…) *Developed countries recognize the responsibility incumbent upon them in the international pursuit of sustainable development given the pressures that their societies exert on global environment and the technologies and financial resources at their disposal*" (Principle 7), "*Women have a vital role in environmental management and development. Their full participation is therefore essential for the achievement of sustainable development*" (Principle 20)[5];

[5] United Nations, 1992, "Rio Declaration on Environment and Development", A/CONF.151/26, Rio de Janeiro, https:// www.un.org/en/development/desa/population/migration/generalassembly/docs/globalcompact/A_CON).

2. The **Declaration of Principles for Sustainable Forest Management** includes principles for the management, conservation and sustainable use of forests[6];
3. **Agenda 21** is a global action program to be undertaken in all sectors to pursue sustainable development. It is divided into forty chapters divided into four sections (economic and social dimensions, conservation and management of resources for development, strengthening the role of social forces and implementation tools;
4. The **United Nations Framework Convention on Climate Change** is an international treaty with the aim of promoting policies to address climate change issues[7];
5. The **Biodiversity Convention** aims to preserve and promote long-term sustainable use of biodiversity.[8]

These documents have laid the foundations on which to build new sustainable development policies, based on three dimensions (economic, social and environmental).

In 1999 the United Nations (UN) announced the introduction of the **UN Global Compact**, formerly introduced on July 26, 2000, with the objective of encouraging businesses to align their strategies to implement 27 sustainable goals. Its aim is to promote greater environmental responsibility and respect for human rights, the abolition of child labor and all types of discrimination and corruption. It is also known as the largest voluntary initiative to support corporate sustainability. It invites member companies to change their actions and strategies in compliance with ten universal principles for human rights, rights at work, the fight against corruption and respect for the environment. Participating entities are required to publish annually a Communication on Progress

---

[6] United Nations, 1992, "Report of the United Nations Conference on Environment and Development, Forest Principles", Rio de Janeiro, https://digitallibrary.un.org/record/160453?v=pdf.

[7] United Nations, 1992, "United Nations Framework Convention on Climate Change", Rio de Janeiro, https://unfccc.int/resource/docs/convkp/conveng.pdf.

[8] United Nations, 1992, Convention on Biological Diversity, Rio de Janeiro, https://www.cbd.int/

(CoP) to provide stakeholders with information on the activities implemented consistent with the aforementioned principles and on the results achieved.

Other important outputs of the Earth Summit were represented by the United Nations Framework Convention on Climate Change (UNFCCC), the Declaration on the Principles to foster management, the Convention on Biological Diversity and the appointment of the Commission for Sustainable Development (United Nations, 2022).

In 2002 the **Johannesburg World Summit on Sustainable Development** took place. On this occasion, further emphasis was placed on the importance of the use of renewable energy and the need to reduce greenhouse emissions, consistently with the Kyoto protocol. Other initiatives were envisaged with reference to agriculture, water use, intellectual property rights and so on.

In 2012 the **United Nations Conference on Sustainable Development** was held in Rio de Janeiro. Long-term programs for sustainable production and consumption were also promoted during the summit. This Conference concluded with the drafting of the document "*The Future We Want*". It essentially addressed two themes: the green economy, or the new economic paradigm aimed at mitigating environmental threats to society, and the definition of an action plan for sustainable development. Consistently, an intergovernmental working group was established which began the process of defining **17 Sustainable Development Goals** (SDGs).

The 2015 **United Nations Summit on Sustainable Development** led to the 2030 Agenda for Sustainable Development. The Agenda was signed by 193 Nations and defines 17 SDGs and 169 targets to be achieved by 2030. The principles concern topics such as climate change, poverty, health, education, equality, peace, partnerships and economic growth. It is based on five fundamental pillars:

1. **People** (i.e., fighting poverty and hunger in the world, guaranteeing every individual the possibility of expressing their potential with dignity and equality in a healthy environment);
2. **Peace** (promoting just, inclusive and peaceful societies);

3. **Partnership** (implementing the actions envisaged by the Agenda through global collaboration for sustainable development);
4. **Planet** (preserving the Earth's natural resources and climate for future generations by taking action against climate change);
5. **Prosperity** (ensuring satisfying lives for all people, promoting progress in harmony with nature).

The Agenda recognizes how the three dimensions of development (economic, social and environmental) are interconnected. Therefore, each objective cannot be considered independently but as part of a coordinated and interrelated system. This integrated approach ensures that the achievement of the objectives of one area does not occur to the detriment of the others, but synergies are created to ensure global development. Each country is called upon to provide its own contribution and is subject to periodic checks to monitor the achievement of results.

Also in 2015 the **Paris Agreement**, a treaty in favor of the environment with a focus on climate change, was signed by 196 countries. It aims to prevent rapid climate change before it becomes irreversible. The provisions of the agreement should lead to a reduction in emissions until reaching climate neutrality by 2050. Its main goal is to limit global warming to below 2°, preferably 1.5°, degrees compared to pre-industrial levels.

From this moment on, numerous conferences and related initiatives on sustainability have been promoted at an international level to encourage the commitment of different countries towards environmental and social objectives, and both public and private organizations have moved in this direction over time.

1.3 The Main Non-financial Reporting Frameworks

The relevance of the "*sustainability*" topic for businesses and the consequent communication of the results achieved to all stakeholders is now clear. To improve their transparency and relationships with their stakeholders, companies are required to report their financial, social and environmental performances, meticulously highlighting their positive and negative impacts (Verburg, 2019). Precisely to promote greater transparency and responsibility of companies towards the environment, society and the economy, specific regulation has become necessary, with the introduction of specific rules and the adoption of reporting frameworks to establish clear guidelines for businesses. Among the objectives there is also that of promoting greater harmonization between reporting standards at an international level.

For many years, the communication of companies' sustainability performance has been characterized by high levels of information asymmetry. Furthermore, non-financial reporting has been the focus of attention exclusively on the part of large companies.

For this reason, over the years numerous frameworks, standards and guidelines have emerged to better define the scope and structure of non-financial reporting. Numerous organizations, in fact, have tried to increase the credibility of non-financial reports and the information contained therein through the publication of internationally accepted standards. Some examples will be covered later in this paragraph.

1.3.1 The United Nations Global Compact

The official launch of the **United Nations Global Compact** took place on 26 July 2000. It is based on ten universal principles deriving from existing international documents, such as the Universal Declaration of Human Rights, the Declaration of the International Labor Organization on Fundamental Principles and Rights at Work and the Convention of the United Nations against corruption. The principles refer to four main areas: human rights, labor, environment and anti-corruption. The first principle states that the organization should support the protection of recognized human rights. The second principle avoids the possibility of being complicit in the abuse of human rights. The third principle supports free association, the fourth the elimination of any form of coercion or corruption at work. The fifth principle concerns the objective of eliminating child labor and the sixth principle is committed to eliminating all forms of discrimination in the workplace. The seventh and eighth principles concern the attention that companies must have for the environment; the ninth principle encourages the development and progress of sustainable technologies and finally the tenth principle underlines the importance of the fight against corruption in all its facets. It requests companies to publish an annual **Communication on Progress (CoP)**, as a way of expressing their ongoing support for the initiative (Anderson & Abensour, 2017).

In January 2003 it introduced new directives relating to the Communication on Progress (CoP) of companies in the implementation of the principles and actions undertaken to promote social responsibility and sustainability. This document consists of a statement from the CEO renewing the commitment to the initiative and the Ten Principles and a questionnaire relating to five areas (Governance, Human Rights, Labor, Environment and Anti-corruption) for monitoring the results. For non-business companies, however, the **Communication on Engagement** (CoE) is envisaged to inform stakeholders on the efforts made to support the principles and involvement in the initiative and the measurement of both qualitative and quantitative goals achieved. Also in this case, a declaration from the CEO regarding the commitment and application of the principles is required.

1.3.2 The SASB and the International Organisation for Standardization (ISO)

Standards provide guidelines for best-in-class practices and the most distinguished ones are the SASB standards, AA1000, ISO and SA8000. The **Sustainability Accounting Standard Board** (SASB), founded in 2011, manages the outcome and ratification of the SASB standards, which provide specific guidance on the disclosure of financially material sustainability information related to ESG issues by corporations to their capital providers.

On the other hand, the **International Organization for Standardization (ISO)** formally created the International Organization for Standardization 26,000 (ISO 26000) in 2010 with the aim of delivering voluntary consultation on social responsibility to any organization regardless of size or type. ISO in general was born in 1946 to create new global standards and over the years it has become a world leader in this, introducing standards for each type of business activity and helping companies reduce their costs and waste.

1.3.3 The AccountAbility 1000

The **AccountAbility 1000**, or AA1000, standards are standards introduced for the first time in 1999 by the Institute of Social and Ethical Accountability (ISEA), to improve the quality of accounting, auditing and social reporting of organizations. The AA1000 standard provides companies with useful guidelines to improve the quality of sustainability performance reporting, increasing the authenticity, reliability and effectiveness of the reports drawn up and the performance achieved by companies and at the same time guaranteeing the correct degree of adherence to AA1000. This standard involves a process divided into five main phases:

1. *Planning*—definition of the values, social and ethical objectives of the company and identification of stakeholders;
2. *Accounting*—analysis of the information collected and definition of an improvement plan;
3. *Audit and reporting*—drafting a communication to be presented to stakeholders;
4. *Embedding*—integration of the process into the management system;
5. *Stakeholder engagement*—involvement of the company's stakeholders.

The principle then finds application in the following three macro-categories:

- **AA1000 AccountAbility Principles**: these are the principles that companies must pursue for sustainable development, i.e., inclusiveness (incentivizing and stimulating the direct participation of stakeholders to define a clear strategy for sustainability issues), materiality (identification of significant issues for the organization and stakeholders), responsiveness (organizations should act transparently towards sustainability, presenting actions and feedback to their stakeholders), impact (organizations should monitor, measure and take responsibility for their actions that affect larger ecosystems);

- **AA1000 Assurance Standards**: these provide guidelines for assessing and assuring sustainability information reported by organizations based on the AA1000 principles. In particular, they aim to provide a structured and rigorous process for sustainability assurance, helping to ensure that sustainability information is reliable and usable by stakeholders. The presence of an Assurance Provider is expected to evaluate the level of assurance present. This person intervenes only for tasks that need to be evaluated in an impartial and independent manner;
- **AA1000 Stakeholder Engagement Standard**: this provides a methodology to increase the effectiveness of stakeholder engagement and enables organizations to better understand relevant issues, manage risks and seize opportunities associated with sustainability and social responsibility. The application of these standards must follow a process divided into three phases: identification and mapping of stakeholders and management of relationships with the preparation of an involvement plan, preparation and implementation of the involvement according to needs (in terms of financial resources and skills) of interlocutors, definition (based on involvement) of sustainable strategies and actions.

1.3.4 Social Accountability 8000

Social Accountability 8000 is a voluntary standard drawn up by the Council of Economic Priorities Accreditation Agency (CEPAA) in 1969 to provide information regarding social-corporate performance inherent to the Universal Declaration of Human Rights, ILO documents and standards for human rights and Work. As in the case of the AA1000, here too we are dealing exclusively with universal principles to be followed when drafting sustainability reports.

The **SA 8000 Ethics certification** is a globally recognized standard for guaranteeing optimal working conditions and responds to the needs of companies that want to differentiate themselves for their commitment to sustainability regarding social issues. It is developed into a list of nine social responsibility requirements and each of them presents guidelines to follow. An organization that holds this certification demonstrates careful management and monitoring of processes relating to worker conditions. The latest version of the standard, introduced in 2014, pays particular attention to the issue of child exploitation. Furthermore, the social fingerprint is a further tool introduced with the new SA8000 2014 version and it is a self-assessment method of ethical performance that can be used by certified companies. The company must carry out a self-assessment to analyze its situation in accordance with and respecting ethical standards. Finally, auditors have been envisaged, i.e., responsible external individuals who undertake to follow the level structure principle: the 'high level structure'. This action involves recurring and unexpected inspection activities in which the auditor verifies the status and compliance with the rules that protect work, safety and health. In other words, a stress test is performed on the quality of the company's ethical and social compliance.

1.3.5 The Organization for Economic Cooperation and Development (OECD)

The **Organization for Economic Cooperation and Development (OECD)**, founded in 1961, currently includes 30 nations that have joined the cause of considering the effects of globalization and economic expansion on the environment and people. The OECD provides a forum in which countries can develop best practices relating to sustainable growth and, therefore, supports attention towards the environmental impacts of economic and social development, sharing the information collected also with the governments of various countries (OECD, 2012).

1.3.6 The Carbon Disclosure Project (CDP)

The **Carbon Disclosure Project (CDP)** is a non-profit organization which scores corporations or cities through an environmental disclosure system solely on the quality and completeness of their disclosures of greenhouse gas emissions, water strategies and climate change. As such, the CDP aims to incentivize companies towards achieving leadership in environmental transparency. Moreover, the **Prince's Accounting for Sustainability Project (A4S)** seeks to drive a fundamental shift towards highly sustainable business models and towards an integrated decision-making process, which addresses the scale of opportunities and risks posed by environmental and social issues.

1.3.7 More Recent Initiatives: The Global Reporting Initiative and the International Integrated Reporting Framework

More recently, two initiatives have stood out for their relevance and degree of diffusion compared to the others. These are the **GRI Standards** for Sustainability Reporting developed by the Global Reporting Initiative and the **International Integrated Reporting Framework**, which regulates the drafting of a new type of reporting called Integrated Reporting. Both of these initiatives will be covered respectively in the second and third chapters of this volume.

1.4 Regulation of Non-financial Reporting at European Level

The regulation of the communication of non-financial information has been the subject of a slow process, which has required many years of evolution and which has not yet come to an end (Rimmel, 2020). Its development began with employee reporting, which was followed by more complete social reporting, then environmental reporting and, finally, the sustainability report.

Employee reporting was used to analyze and communicate employee conditions, for example in terms of safety at work. It consisted mainly of a publication of a voluntary nature, with a few exceptions. An example is France, which made its publication mandatory with law 77–769 of 1977 for companies with more than 750 employees (subsequently updated to 300 in 1982).

Between the 1960s and 1970s this tool was subsequently integrated into **social reporting**, which addressed all the social issues of each company.

Starting from the 1980s, companies began to show a greater interest in environmental issues (also following the numerous international initiatives on the topic) and the need to create greater integration between economic performance and social and environmental issues emerged. Companies, therefore, began to produce the first **environmental reports**.

Finally, we have more recently arrived at the **sustainability report** which integrates the three spheres of the Triple Bottom Line within a document that is separate from the traditional financial statement.

On an international level, the European Union has for years shown great interest in and commitment to building a sustainable economic system. Some of the main regulatory provisions introduced at European level are outlined below.

The first legislation that concerns the communication of non-financial aspects is **Directive 2013/34/EU** which provides for the obligation to communicate within the management report "*fundamental financial result indicators and, where appropriate, the relevant non-financial ones for the specific activity of the company, including information relating to the environment and personnel.*"[9]

On 22 October 2014, the European Parliament issued **Directive 2014/95/EU**, known as the **Non-financial Reporting Directive**

[9] Official Journal of the European Union, 2013, "*Directive 2013/34/EU of the European Parliament and of the Council of 26 June 2013, relating to financial statements, consolidated financial statements and related reports of certain types of companies, amending Directive 2006/43/EC of the European Parliament and of the Council and repealing Council Directives 78/660/EEC and 83/349/EEC*", L182/19, https://eurlex.europa.eu/legal-content/IT/TXT/PDF/?uri=CELEX:32013L0034.

(NFRD). This Directive regulated the non-financial reporting of listed companies and public entities (such as banks and insurance companies) with at least 500 employees or a total balance sheet of EUR 20 million or total revenues of EUR 40 million (Commission of the European Communities, 2002). These companies, therefore, are required to communicate information relating to the social and environmental area, employees, respect for human rights, anti-corruption and diversity in corporate governance bodies. They must adopt a dual materiality perspective, describing how sustainability issues impact their business and how their activities in turn impact the environment and society. EU member countries were required to transpose this Directive at local level: in Italy, for example, Legislative Decree 254/2016 was issued, which specifies the type of information to be included in non-financial reports (e.g., relating to management, business models, policies and risks and opportunities relating to the environmental and social sphere).

In 2019 the European Commission, in line with the Paris Agreement and the SDGs, developed various guidelines to report information relating to the impacts of economic activities on the climate and the risks and opportunities connected to this topic (European Commission, 2019). One of these is the **European Green Deal**, a new strategy that aims to achieve climate neutrality by 2050.[10]

In 2020, **EU Regulation 2020/85219** introduced the taxonomy of eco-compatible economic activities at the level of European legislation. The "***Taxonomy Regulation***" is a useful guide for investors as it allows the integration of sustainability into investments, for companies for the structuring of corporate policies on environmental sustainability and for public institutions, which can use it to guide the ecological transition.

In April 2021, the European Commission approved a sustainable finance package, including **EU Taxonomy** and a **proposal for a Corporate Sustainability Reporting Directive (CSRD)**. In the first case it is a real classification of environmentally sustainable economic activities. One of the objectives is to protect investors from the risk of greenwashing

[10] European Commission, 11 December 2019, Communication from the Commission to the European Parliament, the Council, the Economic and Social Committee European Union and the Committee of the Regions, https://eur-lex.europa.eu/legal-content/EN/ALL/?uri=CELEX%3A52012DC0673.

and support the transition of companies towards sustainable practices (European Commission, 2021). Six sustainable objectives have been defined (climate change mitigation, climate change adaptation, sustainable use and protection of marine resources, transition to a circular economy, pollution prevention and control, protection and restoration of ecosystems) and three pre-requisites that any economy activity has to meet in order to qualify as environmentally sustainable (substantially contribute to at least one of the six sustainable objectives; do no significant harm to any of the other five sustainable objectives; comply with minimum requirements). The CSRD proposal, however, derives from a request from investors to increase the quality of non-financial reports, which are usually not very complete, accurate or detailed. It expands the adoption of this type of disclosure to all large companies with more than 250 employees, with a balance sheet of a total of EUR 20 million or net turnover of EUR 40 million. Furthermore, audit and assurance of the information included in the reports are required (European Commission, 2021).

2021 was also the year of the introduction of the **Sustainable Finance Disclosure Regulation (SFDR)**, which regulates disclosures in the field of sustainable finance and standardizes information on the environmental and social characteristics of financial products.

On 16 December 2022 the Official Journal of the European Commission published the new **European Directive 2022/2464** regarding the **Corporate Sustainability Reporting Directive (CSRD)** which makes important changes to the Accounting, Transparency and Audit directives. The CSRD replaces the Non-Financial Declaration (DNF). Among the main innovations is the expansion of the scope of application. In this regard, the aforementioned Directive is no longer intended only for public interest entities with at least 500 employees, but the following criteria are added:

- Average number of employees during the financial year equal to at least 250 units;
- Revenues of at least 40 million and/or
- Total assets equal to at least 20 million;
- All listed companies with the exception of micro-enterprises;

- Companies with non-EU parent companies that generate a turnover in EU countries exceeding 150 million for two consecutive years.

New standards for the reporting of non-financial information developed by the European Financial Reporting Advisory Group (EFRAG) are also introduced. They are called **European Sustainability Reporting Standards (ESRS)** for the reporting of non-financial information, with the aim of increasing the transparency of sustainability reports. The body cited in November 2022 released a first series of drafts aiming to disseminate the specific information by October 2023, allowing greater comparability of information between different companies. A further new element introduced by the Directive is the review of the information disclosed according to the "*limited assurance*" method. In particular, since the standards have not yet been released, a complete revision would burden companies excessively. Once the standards have been introduced it will be possible to apply the "*reasonable assurance*" method, already applied to financial information, which will guarantee a more reliable audit.

Regarding publication, the Directive requires the inclusion of information in the management report. Finally, article 5 regulates its transposition. It will take place in four stages:

- For financial years starting on 1 January 2024 or on a subsequent date, the reporting obligation on the 2024 financial year will apply to large public interest companies (more than 500 employees) already subject to the previous Directive;
- For financial years starting on 1 January 2025 or on a subsequent date, the reporting obligation on the 2025 financial year will apply to large companies not subject to the previous Directive (more than 250 employees and/or 40 million euros in turnover and /or 20 million euros in total assets);
- For financial years starting on 1 January 2026 or on a subsequent date, the obligation to communicate on the 2026 financial year will apply to small/medium-sized listed companies, small and non-complex credit institutions and captive insurance and reinsurance companies. In

particular, SMEs can choose not to participate until 2028, adequately justifying why in the management report;

- For financial years starting on 1 January 2028 or on a subsequent date, the reporting obligation on financial year 2028 will apply to third-country companies whose subsidiaries or branches generate revenues exceeding EUR 150 million in countries of the European Union.[11]

1.5 Introduction to Non-financial Reporting

According to the concept of sustainability, companies have the objective of achieving an economic, financial and social balance to increase well-being at a global level. Stakeholders have recently shown themselves to be much more interested in social and environmental corporate practices and CSR in general and have started to request more information and transparency in this regard. As a result, companies have been incentivized to commit to sustainability and to integrate this vision into organizational strategy and daily management, as well as to publish increasingly detailed reports (Hart & Milstein, 2003). Only by pursuing social, environmental and governance issues can companies develop and survive in the long term, creating value for the community.

Consistent with this new vision of company performance, financial reporting is no longer sufficient. The company balance sheet, in fact, does not deal exhaustively with green and social issues and does not describe the effects of the company's activity on society and the environment. It is no longer sufficient to communicate the economic result achieved, but how it has been achieved in terms of future sustainability. For these reasons, **sustainability accounting** was born, i.e., a series of internal and external accounting practices that take environmental, social and economic issues into consideration. These practices act in coordination with new Management Control Systems (MCSs),

[11] Official Journal of the European Union, 2022, Directive (EU) 2022/2464 of the European Parliament and of the Council of 14 December 2022 amending Regulation (EU) No. 537/2014, Directive 2004/109/ EC, Directive 2006/43/EC and Directive 2013/34/EU regarding corporate sustainability reporting, L 322/15, page 63, https://eur-lex.europa.eu/legal-content/IT/TXT/?uri=CELEX%3A32022L2464.

suitable for measuring sustainability performance and integrated into the corporate strategy to support the conversion of the business in a sustainable way. Examples are the sustainable balanced scorecard (SBSC) or key performance indicators (KPIs), that include environmental KPIs (primarily related to emissions, renewable resources, resource consumption and waste), social KPIs (closely tied to the respect for human rights, fair working conditions and level of corporate social responsibility) and economic KPIs (Hristov & Chirico, 2019).

Even in the case of the communication of non-financial information, a distinction must be made between reports for internal or external use. The former are aimed at internal stakeholders (e.g., top management, boards of directors and employees) and provide quantitative and qualitative information on the sustainability performance achieved thanks to different activities and departments so as to monitor the results over time, comparing them with the main reference benchmarks, to compare actual results with budgets, forecasts and plans (Doxey, 2019). However, sustainability reporting is mostly used by external stakeholders, such as investors and customers. Thanks to this information they can obtain a more transparent and complete vision of the company's environmental, economic and social performance (White, 2015).

It is possible to identify two approaches to sustainability accounting and reporting: outside-in and inside-out (Schaltegger, 2012). The former (**outside-in**) refers to the fact that the measurement, management and reporting of sustainability performance derives directly from the requests and expectations of stakeholders external to the company. With the outside-in approach, the company develops appropriate management, accounting and reporting systems and aligns internal processes according to the external context. Whereas the latter (**inside-out**) derives from the inclusion of sustainability within the corporate strategy, an element that determines the creation of an integrated performance management and measurement system. In this process, reporting is only the last useful step to communicate the results achieved. It represents the tool with which companies interact with their stakeholders, communicating key information and assisting them in their decision-making process. For this to happen the information must be relevant and must provide faithful representation of the company (IFRS, 2018). The Conceptual Framework for Financial Reporting (IASC, 1989) provides guidelines on the characteristics that disclosed financial information must hold; the same attributes can be transferred to non-financial reporting. They are the following:

- **relevance** (for information to be relevant, it must be valuable and material and it must support decision-makers in the evaluation of the company's outcome. Information is material only if by omitting or misstating it, it is expected to negatively influence the decision-making process of users);
- **faithful representation** (information should faithfully depict a given phenomenon and thus, it should be complete, neutral and free from error);
- **comparability** (it enables the comparison of information and the identification of similarities and differences);
- **verifiability** (it assures users that information disclosure provides a faithful representation of a given event);
- **timeliness** (stakeholders get all the information they need in time to influence their decisions);
- **understandability** (it requires that users of information can fully comprehend its meaning).

1.5.1 Evolution of Sustainability Reporting

Traditionally, the concept of corporate reporting referred to traditional financial reporting, which contains financial information relating to the resources used by companies and the economic-financial performances achieved. Such information is relevant for investment decision-making. This practice has spread since the beginning of the 1900s and was based on tools such as the International Financial Reporting Standards (IFRS) and the International Accounting Standards (IAS), introduced in the 1980s to guide corporate communication and support shareholders, financial analysts and lending institutions or banks in the analysis of company performance.

However, nowadays, thanks to the attention towards sustainability and also to the spread of the aforementioned stakeholder theory, it has become necessary to also include information on non-financial performance addressed to all stakeholders in the reporting. In fact, there has been widespread awareness that companies have a broader purpose than simply maximizing shareholder returns (Ghio & Verona, 2020). For this reason, non-financial reporting has spread, understood as the practice of communicating, on a voluntary or mandatory basis, information on economic, social, environmental and governance issues.

As a result, the evolution of corporate reporting practices has gone through three main phases:

1. Financial reporting;
2. Non-financial reporting (social, environmental and sustainability reporting);
3. Integrated reporting.

In fact, since the 1970s, due to the greater interest in social responsibility, financial reporting has been accompanied by **social reporting**. Many organizations in Western Europe, primarily in Germany and the Netherlands, voluntarily adopted a social balance sheet to report on the company's social performance and on the social effects, namely labor practices, human rights, product responsibility and society, arising from organizational operations. Subsequently, towards the end of the 1980s there was a decline in the adoption of this type of reporting, also influenced by the spread of a new type of corporate communication: **environmental reporting**. This is a useful tool for describing the relationships between a company and the environment through an analysis of the environmental impacts of the production process and the management of resources as well as the waste generated. Its dissemination mainly concerned sectors with a high environmental impact, as this information has become fundamental for improving understanding of the environmental impacts of the business and the line of action pursued to improve its environmental performance. For this reason, numerous guidelines and principles have emerged on the international scene to define the structure and content of this information. However, from the analysis of the reports it has often emerged that they do not represent an actual commitment of companies towards the environment but are often used as a tool to legitimize corporate behavior (Gray et al., 1995; Killian & O'Regan, 2016) and improve corporate reputation (Cho & Patten, 2007).

In the late 1990s and early 2000s, reporting began to consider sustainability from environmental, economic and social perspectives, becoming the so-called **sustainability reporting**. It is based on the TBL concept (Elkington, 1998) and represents the first integrated version of a voluntary environmental and social report. Its main objective is to provide information on corporate sustainability performance (Schaltegger, 2012), supporting companies in defining objectives and measuring performance related to sustainability, identifying related risks and opportunities and describing how value is created for stakeholders.

Finally, more recently, and in particular since 2013 with the publication of the International Integrated Reporting Framework, a further new typology of reporting has spread, **integrated reporting**, with the aim of achieving perfect integration of economic-financial, social and environmental issues within the same document.

Both of these reporting tools (sustainability reporting and integrated reporting) will be explored in depth during the second and third chapters.

References

Anderson, J., & Abensour, J. (2017). Measuring your company's impact: How to make the most of sustainability reporting frameworks. In M. Cronin & T. Dearing (Eds.), *Managing for social impact*. Springer.

Bowen, H. R. (1953). Graduate education in economics. *The American Economic Review, 43*(4), iv–223.

Bowen, H. R. (2013). *Social responsibilities of the businessman*. University of Iowa Press.

Carroll, A. B. (1979). A three-dimensional conceptual model of corporate performance. *The Academy of Management Review, 4*(4), 499–502. https://doi.org/10.5465/amr.1979.4498296

Cho, C. H., & Patten, D. M. (2007). The role of environmental disclosures as tools of legitimacy: A research note. *Accounting, Organizations and Society, 32*(7–8), 639–647. https://doi.org/10.1016/j.aos.2006.09.009

European Commission (2019). Guidelines on reporting climate-related information. Retrieved from https://ec.europa.eu/finance/docs/policy/190618-climate-related-information-reporting-guidelines_en.pdf

European Commission (2021, April 21). *Questions and answers: Corporate sustainability reporting directive proposal*. Retrieved from: https://ec.europa.eu/commission/presscorner/detail/en/QANDA_21_1806

Commission of the European Communities (2002). *Communication from the commission concerning corporate social responsibility*. Commission of the European Communities.

Correia, M. S. (2019). Sustainability: An overview of the triple bottom line and sustainability implementation. *International Journal of Strategic Engineering, 2*(1), 29–38. https://doi.org/10.4018/IJoSE.2019010103

Davis, K. (1960). Can business afford to ignore social responsibilities? *California Management Review, 2*(3), 70–76. https://doi.org/10.2307/41166246

Davis, K. (1973). The case for and against business assumption of social responsibilities. *Academy of Management Journal, 16*(2), 312–322. https://doi.org/10.5465/255331

Doxey, C. (2019). Internal and external reporting. In *The fast close toolkit* (pp. 171–180).

Dyllick, T., & Hockerts, K. (2002). Beyond the business case for corporate sustainability. *Business Strategy and the Environment, 11*(2), 130–141. https://doi.org/10.1002/bse.323

Eccles, R., Ioannou, I., & Serafeim, G. (2012). *The impact of corporate sustainability on organizational processes and performance*. National Bureau of Economic Research.

Elkington, J. (2018). 25 years ago I cointed the phrase "Triple Bottom Line." Here's why it's time ro rethink it. *Harvard Business Review*. Retrieved from https://hbr.org/2018/06/25-years-ago-i-coined-the-phrase-triple-bottom-line-heres-why-im-giving-up-on-it

Epstein, M. J., Rejc Buhovac, A., Elkington, J., & Leonard, H. (2014). *Making sustainability work: Best practices in managing and measuring corporate social, environmental and economic impacts*. Berrett-Koehler Publishers, Incorporated.

Friedman, M. (1912). *Capitalism and freedom* (p. 133). University of Chicago Press.

Ghio, A., & Verona, R. (2020). *The evolution of corporate disclosure: Insights on traditional and modern corporate communication*. Springer Nature.

Gray, R., Kouhy, R., & Lavers, S. (1995). Corporate social and environmental reporting: A review of the literature and a longitudinal study of UK disclosure. *Accounting, Auditing & Accountability Journal, 8*(2), 47–77. https://doi.org/10.1108/09513579510146996

Hart, S. L., & Milstein, M. B. (2003). Creating sustainable value. *Academy of Management Perspectives, 17*(2), 56–67.

Hristov, I., & Chirico, A. (2019). The role of sustainability key performance indicators (KPIs) in implementing sustainable strategies. *Sustainability, 11*, 2–19. https://doi.org/10.3390/su11205742

IFRS (2018, March). *IFRS conceptual framework for financial reporting*. Retrieved from IFRS. https://www.ifrs.org/content/dam/ifrs/project/conceptual-framework/fact-sheet-project-summary-and-feedback-statement/conceptual-framework-project-summary.pdf

Ikerd, J. (2012). *The essential of economic sustainability*. Lynne Rienner Publishers.

Miller, K. (2020). *The triple bottom line: What it is & why it is important*. https://online.hbs.edu/blog/post/what-is-the-triple-bottom-line

Killian, S., & O'Regan, P. (2016). Social accounting and the co-creation of corporate legitimacy. *Accounting, Organizations and Society, 50*, 1–12. https://doi.org/10.1016/j.aos.2016.02.004

Moffat, K., Lacey, J., Zhang, A., & Leipold, S. (2015). The social licence to operate: A critical review. *Forestry*.

Porter, M., & Kramer, M. (2006). Strategy and society: the link between competitive advantage and corporate social responsibility. *Harvard Business Review*.

Porter, M., & Kramer, M. (2011). Creating shared value. *Harvard Business Review*.

Schaltegger (2012). Sustainability reporting beyond rhetoric: Linking strategy, accounting and communication. In Jones & Ratnatunga (Eds.), *Contemporary Issues in sustainability accounting, assurance and reporting* (pp. 183–195). Emerald.

United Nations (1972). *Report of the United Nations on the human environment, Stockholm* (p. 6). https://digitallibrary.un.org/record/523249

United Nations (1992). *Report of the United Nations Conference on Environment and Development, Forest Principles, Rio de Janeiro.*

Venkatraman, S., & Nayak, R. R. (2015). Relationships among triple bottom line elements. *Journal of Global Responsibility, Bingley, 6*(2), 196. https://doi.org/10.1108/JGR-04-2012-0013

Verburg, R. (2019). Leadership, innovation and sustainability. In N. Bocken, P. Ritala, L. Albareda, & R. Verburg (Eds.), *Innovation for sustainability* (pp. 117–133).

White, G. (2015). *Sustainability reporting: Getting started* (2nd ed.).

Zimmerli, W. C., Holzinger, M., & Ritcher, K. (2007). *Corporate ethics and corporate governance* (pp. 173,174). Springer-Verlag.

2

Sustainability Reporting (SR)

This chapter explores the tool of Sustainability Reporting, with its definition, principles and purposes. It provides a description of the main framework used to prepare this kind of report, highlighting the strengths and critical issues of the document, as well as the main factors that favor its adoption.

2.1 The Diffusion of Sustainability Reporting: Definitions, Principles and Theories

Sustainability Reporting is undoubtedly one of the most widespread forms of non-financial reporting. In the late 1990s and early 2000s it developed out of the considerations expressed by the Triple Bottom Line approach and the description provided in the proposal prepared by the Global Reporting Initiative (GRI) It is the first integrated form of disclosure of environmental and social information. It represents a fundamental step towards a sustainable global economy and can provide valid

V. Minutiello, *The Fusion of Accounting and Accountability*,
https://doi.org/10.1007/978-3-031-81385-6_2

support to the corporate communication process thanks to the attention to economic, environmental and social performance.

Sustainability Reporting became increasingly important following the spread of the concept of corporate responsibility and the need for-profit organizations to recognize the impacts of their business on society and the external environment, taking on responsibility for actions taken. Producing this type of report implies the management, measurement and reporting of impacts not only for shareholders, but also for all other stakeholders.

In the literature, Hunt and Auster (1990) identified two fundamental aspects of the management of sustainable issues by a company: the design of the program and the reporting structure, with the involvement and support of top management. The commitment of the Board of Directors and management to sustainability is, in fact, essential to ensure the development of the company in this direction.

Examples of tools used in measuring sustainable performance are, for example, the **Sustainable Balanced Scorecard** (SBSC) or **the Key Performance Indicators** (KPIs), which include environmental KPIs (mainly related to emissions, renewable resources, resource consumption and waste), social KPIs (closely linked to the respect for human rights, fair working conditions and the level of corporate social responsibility) and economic KPIs.

Just as there is not yet a univocal definition of sustainability and sustainable development, as could be seen in the previous chapter, it is not even possible to affirm the existence of a single definition for Sustainability Reporting.

One definition of sustainability reporting was provided by the **European Union** in 2001: "*The voluntary integration of companies' social and ecological concerns into their business operations and their relationships with interested parties*".[1]

According to the **Global Reporting Initiative** (GRI) it represents "*An organization's practice of measuring, reporting publicly and being accountable to internal and external stakeholders for organizational performance (for*

[1] European Commission, July 2001, Book Green 2001 promoting a European framework for corporate social responsibility, https://www.europarl.europa.eu/meetdocs/committees/deve/20020122/com(2001)366_it.pdf.

the economic, environmental and/or social impacts, and hence the contributions – positive or negative -) towards the goal of sustainable development".[2] The report, therefore, is a means of providing information on corporate sustainability performance and helps companies define goals, measure performance, evaluate risks and opportunities related to sustainability and evaluate their value creation process (Schaltegger, 2012).

The recipients of this document are all stakeholders interested in the impacts generated by the organization. Furthermore, as can be seen from the definition, these impacts can have a dual nature: they can be both positive, as in the case of the objectives achieved and the strategies adopted to achieve them, and negative, for example information regarding pollution and emissions. This increases transparency and information for stakeholders, so they enjoy a complete vision of the company.

In Italy, according to **Legislative Decree 254/2016**, the main objective of the sustainability report is to communicate in a transparent and complete way the commitment and actions undertaken by the organization to address social and environmental challenges. This tool allows stakeholders to evaluate company performance and make informed decisions based on sustainable criteria. Many companies and organizations adopt sustainability reporting as an integral part of their corporate reporting practices and responsible management. In fact, its adoption reflects the commitment to a holistic and far-sighted approach towards managing the social, environmental and economic impacts of corporate activities.

This reporting tool aims to report the company strategy, communicate its mission, vision and sustainability objectives and the activities implemented to achieve them, as well as the consequences of these. It is not limited to simple reporting of non-financial facts, but is also a tool to support companies in the definition, measurement and evaluation of objectives, performance and risks related to the issue of sustainability within the company.

[2] Global Reporting Initiative, 2016, GRI 101: REPORTING PRINCIPLES 2016, https://reportadviser.com/wp-content/uploads/2021/05/GRI-101-foundation-2016.pdf.

To ensure that a SR is considered reliable, certain principles must be respected in its drafting:

- **Neutrality** (ensure maximum accuracy of information which must be impartial and objective);
- **Clarity** (necessary for anyone to understand the document);
- **Consistency** and **completeness** (long-term corporate vision and inclusion of its stakeholders).

Regarding the characteristics that the sustainability report must contain, the guidelines formulated by the **Conceptual Framework for Financial Reporting** for financial information can be considered. In particular:

- **Relevance**: the information must be relevant in order to support the decision-making process and influence the economic evaluations of stakeholders;
- **Faithful representation**: the information must be reliable, i.e., free from material errors and faithfully represent the economic reality of the company. This requires compliance with accounting standards;
- **Comparability**: information must be presented in a way that allows users to compare the company's performance and financial position over time and compared to other entities;
- **Verifiability**: the information must be based on objective sources available to users so as to allow them, by observing a phenomenon, to reach similar conclusions. This aspect can be guaranteed through audit procedures that certify the validity of the information;
- **Timeliness**: financial information must be available in a timely manner to allow users to make informed economic decisions. This is a fundamental aspect as any delay could compromise the relevance or usefulness of the information;
- **Understandability**: financial information must be presented in a clear and understandable way for users through the use of clear language, the logical structuring of information and the presentation of explanations, if necessary (IFRS Foundation, 2018).

Sustainability Reporting can be adopted on a **voluntary** or **mandatory basis**. In the first case, the decision to prepare the report is essentially based on the stakeholders' request for social and environmental information, in addition to the financial information already contained in the traditional budget. The latter document, in fact, fails to provide a 360° vision of the performance of companies, i.e., including the positive and/or negative social and environmental impacts (Fasan, 2013). The production of a voluntary disclosure necessarily involves additional costs, but it can also bring economic benefits and help companies to signal the quality of their performance; it also reduces information asymmetry and favors higher corporate value (Jensen & Meckling, 1976).

It also finds explanation in a series of theories promoted in the literature. One of these is **institutional theory**: institutional pressures influence corporate practices and the decision to communicate non-financial information depends on external pressures coming from the environment (Herold, 2018). It concerns the fact that companies disclose information on their impact on the environment/society because of political pressures. According to **legitimacy theory**, however, voluntary disclosure provides a social license to operate, legitimizing companies' actions since they demonstrate that they operate according to the requests and needs of their stakeholders (Guthrie & Parker, 1989). Therefore, the report is used as a tool to strengthen a company's relationships with stakeholders (Herold, 2018). "*According to legitimacy theory, a company needs to have legitimacy in the sense of a social license to operate*" (Deegan & Soltys, 2007). The **signaling theory** requires that companies communicate their sustainability performances on a voluntary basis to signal their commitment to environmental and social issues, increasing their success and credibility and attracting investors and society (Weichieh et al., 2016). Finally, for **stakeholder theory**, sustainability reports represent a response from companies to stakeholders' requests for greater transparency, accountability and responsibility and to persuade them that their actions are legitimate (Donaldson & Preston, 1995; Persic et al., 2016). "*Media exposure and stakeholder pressure as external determinants are also consistently found to have a positive influence on sustainability reporting*" (Hahn & Kühnen, 2013).

Moving on to the mandatory adoption of the report, however, in this case companies are obliged by law to report on environmental and social, as well as economic, issues. This approach should "*force*" companies towards greater accountability and avoid more widespread greenwashing phenomena as in the case of voluntary adoption (Zeynep & Cankaya, 2019). If sustainability reports were originally drawn up almost entirely on a voluntary basis, today the regulatory push at an international level for the communication of non-financial information has increased (for more information see Chapter 1, paragraph 1.4). Precisely this phenomenon has made sustainability reporting widespread today.

2.2 The Main Framework for Sustainability Reports: The Global Reporting Initiative (GRI)

The **Global Reporting Initiative (GRI)** is one of the major organizations that over the years has worked on the development of shared standards and guidelines for the preparation of non-financial reports. Currently its standards are used by most companies around the world. The GRI is an independent international organization, founded in 1997 in Boston by Robert Massie and Allen White and developed by the Coalition for Environmentally Responsible Economies (CERES). In 2002 it was defined as an independent body by the executive committee and in the same year the United Nations Environment Program (UNEP) formally approved the principles of the GRI in front of the former United Nations secretary Kofi Annan. The purpose of the organization is to create global standards for non-financial reporting to allow businesses to achieve the accountability and the transparency requested by their stakeholders.

In the first phase, therefore, the body supported the development of environmental reporting and, later, developed the **Sustainability Reporting Standards** to help communicate sustainability issues. A distinctive element emerges among the standards: the multi-stakeholder inputs, i.e., the need to consider the widest possible number of stakeholders' interests. Furthermore, a fundamental characteristic is the non-static nature and continuous evolution of standards; they reflect the impacts of the changes that occur in the contexts in which they are applied to take into account all the emerging needs of the stakeholders. In this way, they help the business world, the government and other organizations to understand and communicate the impacts generated by companies.

The mission of the GRI has allowed Sustainability Reporting to be transformed from a niche practice in the 90s to a practice that is now widely adopted by organizations. Its vision concerns the creation of a future in which the concept of sustainability is fully integrated into any decision-making process undertaken by an organization.

It currently represents the most widespread and adopted framework in the world. The GRI's mission, in fact, is the following: "*The GRI imagines a sustainable future made possible by transparency and open dialogue on impacts. This is a future where impact reporting is common practice for all of the world's largest companies by revenue (G250) and 68% of the top 100 companies in each country (N100) use GRI standards organizations around the world. As the provider of the world's most widely used sustainability disclosure standards, we are a catalyst for that change*".[3]

The first version of the GRI guidelines (G1) was released in 2000. Subsequently there were several updates: in 2002 (G2), in 2006 (G3) and in 2011 (G3.1). The most important revision was that of 2016 (G4) and involved the transformation of the guidelines into actual reporting principles or standards.

The principles are divided into **universal standards** and **specific standards**. The first are the following:

- **GRI 101 Foundation** contains the guidelines for the application of the standards in the report and are divided into principles for the definition of the contents of the report (stakeholder inclusiveness, sustainability context, materiality and completeness) and principles

[3] Global Reporting Initiative, Our mission and our history, https://www.globalreporting.org/.

for the definition of quality of the report (accuracy, balance, clarity, comparability, reliability and timeliness);
- **GRI 102 General Disclosure** provides information on the context of organizations in terms of profile, strategy, ethics, integrity, governance, stakeholder involvement and the reporting process;
- **GRI 103 Management Approach** describes the management of material issues by companies.

The specific standards are as follows:

- **GRI 200 Economic** (from GRI 201 to GRI 207) concerns economic performance, market presence, indirect economic impacts, procurement practices, anti-corruption, anti-competitive behavior and taxes;
- **GRI 300 Environmental** (from GRI 301 to GRI 308) concern materials, energy, water and water discharges, biodiversity, emissions, water discharges and waste, waste, corporate compliance and environmental assessment of suppliers;
- **GRI 400 Social** (from GRI 401 to GRI 419) concern employment, relations between workers and management, health and safety at work, training and education, diversity and equal opportunities, non-discrimination, freedom of association and collective bargaining, child labor, forced or compulsory labor, safety practices, indigenous peoples' rights, human rights assessment, local communities, social assessment of suppliers, public policy, customer health and safety, marketing and labeling, customer privacy, socioeconomic compliance.

The 2016 update also provided the possibility for companies to choose between two reporting options: "*core*", which includes all the essential elements, and "*comprehensive*", with a focus on integrity, ethics, governance and company strategy.

The latest update of the GRI of 2021 was the result of the multi-stakeholder consultation by the Global Sustainability Standards Board (GSSB), an independent body that defines the GRI standards, and came into force on 1 January 2023. This update included the division between **universal standards**, **sector standards** and **topic standards**. The previous GRI 101, 102 and 103 are replaced by GRI 1, 2 and

3, which respectively concern the nine drafting requirements, general information and a more detailed explanation of the concept of double materiality. Regarding sector standards, the GRI provides guidelines for 40 different sectors in order to streamline the identification of the most significant impacts of the sector and, consequently, the relevance of the information. Finally, standard topics allow organizations to report specific information regarding their respective material topics. Furthermore, the "*core*" and "*comprehensive*" options are replaced by "*in accordance*", in cases where the nine requirements of GRI 1 are respected or "*with reference to*", if the organization is not able to report the totality of the information requested, while respecting at least the last three requirements.

GRI sustainability reporting guidelines include principles for defining report content and principles for guaranteeing report quality. The former are composed of:

- **materiality** (the significance of economic, environmental and social impacts and the influence on stakeholder assessments and decisions);
- **stakeholder inclusiveness** (achieved through the identification of stakeholder expectations);
- **completeness** (stakeholders have all the information required to assess the organizational performance);
- **sustainability context** (firm performance in terms of sustainability).

As far as the principles for ensuring reporting quality are concerned, the quality of a report is commonly defined by its balance, accuracy, comparability, reliability and timeliness (White, 2015).

In more detail, **GRI 1** defines the fundamental principles and illustrates the purposes of the GRI standards by presenting the essential concepts of sustainability reporting. In addition, it outlines the reporting principles and requirements that companies must follow to provide reports in compliance with the GRI standards guidelines. GRI 1 Fundamental Principles is structured into several sections as follows:

- Section 1 indicates the purposes and system of the GRI Standards;

- Section 2 illustrates the fundamental principles adopted within the Standards;
- Section 3 highlights the conditions for reporting in compliance with the GRI Standards;
- Section 4 explains the reporting principles, fundamental to ensuring the truthfulness and reliability of the information;
- Section 5 provides recommendations to companies to make reporting consistent with other types of reporting, strengthening the credibility of their report;
- The last 3 sections include the glossary, the bibliography and the appendices which provide information on how to draw up the GRI index.

The GRI that illustrates the General Information is **GRI 2**. It presents useful information to inform the market on the reporting procedures, governance, strategy and involvement of an organization's stakeholders. This type of information describes the framework and dimensions of the organization to understand its impact. The standard is in turn composed of further sections:

- Section 1 contains five points of general information on sustainability reporting practices;
- Section 2 concerns information on employees, other workers in the company and further information on the business;
- Section 3 presents thirteen disclosures regarding the organization's governance structure, composition, roles and compensation policy;
- Section 4 presents information on the strategy, policies and actions adopted by the company to have responsible behavior;
- Section 5 illustrates the organization's procedures for involving stakeholders and employees.

GRI 3 concerns the material topics that allow the company to be guided on those fundamental issues that include materiality. Additionally, it explains how industry standards are used in this process. By material topics we mean those corporate activities that represent the most significant impacts of an organization at an economic, social and environmental level. The GRI 3 also contains guidelines on how to report the information for determining the material topics, the list and the way in which the organization manages each topic. This standard is also structured in this way:

- Section 1 defines detailed guidelines on how to establish material topics and is developed in four phases: understanding the context of the organization, identifying potential impacts, assessing the scope of impacts and prioritizing the most significant impacts. This section plays a role in supporting the organization in determining the material topics;
- Section 2 defines the organization's processes for determining material topics, the list and how they are managed. The information in this section illustrates the process for identifying potential positive and negative impacts and specifies the priorities for managing them at an economic, environmental and social level.

The **GRI Sector Standards** were developed to increase the completeness, quality and accuracy of reporting by companies. Standards will be developed for 40 sectors, starting with those that have the greatest impact, such as gas, oil, coal, agriculture and fishing. In fact, in 2021 the industry standards for oil and gas were launched, in 2022 the industry standards for coal, agriculture and fishing were published. The standards relating to mining, financial services, textiles and clothing are still in the development phase. The Sector Standards define the issues of greatest importance to most organizations in a specific sector and illustrate the fundamental information to be reported to the market on these issues. The GRI standards guidelines state that if an applicable industry standard is available, the organization is obliged to use it. Each sector standard has an initial section offering an overview of the particularities of the sector, taking into account the activities, actions and commercial relationships that may have an impact on that sector. There is also a main section for each industry standard that defines the material topics related to the specific industry. This section illustrates, topic by topic, the most significant impacts relating to the reference sector. Each description of the topic refers to the information present in the thematic Standards that the company must report. An industry standard may provide additional information that is not illustrated in the Topic Standards, for example, when the information in the Topic Standard is not sufficient to determine the company's impacts on that topic. The themes and information are determined thanks to sector evidence, international tools and expert considerations. Therefore, the GRI standard sectors represent the expectations and broad interest that stakeholders have in the environmental impacts of each sector.

The **GRI Topic Standards** include information on material topics. These Standards address the issues of waste, health and safety at work and each of them has an overview of the topic and specific notes. The standards also indicate how an organization monitors and manages the impacts related to the topic in question. The GRI Topic Standards are selected by the organization based on the material topics and consequently used to prepare the sustainability reporting. It must be said that there is not a dramatic change regarding the Topic Standards in the new project since they are composed of the GRI 200, GRI 300 and GRI 400 of the previous version. As regards the GRI 200 standards, they are recognized for the treatment of the economic issues of the organization, reprocessing the final data in order to verify the impact of the economic-strategic choices on the stakeholders and on the economy in which the company operates. The GRI 200 are divided into six standards and in total are made up of twenty-three reporting principles. The ones that are commonly used by most by companies are outlined below:

- GRI 201-1: The organization must provide information regarding the objectives and economic results achieved, i.e., the revenues and economic values distributed to all subjects directly and indirectly interested in the company activity. Furthermore, the organization must inform the market about the value created locally, nationally or internationally;
- GRI 202-1: The organization has the obligation to present the minimum wage for entry into the company, especially if there is already a good number of employees who receive the minimum wage.

In the absence of a local/national minimum wage the organization can justify its own minimum wage;

- GRI 203-1 and 2: The organization has the duty to illustrate all investments made in terms of sustainability and the direct and indirect results of their impacts on the community;
- GRI 205-1, 2, 3: To discourage corruption, the organization must provide the percentage of operations that have a high risk of corruption. The organization subsequently illustrates the policies and actions to be applied to combat this phenomenon, communicating concrete episodes;
- GRI 206-1: The organization must clearly illustrate any legal actions completed during the reporting period on issues related to corruption, unfair monopoly, unfair competition and dumping.

The GRI 300 are the standards dedicated to the examination of the environmental policies and impacts generated by the organization. The GRI 300, together with the GRI 400, certainly represent the core of sustainability balance sheets and reports. The GRI 300 are divided into eight standards as follows:

- GRI 301 addresses the topic of materials used by the organization throughout the production chain and the percentages of recovered and recycled material are illustrated;
- GRI 302 are standards that describe the type of energy used by the organization, the sources for obtaining it and the management of energy waste;
- GRI 303 allows organizations to illustrate how they manage the primary resource within the structure, i.e., water, and what water resources and water discharge there are;
- GRI 304 defines and allows the impact of company activity on the environment to be presented to verify and protect respect for biodiversity;
- The GRI 305 are standards that define the direct and indirect emissions of the organization based on the activity carried out;

- The GRI 306 take into account the management and operations regarding the waste produced and how the organization manages the disposal of the most toxic and dangerous waste;
- GRI 307 illustrates the company's environmental compliance and must indicate whether it has been subject to sanctions;
- GRI 308 provides an assessment of suppliers regarding their attention to the environment and requires a numerical count of those suppliers sensitive to this issue out of the total number of suppliers of the organization.

Finally, the GRI 400 are standards that address the topic of social policies and actions adopted by the organization. This is the category with the largest number of standards, with nineteen categories divided into forty reporting principles.

The GRI 400 can be defined as the most complete standards in terms of reporting on social policies inside and outside an organization. In fact, following and respecting these standards allows the organization to enjoy an excellent reputation in the eyes of stakeholders, even more so in a context such as the current one characterized by a vast offer of work to cover tasks without any form of protection and rights for workers.

Presenting transparent, clear and precise reporting is an added value for the organization and beyond. Following these guidelines companies create a climate and a positive working environment, where workers feel protected and identify with the company values, encouraging a better commitment to making their own contribution to achieve the set objectives. The GRI defines the information, the elements that must be present in the report, enhancing the positive aspects and solving the problems linked to the violation of human rights, such as:

- Absence of equal opportunities, disfavoring the equality of rights of both a contractual and remunerative nature;
- Any form of discrimination based on race, culture, religion and gender;
- Exploitation of child labor and any other form of workplace abuse, which potentially places workers in dangerous or inhumane situations;

- Lack of safety in the workplace or the total absence of a system that prevents danger;
- Lack of collective agreements, absence of formal employment contracts, inability to receive benefits or any other form of recognition;
- Inability to express one's rights and not being able to freely associate with trade unions, as a form of coercion.

In conclusion, it should be clarified that in practice a transition period could be observed in which companies jointly applied the GRI standards according to the 2016 and 2021 updates. To date, however, it is necessary to refer only to the most recent update of these standards of 2021.

2.3 Strengths and Criticalities of Sustainability Reporting

Some exponents of the debate on non-financial reporting have pointed out that its adoption by companies can have multiple **benefits**. Among these, the influence exerted in paying greater attention to the issue of sustainability stands out, favoring a lasting commitment of the company towards this issue and the pursuit of new business opportunities in terms of the adoption of sustainable products, new business models or lower costs, deriving from energy saving projects, and the ambition to fully satisfy the information needs coming from a wide range of subjects interested in various capacities in corporate affairs (Bernardi & Stark, 2018; Eccles & Saltzman, 2011; Eccles & Serafeim, 2011; Krzus, 2011). Other studies have also shown a positive effect on company performance (Arguelles et al., 2015; Baboukardos & Rimmel, 2016). Moreover, it produces an improvement of business reputation, employee satisfaction and access to capital. In addition, it can help in addressing environmental and social risks, which could have financial impacts on the business, allowing compliance with not only economic and financial, but also social and environmental values. The same goes for governance risks. Other observable benefits are greater employee involvement which improves the company's performance and attractiveness and the production of a positive impact on local communities.

However, this practice has also been the subject of fierce **criticism**, as the impression that is obtained is that this type of reporting is often in reality little connected with sustainability and finds its main motivation only as a suitable means to create a symbolic link between the image of the company and the concept of sustainability, without actual feedback and repercussions on business operations. In fact, although sustainability reporting can represent an important tool within the corporate communication strategy if used in an authentic and genuine way towards stakeholders, it is often used as a means to manipulate the perceptions of stakeholders. Some authors have highlighted its incompleteness and the distorting effects that can be generated following its adoption (Brown & Dillard, 2014; Cheng et al., 2014; Flower, 2015; Thomson, 2015). In fact, it may happen that companies use this tool with the aim of creating an ideal image of the company. In this sense, companies may seem to use these tools only to improve and/or restore their reputation and acquire legitimacy to operate (Criado-Jimenez et al., 2008; Stacchezzini et al., 2016; Van Bommel, 2014). This results in practices such as greenwashing, the need to deal with harmful events and deal with their possible negative consequences (Lewis, 2016). Another criticality is the complexity of the reporting, due both to the increase in the information to be reported and to the wider audience of readers of the report, which will therefore require different levels of detail, format and type of information (Flower, 2015). Other critical issues concern the lack of a global reference framework that allows for standardization and easier comparison of reports between different organizations, the ambiguity of the performance evaluation criteria used (the attribution of a monetary value to sustainability practices is not an easy operation), the difficulty in obtaining reliable data for the preparation of the report with the need to use significant resources, an aspect that affects the quality and accuracy of the information reported.[4]

[4] Risk&Compliance Platform Europe, A. Moriani, June 2022, The limits and critical issues of non-financial declarations, https://www.riskcompliance.it/news/i-limiti-e-le-criticita-delle-dichiarazioni-non-finanziarie/.

References

Arguelles, M. P. M., Balatbat, M., & Green, W. (2015). Is there an early-mover market value effect for signalling adoption of integrated reporting? Unpublished working paper.

Baboukardos, D., & Rimmel, G. (2016). Value relevance of accounting information under an integrated reporting approach: A research note. *Journal of Accounting and Public Policy, 35*(4), 437–452. https://doi.org/10.1016/j.jaccpubpol.2016.04.004

Bernardi, C., & Stark, A. W. (2018). Environmental, social and governance disclosure, integrated reporting, and the accuracy of analyst forecasts. *The British Accounting Review, 50*(1), 16–31. https://doi.org/10.1016/j.bar.2016.10.001

Brown, J., & Dillard, J. (2014). Integrated reporting: On the need for broadening out and opening up. *Accounting, Auditing & Accountability Journal, 27*(7), 1120–1156. https://doi.org/10.1108/AAAJ-04-2013-1313

Cheng, B., Ioannou, I., & Serafeim, G. (2014). Corporate social responsibility and access to finance. *Strategic Management Journal, 35*(1), 1–23. https://doi.org/10.1002/smj.2131

Criado-Jimenez, I., Fernandez-Chulia, M., Husillos-Carque, F. J., & Larrinaga-Gonzalez, C. (2008). Compliance with mandatory environmental reporting in financial statements: The case of Spain (2001–2003). *Journal of Business Ethics, 79*, 245–262. https://doi.org/10.1007/s10551-007-9375-7

Deegan, C., & Soltys, S. (2007, March). Social accounting research: An Australasian perspective. *Accounting Forum, 31*(1), 73–89. No longer published by Elsevier. https://doi.org/10.1016/j.accfor.2006.11.001

Donaldson, T., & Preston, L. (1995, January). The stakeholder theory of the corporation: Concepts, evidence and implications. *The Academy of Management Review, 20*(1), 65–91. https://doi.org/10.5465/amr.1995.9503271992

Eccles, R. G., & Saltzman, D. (2011). Achieving sustainability through integrated reporting. *Stanford Social Innovation Review, 9*(3), 56–61.

Eccles, R. G., & Serafeim, G. (2011). In F. de Leo, & M. Vollbracht (Eds.), *Accelerating the adoption of integrated reporting. Chap. 2.2 in CSR Index* (pp. 70–92). InnoVatio Publishing Ltd.

Fasan, M. (2013). Annual reports, sustainability reports and integrated reports: Trends in corporate dislosure. In C. Busco, M. Frigo, A. Riccaboni, & P. Quattrone (Eds.), *Integrated reporting* (pp. 41–57). Springer.

Flower, J. (2015). The international integrated reporting council: A story of failure. *Critical Perspectives on Accounting, 27*, 1–17. https://doi.org/10.1016/j.cpa.2014.07.002

Guthrie, J., & Parker, L. (1989). Corporate social reporting: A rebuttal of legitimacy theory. *Accounting and Business Research, 19*(6), 343–352. https://doi.org/10.1080/00014788.1989.9728863

Hahn, R., & Kühnen, M. (2013). Determinants of sustainability reporting: A review of results, trends, theory, and opportunities in an expanding field of research. *Journal of Cleaner Production, 59*, 5–21. https://doi.org/10.1016/j.jclepro.2013.07.005

Herold, D. M. (2018). Demystifying the link between institutional theory and stakeholder theory in sustainability reporting. *Economics, Management and Sustainability, 3*(2), 6–19.

Hunt, C. B., & Auster, E. R. (1990). Proactive environmental management: Avoiding the toxic trap. *MIT Sloan Management Review, 31*(2), 7.

IFRS Foundation (2018). Conceptual framework for financial reporting. www.ifrs.org

Jensen, M., & Meckling, W. (1976). Theory of the firm: Managerial behaviour, agency costs and ownership structure. *Journal of Financial Economics, 3*, 305–360.

Krzus, M. P. (2011). Integrated reporting: If not now, when. *Zeitschrift Für Internationale Rechnungslegung, 6*, 271–276.

Lewis, J. (2016). Corporate social responsibility/sustainability reporting among the fortune global 250: Greenwashing or green supply chain? In M. Bilgin & H. Danis (Eds.), *Entrepreneurship, business and economics*. Springer.

Persic, M., Jankovic, S., & Krivacic, D. (2016). Sustainability accounting: Upgrading corporate social responsibility. In *The dynamics of corporate social responsibility* (pp. 285–303). Springer. https://doi.org/10.2308/ajpt-50849

Schaltegger (2012). Sustainability reporting beyond rhetoric: Linking strategy, accounting and communication. In Jones & Ratnatunga (Eds.), *Contemporary issues in sustainability accounting, assurance and reporting* (pp. 183–195). Emerald.

Stacchezzini, R., Melloni, G., & Lai, A. (2016). Sustainability management and reporting: The role of integrated reporting for communicating corporate sustainability management. *Journal of Cleaner Production, 136* (Part A), 102–110. https://doi.org/10.1016/j.jclepro.2016.01.109

Thomson, I. (2015). 'But does sustainability need capitalism or an integrated report'a commentary on 'The International Integrated Reporting Council: A story of failure' by Flower J. *Critical Perspectives on Accounting, 27*, 18–22.

Van Bommel, K. (2014). Towards a legitimate compromise? An exploration of integrated reporting in the Netherlands. *Accounting, Auditing & Accountability Journal, 27*(7), 1157–1189. https://doi.org/10.1108/AAAJ-04-2013-1309

Weichieh, S., Peng, M., Tan, W., & Cheung, Y. (2016). The signaling effect of corporate social responsibility in emerging economies. *Journal of Business Ethics*, 479–491.

White, G. (2015). Sustainability Reporting: Getting Started (Second Edition).

Zeynep, S., & Cankaya, F. (2019). The importance of sustainability and sustainability reporting. In *New approaches to CSR, sustainability and accountability* (pp. 45–59).

3

Sustainability and the Process of Corporate Integration: Integrated Reporting (IR)

The chapter explores the tool of Integrated Reporting (IR) with its definition and purpose. It provides a description of the structure of this type of report and considers its strengths and weaknesses, as well as the factors that favor its adoption.

3.1 Introduction to Integrated Reporting

The birth of Integrated Reporting (IR) derives from the need to overcome some obvious limitations of traditional reporting tools used by companies and to fill the existing gap between corporate reporting and the requests of stakeholders.

IR as a new reporting tool was proposed by the **International Integrated Reporting Council (IIRC)**[1] The IIRC developed IR with the purpose of making integrated reporting a practice widely used in both the public and private sectors. Its proposal is the most recent to have

[1] IIRC is a global organization made up of regulatory bodies, investors, companies, and professionals operating in the accounting sector and NGOs, established in 2010 and aimed at conceiving communication as an appropriate means to achieve value creation.

V. Minutiello, *The Fusion of Accounting and Accountability*,
https://doi.org/10.1007/978-3-031-81385-6_3

been developed in professional contexts for the preparation of reports dedicated to the representation of the financial, environmental and social situation of a company. It provides the following definition of IR:

> *Integrated Reporting brings together material information about an organization's strategy, governance, performance and prospects in a way that reflects the commercial, social and environmental context within which it operates. It provides a clear and concise representation of how an organization demonstrates stewardship and how it creates and sustains value. An Integrated Report should be an organization's primary reporting vehicle.*[2]

Integrated Reporting (IR) aims to pursue the following objectives:

- Obtain an **overall representation of corporate performance** (financial, social and environmental) **and the value creation process**. It makes it possible to obtain a holistic representation of a company. Thanks to the union of three dimensions in a single document, it was called "***One Report*** ";
- Adopt a **forward-looking perspective**, highlighting future opportunities for the company and not just its past performances. The past performances are used as starting point to explain the present and predict the future;
- Obtain greater **connectivity** between the information reported and improve the quality of information so as to meet the needs of all the categories of stakeholders, favoring a higher level of responsibility on the part of the company;
- Increase the **clarity** of the report, thanks to the use of a single document;
- Make the **reporting process easier** for companies, thanks also to the use of web technologies and interactive tools;
- Improve the management of **financial, human, social and natural capital** and encourage the correlation and interaction between them;
- Support corporate actions and strategies aimed at **creating value in the short, medium and long term**.

---

[2] http://integratedreporting.org/wp-content/uploads/2011/09/IR-Discussion-Paper-2011_spreads.pdf.

The main purpose certainly consists in providing an exhaustive explanation of the creation of value over time, highlighting the entire range of factors that can influence this for the benefit of those who provide financial capital to a company. Its implementation should benefit all stakeholders, such as employees, customers, suppliers, local communities, politicians and not just some of them. The introduction of Integrated Reporting, in fact, has the potential to make companies more aware of their impact on stakeholder groups and the environment.

This report, therefore, aims to be a response to the challenge taken up by companies to create value and to the need to use company reports to provide useful information to express a judgment regarding the future ability of companies to generate value.

Currently, IR is promoted by the **Value Reporting Foundation (VRF)**,[3] a global non-profit organization that supports companies in studying the process of value creation over the years.

3.1.1 Weaknesses of Previous Corporate Reporting Models

The birth of IR derives from the need to overcome some obvious limitations of the traditional reporting tools used by companies up to now and to therefore fill the gap between corporate reporting, as previously conceived and used, and the emerging needs of stakeholders.

The first limit concerns the **overproduction of information** by organizations, aimed at providing an answer to stakeholders' questions, but which in reality makes communication even more confusing to the detriment of information transparency. It is not uncommon for a large variety of reports to be published, but the information contained in them is disjointed, which increases complexity and hinders understanding. Furthermore, the main focus is often exclusively on **providers of financial capital**, who mostly require economic-financial data, thus neglecting the needs expressed by other stakeholders. Added to this is

[3] This organization was born in 2021 from the merger between the IIRC and the Sustainability Accounting Standards Board (SASB). From 1 August 2022 the VRF became part of the IFRS Foundation.

the **complexity of financial reporting standards** which require knowledge and technical skills to ensure adequate reading and interpretation and not all readers have them. The representation of **data exclusively of a financial nature** represents a very strong limitation that should not be underestimated. Moreover, reports generally include information on the **present of the company**, but not on possible developments and future prospects and what concerns other aspects of the life of the company itself, such as strategy, governance models and relations with the external environment, reported to a limited extent in other documents such as the Notes to the Financial Statements and the Management Report. Before the advent of the IIRC, a framework capable of regularizing and conceptualizing non-financial reports and consequently of making it easier for stakeholders to **compare the data** reported was not available. This represented a serious gap, in light of the importance of the process of creating corporate value, which therefore required adequate representation.

Integrated Reporting, to fully fulfill the role conferred and overcome these limits, should allow the pursuit of the following benefits:

- **connectivity** between the information reported and satisfaction of the stakeholders' need for knowledge;
- **clarity** and **simplicity**, thanks to the use of a single document to report the information;
- telling the **story of the company** to explain to the reader how it works to create value for itself and for the surrounding environment and society;
- reporting that goes **from past to present** and **from present to future**, in which past performances are used as a starting point to explain the present and predict the future.

3.2 The International Integrated Reporting Framework (IIRF)

As already underlined above, the IIRC pursues the following main aim: to promote the most universal adoption of Integrated Reporting through the development and dissemination of a widely accepted and shared Framework.

The Framework, published towards the end of 2013, deals with the topic of creating a single report with financial, environmental and social information included in it. It is nothing more than a tool used by companies during the preparation of the integrated report.

Its adoption should lead to the diffusion within organizations of the so-called "***integrated thinking***", i.e., a change at management level and in the decision-making process relating to the philosophy of "*integrated thinking*". Its development, in fact, must be based on the concept of integration, which is related to various aspects. In this sense, therefore, the interdependencies existing between the multiple factors that affect the creation of value, such as the different types of capital, the governance structure, the business model adopted and the opportunities and risks that arise, take on greater importance. In reality, the concept of integration promoted by the Framework must not be limited to the report, but must pervade the organizational reality in its entirety. This implies that there is:

- Integration between strategy, actions and measures (alignment with strategic objectives);
- Integration of data processing and collection procedures (information technology, databases, etc.);
- Organizational integration between functions, units and roles (accounting, finance and control, etc.);
- Cultural integration between different cognitive models (financial, sustainability, Triple Bottom Line, etc.);
- Integration between the perspectives of the different categories of stakeholders.

The presence of integration in an organization is positive from many points of view: it promotes a common culture oriented towards sustainability, takes into consideration the expectations of stakeholders, creates an explicit link between strategy and performance and favors alignment between the measurement of performance for external communication and within the perspective of internal control.

Finally, the value creation process must not be carried out solely through the actions of the company itself, but also by making use of the relationships that can be built and maintained with the different categories of stakeholders and taking into account a series of external factors that define the context in which the company operates (economic conditions, technological development, environmental and social problems). This process, in fact, derives from the contribution in terms of capital from external and internal actors (such as stakeholders, employees, suppliers, customers) and from its correct use.

The development phase of Integrated Reporting is called "*The Breakthrough Phase*" (2014–2017) and moves from the creation and introduction of the Framework in 2013 to the direct observation of the first adoptions by organizations located all over the world. The Framework was then updated in January 2021. The update does not present any further requirements, but introduces some clarifications aimed at increasing the level of clarity and understandability of the integrated reports. For example, it clarifies the terminological distinction between "***output***" and "***outcome***": the first refers to the products and services offered by companies, while the second concerns the internal and external consequences of the capital used by the company in the value creation process. Therefore, it is possible to distinguish between:

- **internal outcome** (e.g., corporate reputation, economic-financial performance);
- **external outcome** (level of customer satisfaction, social and environmental impacts);
- **positive outcome**, which produces an increase in capital and, therefore, generates value;
- **negative outcome**, which on the contrary implies a decrease in capital with the consequent erosion of value.

Other innovations concern the simplification of the declaration of responsibility and the role of corporate governance in the value creation process.

3.3 The Structure of the Framework and Its Guiding Principles

The IIRF consists of two distinct parts. The first deals with the following topics:

- **use of the Framework** (definition of an integrated report, objectives of the Framework, purpose and recipients, principles, types of reports and relationships with other sources of information, application of the Framework, responsibility of the report);
- **fundamental concepts** (introduction to fundamental concepts, creation of value for the organization and other entities, capitals, value creation process).

In the second part there are the following topics:

- **the guiding principles** (strategic focus and orientation to the future, information connectivity, relations with stakeholders, materiality, conciseness, reliability and completeness, consistency and comparability);
- **the elements of the content** (presentation of the organization and the external environment, governance, business model, risks and opportunity, strategy and allocation of resources, performance, perspectives, basis of preparation and presentation).

In particular, the IIRC's proposal provides a series of guiding principles, the so-called "***Building Blocks***", to be followed in order to obtain an integrated and comprehensive approach:

- **strategic focus**: a company's Integrated Reporting must define its strategic objectives, the methods to pursue them as well as the influence they exert on the ability to create value in the short, medium and long term. This principle guarantees the relationship between financial performance and use of resources;
- **connectivity of information**: the report must highlight the link between the different factors that have an impact on companies' performance. This concept is all the more feasible the more the company is able to adopt the logic of "*integrated thinking*". Some typical forms of information connectivity are those that occur, for example, between the content, inserted within a general framework that reports the activities of the organization as a whole, the past, the present and the future of the company, capital, financial and non-financial information and quantitative and qualitative information;
- **orientation to the future**: it is necessary that the future expectations of managers find expression within the Integrated Reporting, consistently with the representation of the challenges and opportunities that arise on a daily basis and which may derive from the market position and the business model of the company organization. This principle also serves to bring the analysis of the sustainability of the business model to the attention of stakeholders;
- **relations with stakeholders**: there should be a careful description of the ways in which the company usually manages relations with the different categories of stakeholders. This principle is fundamental in light of the observation of how value is not generated exclusively within an organization, but also depends on external relationships. If "*integrated thinking*" is included within the business model, it is more likely that the needs and expectations of key stakeholders will be adequately considered as there will tend to be greater transparency and communication capacity, the basic elements for building well-founded relationships on trust;
- **conciseness, reliability and completeness**: the report must consist of information that is as reliable and concise as possible about the company's ability to create value in the short, medium and long term. Going into specifics, conciseness means avoiding burdening the document with information deemed non-fundamental and therefore

reporting only the information that is essential for understanding the strategy, governance, performance and prospects for the future. This implies the use of clear and not excessively technical language. The reliability of information, however, is influenced by objectivity and the absence of material errors and can be increased by the implementation of control and reporting mechanisms and an internal audit system. Furthermore, the information must be reported in an impartial manner, whether positive or negative, to guarantee the objectivity of the report;

- **coherence and comparability**: the representation of information must take place through a coherent time base and must be such as to allow comparison with other organizations, through the use, for example, of benchmark data or indices;
- **materiality**: Integrated Reporting must report all the issues that in various ways may interest and, above all, influence the decision-making process of management and readers of the information and, therefore, produce effects on strategy, governance, performance and, lastly, on the ability to create value over time.

The guiding principles play a crucial role in the success of Integrated Reporting and pursuing them in the most correct way possible undoubtedly represents the main challenge promoted by the IIRC towards organizations that intend to comply with an integrated vision.

3.4 The Types of Capital and the Process of Value Creation

In the section dedicated to the fundamental concepts, several capitals are identified that, thanks to their use and interactions, contribute to the generation of companies' value, producing returns for the organizations and the stakeholders. The value generated by the company, in fact, is the output deriving from the use of the aforementioned capitals and their mutual interrelationships, taking into account first of all the return generated for the suppliers of financial capital and, then, the impacts on all the other categories of stakeholders. It should be noted, however, that capital also undergoes transformations as a result of external factors (economic climate, technological progress, social changes and environmental problems).

The **capitals** are stocks of value that can be increased, reduced or transformed as a result of the organization's activity or due to external factors (e.g., the economic context, technological progress, etc.); therefore, are not fixed over time. The Framework divides them into the following categories:

- The **Financial Capital** is the set of funds that an organization uses to produce goods or provide services. It can be obtained through different sources of funding (debt, equity, bond loans, etc.);
- The **Manufactured Capital**, is made up of physical assets, such as, for example, buildings, machinery, plant and equipment, various infrastructure that an organization uses to produce goods or provide services; it can be owned directly by the organization or by third parties;
- The **Intellectual Capital** consists of intangible assets, such as intellectual property (patents, software, copyrights, rights and licenses) and organizational capital (implicit knowledge, systems, procedures and protocols);
- The **Human Capital** includes skills, ability, motivation to innovate and experience accumulated by the people who work inside the organization;
- The **Social** and **Relationship Capital** includes the resources created by all the relationships between or within communities, stakeholder groups and network;
- The **Natural Capital** concerns all processes and environmental resources, renewable and non-renewable, which help to enable the provision of goods or services.

As previously mentioned, Integrated Reporting is aimed at representing the **value creation process** in all its phases. In doing this, it is appropriate to start with the analysis of the external environment or the context in which the company operates. This includes economic conditions, technological changes and social and environmental issues.

Corporate governance is derived from the analysis and monitoring of the context and essentially deals with the supervision of the entire process, while the business model, instead, manages the transformation of capitals and inputs of various kinds into outputs (products and services) through the carrying out of company activities. The outputs in turn produce a series of impacts on capital. It is also necessary for the business model to be as flexible as possible to adapt to changes in the external and internal context and to guarantee the sustainability of company activities in the long term. Finally, it is necessary to adopt different methods of measuring and analyzing information and a company strategy that identifies the methods of managing the risks and opportunities that arise. Therefore, the concept of "***connectivity***" plays a fundamental role, understood as the identification of the interdependence between all the elements, internal and external, which materially influence the ability to create value over time. In this sense, Integrated Reporting must be perceived not only as a new way of preparing reports, but also and above all as the spread of an innovative organizational approach. The value creation process is not fixed and immutable, indeed it is essential that there is continuous review and improvement, with constant attention to the evolution of future prospects.

3.5 The Content of Integrated Reporting

The Framework provides indications on the minimum content that must be covered within the report. This is not intended to outline a standard structure for the IR, but rather to try to make the representation of the connections between the various elements of the content more immediate.

The planned topics are the following:

- **presentation of the organization and the external environment**, identifying the mission, vision, characteristics of the organization (culture, ethics and values, ownership structure, main activities carried out, reference markets, competitive context and market position, positioning within the value chain) and the most relevant factors in the external environment (legal, social, environmental and political context);

- **governance**: an integrated report must provide an explanation of the way in which certain issues are connected to the creation of value, such as, for example, the leadership structure and the processes used for strategic decisions and to monitor the organization's culture;
- **business model**, i.e., the system adopted to transform inputs into outputs, achieving the strategic objectives envisaged for the short, medium and long term. The report will describe a number of key elements, such as the inputs used and in particular those that materially influence the value creation process, the business activities, which may include, for example, how the organization distinguishes itself on the market and addresses the need for innovation, the outputs (products and services typical of the organization) and the impacts, whether internal or external, positive or negative. It is fundamental as it constitutes the essence of the company and allows the definition of the processes thanks to which value is created;
- **risks and opportunities**, including those related to the availability, quality and accessibility of capital. It is appropriate to consider their origin, the way in which the organization evaluates the probability that they will materialize and the extent of their effects, the procedures to be followed to contain and manage risks or to make the most of opportunities;
- **strategy and resource allocation**: the report must identify the short, medium and long-term strategic objectives, the strategies that are intended to be adopted, the resource allocation plans to implement the strategy and the methods for measuring the objectives and results;
- **performance**, described by qualitative and quantitative information, which includes quantitative indicators on targets and risks and opportunities, the positive and negative effects produced on capital, the quality of relationships with key stakeholders and the way in which the organization meets their needs, the links between past and current performance and future prospects;
- **prospects**, i.e., the changes expected over time both in relation to the evolution of the external environment and the tools available to the organization to respond to the challenges that may arise;

- **basis of preparation and presentation**: an integrated report must present a description of the materiality definition process, the reporting perimeter and how it was determined, the significant frameworks and the methods used to quantify or evaluate the material topics.

3.6 The Loss of the Supremacy of the Shareholders in Favor of the Inclusion of All Stakeholders

Considering the overall set of all stakeholders can allow us to take into account subjects who are attentive not only to financial performance, but also to the role played by the company in society and the consequences connected to its behavior.

Traditionally, however, the financial statements focus exclusively on the figure of the shareholder, neglecting other stakeholders and this undoubtedly represents a limit to be overcome thanks to the use of reporting forms that support the main information.

IR, as highlighted in the principles reported within the Framework, aims to broaden the vision to satisfy the information requests of a significantly larger and more varied audience. It dedicates the same attention to all stakeholders, without privileging some categories to the detriment of others. From this perspective, therefore, the development of stable relationships with its stakeholders, capable of also directing strategic choices and the business scope, becomes a strong point for the organization and must be cultivated through transparency and high quality of the information provided. The pursuit of this objective is not trivial: taking into account that the One Report is used in the private sector as well as in the public sector, it follows that, by inevitably varying the categories of interested parties, it will be necessary to modify the type and structure of the report, thus adapting the information in the most appropriate way. Some companies, for example, try to overcome the aforementioned problem by involving their stakeholders in the process of reviewing the information published in the report, in such a way as to create a climate of trust, approval and collaboration. In this case we talk about "***social auditing***" (Gao & Zhang, 2006).

There are three perspectives of stakeholder engagement:

- **management perspective**: the involvement of stakeholders is seen from a purely utilitarian perspective as a means to obtain new knowledge and innovation, to establish partnerships and to avoid conflicts;
- **ethical perspective**: contrary to the previous one, in this case the stakeholders are seen according to the typical perspective of the public enterprise as citizens who have the right to determine or influence certain services;
- **social learning perspective**: stakeholders participate in meetings in which they exchange information while respecting the opinions of each other (Mathur et al., 2008).

The best path to pursue is the one that includes all three of the aforementioned perspectives.

To implement this process the following five phases can be followed consecutively:

1. Consider the strategic objectives of the company and their connection with stakeholders;
2. Define the levels of involvement and analyze relationships, available resources and organizational links; this also helps in selecting stakeholder representatives and deciding which relationships to deepen and consolidate;
3. Address problems on issues relating to combined internal and external skills, the capacity for involvement and the methods necessary to guarantee that all subjects actively participate in the process;
4. Expose the involvement techniques and provide a plan of the objectives to be achieved and the needs to be satisfied in each specific situation;

5. Illustrate how it is concretely intended to obtain results on involvement, guaranteeing stakeholder satisfaction, despite the contributions requested.[4]

3.6.1 The Measurement of Intangibles

Intangibles are defined as "*identifiable, non-monetary assets without physical substance that are controlled by an enterprise for use in the production or provision of goods or services, for rental to third parties, or for administrative purposes. They are the result of past decisions or events and from which future economic benefits are expected*".[5]

Intellectual capital, in particular, is made up of:

- **Human Capital**: this is a sort of tacit knowledge linked to the value of the people who work in the company in terms of skills, experience, motivation, etc.;
- **Structural Capital**: this includes organizational capabilities and knowledge institutionalized within the structure, processes and corporate culture;
- **Relational Capital**: this is formed by the set of relationships and the exchange of knowledge between the company and internal and external subjects and represents the perception of value that external subjects derive from integration with the organization.

The statutory budget presents clear limits on the measurement of intangibles, which remain mostly hidden, despite the fact that their importance is now undisputed (and sometimes even greater than that relating to tangible elements) in the process of creating value of a

[4] www.accountability.org, "*Il manuale dello stakeholder engagement*", https://www.yumpu.com/it/document/view/43616716/il-manuale-dello-stakeholder-engagement-accountability.

[5] Definition of the International Accounting Standards Board, 2005, https://www.ifrs.org/issued-standards/list-of-standards/ias-38-intangible-assets/#:~:text=An%20intangible%20asset%20is%20an,contractual%20or%20other%20legal%20rights.

company. However, their evaluation is usually useful to provide an explanation of the difference between the book value and the market value of an organization.

The integrated report, however, accepts the challenge of trying to report the values of intangibles and, although no methodologies are defined to be used to facilitate this representation, organizations proceed with the adoption of those deemed most appropriate, such as, for example, the following:

- **Return On Asset**: concerns the ratio between the average value of the income of tangible assets before taxes estimated over an average period of three to five years and the average value of the assets over the same period of time. This result is compared with the industry average and the difference is calculated. If this is positive, the company holds intangibles and can multiply it by the value of tangible assets to find the average profitability that intellectual capital can produce. Furthermore, dividing the profitability by the average cost of capital can obtain the value of intangible assets. It is part of the Economic Value Added (EVA) approach;
- **Balanced Scorecard (BSC)** (Kaplan & Norton, 1996): the business model is divided into different perspectives. Each perspective is connected to the others according to a cause-effect logic and is measured with specific indicators.

3.6.2 Materiality in Integrated Reporting

The concept of **materiality** is fundamental with regard to the preparation of reports, as only what is considered material is reported within them. In other words, the report must present a focus on those factors that have a significant impact on the long-term financial performance of the organization and must be concise and meaningful. Information is significant if it can influence the decisions of an organization's highest governing bodies and/or its capital providers.

On this topic, a different definition has been provided in the financial field compared to the non-financial one. In the first case, in fact, it is argued that information is material if its incorrect presentation or its omission would impact the decision-making behavior of investors (Faux, 2012). In the second case, however, materiality refers not only to the category of investors, but to all the various stakeholders (Mio, 2013). Always in this context, various realities have expressed themselves in reference to this concept: in 2013 AccountAbility, for example, expressed the need for adequate communication of information classified as material and proposed a framework divided into three steps to be followed to identify the issues actually relevant in a non-financial communication:

- Identify what could be material for stakeholders and collect data about it;
- Prioritize certain issues based on materiality thresholds and internal and external criteria, through qualitative analyses or discussions or scoring systems;
- Ensure that the process determining the relevant issues is based on valid sources and is supported both internally and externally (AccountAbility, 2006).

The GRI, however, in providing its definition of materiality, maintains that not only can objects that have an influence on the financial result be assessed as significant, but it is also appropriate to take into account the impacts in the environmental and social fields.[6]

In the IASB Conceptual Framework for Financial Reporting[7] mention is made of the definition of "*relevance*", as in the "*ability to influence decisions made by users of the financial statements*". To influence decisions, information must have a predictive value, i.e., it can be used as input in a process of predicting future results, and/or value confirmation, if it informs on previous evaluations. One aspect of relevance is precisely "*materiality*": information is significant if its omission or inaccuracy is capable of influencing the decisions of users taken on the basis of the financial information concerning a particular company.

---

[6] GRI, " G4 Guidelines", pp. 11–12 https://respect.international/g4-sustainability-reporting-guidelines-implementation-manual/.

[7] https://www.ifrs.org/issued-standards/list-of-standards/conceptual-framework/.

With the spread of Integrated Reporting, materiality takes on importance to the point of becoming one of the Guiding Principles of the Framework, which provides the following definition: "*an integrated report should disclose information about matters that substantively affect the organization's ability to create value over the short, medium and long term*".[8] It concerns the entire extension of the company strategy.

The process of determining what is material and must, therefore, be reported within Integrated Reporting is based on three criteria:

- **relevance**: issues that have already impacted the company strategy, business model or strategic capital or may do so in the future; it is the starting point for determining what is material;
- **significance**: assessing the significance of issues requires evaluation of the magnitude of the impact (both for past, current and future issues) and the probability of occurrence (for issues that are not necessarily guaranteed to occur);
- **prioritization**: people as well as an organization need to prioritize issues based on their relevance and significance.

The Framework also provides for the identification and evaluation of material issues that impact the creation of value. The process of identifying these elements presents, however, some difficulties:

- The relationship between the occurrence of the event and the impact on company value is not easy to identify;
- The number of stakeholders to take into consideration is much larger;
- It is not always possible to determine a monetary value of non-financial aspects;
- Difficulties arise in the assessment due to the adoption of a long-term perspective.

[8] http://integratedreporting.org/wp-content/uploads/2013/12/13-12-08-THE-INTERNATIONAL-IR-FRAMEWORK-2-1.pdf.

3.6.3 The Business Model

The **business model** is the tool that defines and contributes to the implementation of the corporate strategy, to the mapping of the processes of sustainable creation of value over time and helps to express an evaluation of the organization in the long term as well as its elasticity.

To achieve the creation of value it is necessary to refer to a series of resources in terms of capital: tangible elements such as financial and manufacturing capital, intangible elements such as relationships with the reference community and human and intellectual capital and other inputs such as services that derive from natural capital.

The business model has the specific purpose of identifying all the key resources that contribute to the creation of value of a company, illustrating how to organize their management.

A study conducted by Ernst&Young (EY, 2014) provides the main questions to take into consideration for its correct definition:

- How does the organization define value?
- What are the mission and vision of the organization?
- What is the environment of the organization?
- How does the organization define the strategy and what resources does it use?
- What are the main opportunities and challenges of the organization?
- Which indicators are most significant in terms of measuring the effort with which the organization achieves its objectives in creating value?
- What are the inputs, resources and capitals on which the organization depends?
- What are the outputs produced?
- What is the revenue?
- What are the activities that add value?

Finally, the business model must be aligned with the mission, i.e., with the main purposes of the organization, with the vision, which reflects the aspirations for the future, and with the operating context and the external factors that shape it (e.g. macroeconomic situation, availability of natural resources, technology, etc.).

3.7 The Process of Adoption of the Integrated Report

Eccles and Krzus (2014) identified four phases in the development of Integrated Reporting, which help to understand its significance.

The first was called "***Company Experimentation***" and has developed since the 2000s with the first attempts by companies to put integrated reporting into practice. Examples are Natura and Novo Nordisk, which published their first integrated reports in 2002 and 2004, respectively.

The second phase, "***Expert Commentary***", is characterized by the manifestation through publications in books and magazines of a growing interest on the part of academics and professionals aimed at this new practice and by the expansion of the number of companies that use it.

The third phase is called "***Codification***". Having reached this point, we proceed with the effective establishment of the report and with the observation of its first effects, and new subjects find room in the debate, such as various NGOs, the Integrated Reporting Committee of South Africa (IRC of SA) and, finally, the IIRC, motivated to provide a complete and shared definition of this new reality.

Finally, the fourth phase, called "***Institutionalization***", is characterized by the involvement of regulatory and market entities and is distinguished from the previous ones by a more international adoption of the integrated report. In reality, this phase does not end the process of evolution of Integrated Reporting, which still continues today and is increasingly moving towards its adoption as universally as possible.

Wendy Stubbs and Higgins Colin (2014) have highlighted how, in concrete terms, organizations use some specific mechanisms to facilitate the implementation of Integrated Reporting:

- **"*push*** or ***pull*" approach**: these are two different strategic approaches. In some cases, Integrated Reporting is used to explicitly guide change within the organization itself ("*push*" strategy), in others it is seen as the product deriving from an integrated business itself ("*pull*" strategy), in still other cases both of these two approaches are put into practice. The "*push*" strategy serves to better integrate the issue of sustainability with the core business. This is achieved with the support of a sustainability team, which uses the report as an internal tool to push all members of the organization to become an active part in the process that will lead to the use of Integrated Reporting, through continuous comparisons and internal discussions. Larrinaga-Gonzalez and Bebbington (2001), commenting on this strategy, argue that in this case it is the people who deal with sustainability that lead the change, but there is no "*uncontrollable shock*" which could, instead, be caused by external pressures, such as those exercised by stakeholders or regulatory bodies, to force change in the organization. Here there is the desire of the sustainability team to integrate sustainability into the organization more deeply. The aforementioned authors consider internal pressures as factors that tend to be weaker than the pressure that can come from outside. The "pull" strategy sees Integrated Reporting as the result of a business that is already integrated in itself or is gradually becoming more integrated. The concept of sustainability, precisely because it is fundamental for guiding one's business and for holding oneself responsible for externalities of a social and environmental nature, is already included in the policies promoted by the organization;

- **cross-functional teams and stakeholder involvement**: Integrated Reporting requires planning and coordination between business areas. To achieve this objective, we use the help of cross-functional teams, which include representatives from the finance, strategic, legal, accounting and sustainability functions. Furthermore, the involvement of stakeholders is relevant for the identification and monitoring of the topics of interest to them.
- **sustainability committees**: this is one of the most commonly used mechanisms to manage sustainability reports. The committee includes the CEO and/or representatives of the entire organization and is responsible for defining the strategic direction to be taken;
- **materiality analysis**: identifying material issues is a key step. Organizations traditionally had processes used to identify environmental issues, but integrated reporters are changing them in order to focus on a few more strategic issues. Some organizations have taken advantage of the GRI Sustainability Reporting guidelines, while others

believe that they are not suitable for managing the transition from Sustainability Reporting to Integrated Reporting;
- **integrated measures**: developing mechanisms that identify some value creation processes, particularly around the social area, and developing efficient measurement systems are considered necessary changes.

In July 2015, however, PwC published a "practical guide"[9] which provides some useful indications for management teams on the adoption of the integrated report by companies to make up for the lack of practical advice in relation to its implementation. The guide is developed through a roadmap in three main phases:

- **maeriality analysis**: the importance of materiality has already been highlighted by the GRI and the IIRC Framework, but the definitions that have been given differ from each other. In defining issues as material, according to PwC, the role played by dialogue with investors and stakeholders is important, to also understand how they perceive the impact exerted by the business in financial and non-financial terms;
- **value creation**: this is the second key component. The company must develop a qualitative understanding of the value creation process. Furthermore, this process depends on a series of building blocks (stakeholders, their key messages, risk, strategy, value drivers, i.e., the activities that influence the achievement of strategic objectives, performance and impact) and cannot ignore an intense dialogue with stakeholders;
- **evaluating impact**: this is achieved by translating the value creation process into the information management system, so that the organization monitors performance and makes informed decisions (in this case we speak of "*integrated dashboard*").

The guide also provides the following suggestions to ensure the success of the process:

[9] https://www.pwc.com/gx/en/audit-services/publications/assets/pwc-ir-practical-guide.pdf.

- **Observe the external world and relate to all the stakeholders**: the organization cannot function independently of the environment to which it relates, which can express factors worthy of consideration such as demographic trends, urbanization, technological evolution, resource scarcity and climate change. From this relationship risks and opportunities for the company arise, which can also have an impact on customers, competitors and other subjects operating within the value chain;
- **Determine a value proposition for stakeholders and renew the strategy**: implementing Integrated Reporting often involves a renewal of the strategy adopted by the company. It will be necessary to identify, on the basis of the dialogue with its stakeholders, the areas that can create greater value, with what methods, and the proposal to be submitted to the attention of the stakeholders will have to be formulated, through the development of a matrix that reports the definition of value for each of them. The risk lies in the fact that, just as value can be generated, it can also be destroyed;
- **Align internal processes with the strategy**: the basis of the integrated report is integrated information management aligned with the organization's sustainable strategy. Integrated information management means a well-balanced and connected set of key performance indicators (KPIs), incorporated into systems and processes and aligned with the value drivers and in support of the organization's culture;
- **Develop an integrated dashboard**: it is an organization-specific tool developed by PwC to monitor stakeholder value with information management, showing the impacts produced by the organization, its mission and vision, as well as its dialogue with the outside world. The use of an interface helps to collect all the relevant data from different sources and, in this way, guarantees management access to dynamic and significant information so as to be able to evaluate past performances and predict the future developments of the organization;
- **Integrate your reporting to obtain an effective and complete dialogue with investors**.

It is important that this operation takes on a circular and iterative trend of continuous improvement, starting with the dialogue with the stakeholders and ending with the production of the Annual Report, which in turn has the task of stimulating the dialogue with the stakeholders. Corporate reporting is fundamental because, if it is of good quality, it can exert an influence on the perception and trust of investors, helping them to understand how management is managing the main drivers of value creation.

3.8 The "*One Report*": Lights and Shadows Behind the Tool

The IR adoption can bring about multiple **benefits**.

Among these, it enhances the attention to sustainability themes, fostering a commitment of the company and the pursuit of new business opportunities in terms of adoption of sustainable products and new business models. From the point of view of organizations, it should produce lower costs (due to the creation of a single report and the reduction of the risks associated with the activities carried out by the organization) and facilitate the search for financial resources.

The ambition is that a single report can fully satisfy the information needs coming from a wide range of parties, reducing the amount of information reported. This results in higher quality and transparency of corporate communication.

Some academic studies have, then, attributed the following potentialities to the integrated report, which can:

- Allow reporting of information no longer only on historical data, but also on future perspectives;
- Guarantee an effective representation of the process of companies' value creation for a company;
- Facilitate the decision-making process, as it makes more information available;
- Provide a representation of the risk factors to be neutralized thanks to their evaluation and constant monitoring;
- Allow for a reduction in the cost of capital;

- Favor positive impacts on the market, through the reduction of reputational risk, the strengthening of the brand and stakeholder satisfaction (Adams & Simnett, 2011; Hampton, 2012; Roberts, 1992).

An opposite side also emerged from the debate on IR, which highlighted its incompleteness and the **distorting effects** that its adoption can generate. In fact, not infrequently there is the impression that this type of report has as its effective purpose the creation of a "*fictitious*" company image. For this reason, it was defined as "*a masterpiece of obfuscation and avoidance of any recognition of the prior 40 years of research and experimentation that threaten to push even further away from any plausible possibility that sustainability might be seriously embraced by any element of business and politics*" (Milne & Gray, 2013).

Some authors have pointed out the presence in the integrated reports (even in the most structured of them) of a considerable number of repetitions and the lack of strong integration between financial and non-financial topics. The real risk that may result from the dissemination of this report is the tendency for it to become a mere exercise in reporting (Solomon et al., 2013). Furthermore, although the integrated report was born with the goal of providing useful information for all the stakeholders, it actually ends up mostly satisfying only the shareholders' interest. If, on the one hand, it allows the reduction of some costs thanks to the creation of a single report and of the typical risks of the activities carried out by the organization, on the other hand, it implies problems and costs necessary to obtain the effective integration process within the organization, such as the risk associated with dissemination of sensitive information and strategic data, investments in training functional to the spread of the new culture and skills among personnel and investments in technology and data processing systems.

The One Report also has limitations on the side of comparability between companies due to the absence of a standard structure that makes the comparison possible.

Moreover, to date, such a tool is more suitable for large size businesses, finding little use and interest on part of small and medium-sized companies: they find it more difficult to recognize the IR potential and feel more penalized by the necessary costs of its introduction (lack of data to produce the report, absence of skilled personnel, etc.).

3.9 Integrated Reporting and Sustainability Reporting

Integrated Reporting was not presented as an evolution of Sustainability Reporting, but as an attempt to promote a more cohesive and efficient approach to corporate reporting to avoid the production of a large amount of static and disconnected information.

Both tools make it possible to increase the attention paid to ESG criteria and sustainability, towards which companies demonstrate a lasting commitment. This commitment allows for rationalization in the management of resources and the possibility of seizing new business opportunities. Despite this, some companies maintain their focus on profitability. A further advantage shared between the two tools is the improvement of company reputation. This, however, is an aspect to which greater attention should be paid, as many companies could use the tools analyzed to create a fictitious image (a criticality the two tools have in common) and restore, or improve, their reputation towards stakeholders. In addition to this, the integrated report and the sustainability report share other critical issues; in particular, both tools increase the complexity of reporting (especially in the case of integrated reporting) and this makes the process more onerous.

The main differences between these two types of reporting fall into two categories: **conceptual differences** and **structural differences**. As regards the former, with Integrated Reporting the distinction between shareholders and stakeholders is totally eliminated, since upon closer inspection the shareholder is nothing more than a stakeholder like the others, without a condition of primus inter pares, a state which, instead, it fully maintains in Sustainability Reporting. As regards the structural differences, we can observe how the great novelty of Integrated Reporting lies precisely in its content, which includes all the information useful for adequately evaluating the company's ability to create value for stakeholders not only in the short, but also and above all in the long term.

According to Eccles and Krzus (2010), the added value provided by this report is evident precisely in its output, consisting of a holistic and complete representation of the company's performance, which shows both the results achieved by the business itself and the factors that determined them. Furthermore, the responsibility for the data reported therein lies solely with the Board of Directors and the certification of the documents goes from optional to mandatory and is entrusted to an external party.

Sustainability Reporting focuses on economic, social and governance performance of an organization in a sustainable global economy, while Integrated Reporting aims to offer an organization's financial capital providers an integrated representation of the key factors essential for the current and future creation of value. Despite these divergences, the IR is a key tool for the development of the integrated culture and reporting processes of a company since it provides, in addition to financial data, input for the identification of "*material issues*" and strategic objectives for evaluating the ability to achieve these objectives and create value.

In conclusion, the IR consists of a hybrid practice that extends between the two different worlds of financial reporting on the one hand and Sustainability Reporting on the other, with the aim of providing a correct and truthful vision of the value of the company and thus estimating the level of sustainability achieved. What exactly this value represents remains a topic to be clarified and on which much has been debated and is still being debated today. To summarize, therefore, how to effectively define Integrated Reporting, we could undoubtedly talk about a set of different evaluation logics and their application aimed at obtaining a state of legitimacy for the company that draws up the report. One of the main concerns of companies is, in fact, being able to obtain and maintain a condition of legitimacy over time through the alignment of the typical activities of their personal business with the most widely spread social values. As supported by Legitimacy Theory (Suchman, 1995), companies must stipulate a sort of "*social contract*" with the company with which they interact and strategically pursue a kind of balance between their own values and those of the company, trying to fully satisfy the needs of stakeholders. Legitimation must come through the use of reporting and must involve the company as a whole.

To achieve this, it is advisable to implement a management model that requires all the parts that make up a company to cooperate with each other to define objectives and strategies to be pursued, so that the company is integrated within itself.

3.10 A Final Reflection on IR

The proposal of the IIRC of an integrated report, although moved by "*right*" principles and purposes, would seem still impractical, idealistic and incomplete, as the presence of relevant costs is not counterbalanced by similar benefits.

From the above-mentioned analysis, it emerges that the IR is still an incomplete instrument and with imperfections. The integration of the three dimensions (financial, environmental and social) should not stop at the simple content of the report but, instead, should take place within the whole organization. The more widespread perception is that it only serves to enrich the quantity of the information reported, not guaranteeing effective cohesion between the different types of information.

Therefore, to date, it has not been widely adopted. Three main reasons can justify this imperfection of the reporting tool. First, the recent birth of this type of reporting makes it an instrument that is still experimental. Secondly, its voluntary nature does not foster the creation of universally recognized and adopted standards. Finally, there is the fear on the part of businesses of disclosing strategic information to their competitors.

A possible solution to these problems could be its further improvement and the introduction of incentives that favor its adoption and allow the development of detailed standards that can concretely guide companies in its adoption. In conclusion, Integrated Reporting could represent a real revolution in terms of reporting, but its future depends on its evolution and improvement. Thanks to the introduction of a series of improvements and adjustments, in fact, the so-called *One Report* will fulfill the purposes for which it has been generated and become a new frontier for corporate communication.

3.11 In-depth Analysis: Intellectual Capital Disclosure Within the Integrated Reporting

The following paragraph aims at thoroughly analyzing the concept of intellectual capital (IC), its characteristics and what it represents within the Integrated Reporting.

3.11.1 Intellectual Capital

Intangible assets are a fundamental resource for any organizations in the process of value creation: they provide an important competitive advantage and are a source of business success (Augier & Teece, 2005; Cohen, 2005; Hsu & Fang, 2009; Itami, 1987; Kong, 2010; Li et al., 2010; Lin & Huang, 2011; Martín et al., 2011; Roulstone, 2011; Skoog, 2003; Teece, 2000).

In general, the term "***intangible assets***" refers to company resources that do not possess the attribute of physical substance that produces future long-term positive returns for the company (Abhayawansa & Guthrie, 2014; Castilla-Polo & Gallardo-Vázquez, 2016; Li et al., 2010; Singh & Narwal, 2015). Some examples of this are know-how, the ability to innovate with new products and services, customer and supplier satisfaction, loyalty and trust, company reputation and image and employee motivation.

However, we can't find a unique definition of intangibles in the literature (Kaufmann & Schneider, 2004; Keong, 2008) and it is possible to distinguish between accounting and non-accounting research. Following an accounting perspective, we consider intangibles only the items presented in the financial statements in accordance with the mandatory accounting regulations (for instance, IAS 38 Intangible Assets or SFAS 142 Goodwill and Other Intangible Assets), while the non-accounting field defines intangibles also those assets not recognized formally (Cuozzo et al., 2017). In the latter case, organizations can publish the value and the composition of intangible assets on a voluntary basis.

There is also a strong debate on how to recognize the accounting value of intangible assets (Lev et al., 2005; Powell, 2003; Wallman, 1996). Some studies suggested that their value derives from particular attributes: the possibility of simultaneous uses, and their uniqueness, which also implies that they are difficult to replace or copy (Giustina et al., 2010; Keong, 2008; Kong, 2010; Lev, 2001). A company can receive a series of benefits such as the creation of a learning process related to operations with intangibles (Sveiby, 2001, 2010).

All the intangible assets are grouped under the concept of **Intellectual Capital (IC)**. Consequently, Intellectual Capital is an aggregation of individual intangible assets (Castilla-Polo & Ruiz-Rodríguez, 2017) that includes all the knowledgebase resources that are useful to give a competitive advantage to an organization (Cinquini et al., 2012). Also in the case of Intellectual Capital, we found many different definitions in previous contributions (An et al., 2015; Chiucchi & Dumay, 2015; Dumay, 2014; Schneider & Samkin, 2008; Sveiby, 1997; Yi & Davey, 2010). For instance, Stewart (1997: p. 10) defined it as "*the sum of everything everybody in a company knows that gives it a competitive edge […] Intellectual Capital is intellectual material, knowledge, experience, intellectual property, information […] that can be put to use to create wealth*". Dumay (2016) modified the above-mentioned definition by replacing the word "*wealth*" with "*value*". He proposed four different dimensions of value: monetary, utility, social and sustainable. The first dimension (monetary) refers to the fact that it is essential for companies to obtain monetary returns (Dumay & Lu, 2010). The utility value concerns the value of company goods and services for consumers and the price they are willing to pay for use and consume them (Marshall, 1920). The third dimension (social) is related to the construction of social capital by providing a series of benefits to society (Nahapiet & Ghosal, 1998). Finally, for the last dimension (the sustainable one) Dumay (2016) considered the fact that organizations are required to provide sustainable value due to an increasing sensitivity to sustainability issues, even if still today many organizations do not address them yet.

Other definitions of Intellectual Capital are the following:

- Stewart (2001: p. 13): "*It has become standard to say that a company's intellectual capital is the sum of its human capital (talent), structural capital (intellectual property, methodologies, software, documents, and other knowledge artifacts), and customer capital (client relationships)*";
- Edvinsson (2002: p. 8): "*Intellectual capital is a combination of human capital— the brains, skills, insights, and potential of those in an organization—and structural capital—things like the capital wrapped up in customers, processes, databases, brands, and IT systems. It is the ability to transform knowledge and intangible assets into wealth creating resources, by multiplying human capital with structural capital*".

Finally, Kwee (2008) performed a review of the literature on Intellectual Capital and concluded that several authors used different terms (intellectual assets, intangible assets, intangibles, intangible resources, IC, intellectual property and intellectual knowledge) as synonyms to identify the same concept. However, there is a shared opinion about its crucial role for the company in terms of competitive advantage (Kujansivu, 2008; Schiuma et al., 2008).

The IC concept has been subject to an evolution over time. Traditionally, the Intellectual Capital was divided into two macro-categories (Edvinsson & Malone, 1997): human capital and structural capital, in turn split into organisational and customer capital. Then, Bontis (1998) suggested that the concept of relational capital is an evolution of customer capital, which includes the importance for an organization to interact with external stakeholders (such as, but not only, customers). This concept is also known in the literature as social capital (Nahapiet & Ghosal, 1998). As an ending point of this process, other authors proposed dividing Intellectual Capital into three categories (Castilla-Polo & Gallardo-Vázquez, 2016; Guthrie & Petty, 2000; Meritum, 2002; Stewart, 1997; Sveiby, 1997):

- **human capital**: in general, refers to human resources (such as employees' education, competencies, skills and motivation);
- **structural** or **organisational capital** (refers to the organization's processes, infrastructures, systems and culture);

- **relational capital**, related to the external relationships of the organization (for instance, with customers, suppliers and partners and other stakeholders).

There is also an extended version of this classification that provides seven different classes (Gerpott et al., 2008): human capital, customer capital, supplier capital, process capital, innovation capital, location capital and investor capital.

Previous contributions also paid attention to how to measure Intellectual Capital for different reasons (Holmen, 2005):

1. It helps in formulating the right business strategy;
2. It supports the development of key performance indicators that are useful in evaluating the company's strategy;
3. It helps in determining the price for acquiring firms during operations of merger and acquisition;
4. It is useful in the development of the company's incentive and compensation plan;
5. It improves communication with the external stakeholders regarding the company's intellectual property.

3.11.2 Intellectual Capital Disclosure (ICD)

Even if literature on Intangible Assets began being published during the early 1990s, contributions on Intellectual Capital Disclosure (ICD) are more recent (FASB, 2001: Improving Business Reporting: Insights into Enhancing Voluntary disclosures).

Nowadays firms are under high pressure to disclose not only their financial information, but also that of a non-financial nature so that their stakeholders understand how the creates value over time (Beattie & Thomson, 2010; Lev, 2001) and how their knowledge is managed (Bukh et al., 2001).

In this scenario, previous research suggested that disclosure related to the Intellectual Capital plays a crucial role depending on its influence in value creation (Abhayawansa & Guthrie, 2010; Ariff et al.,

2014; Curado et al., 2011; EY, 2014; Gamerschlag, 2013; Lev, 2001; Zambon & Marzo, 2007). Even the resource-based view theory supports the assumption that intangible assets are the resources most valuable in producing a competitive advantage (Dierickx & Cool, 1989). However, some previous contributions (Beattie & Thomson, 2007; Bontis, 2003; Brennan, 2001; Firer & Williams, 2005; Guthrie & Petty, 2000; Guthrie & Ricceri, 2004; Mahesh et al., 2012; Mat et al., 2012; Sharma & Kaur, 2016; Singh & Kansal, 2011; Xiao, 2008) highlighted still a low level of Intellectual Capital Disclosure (ICD). This result could depend on the absence of a shared framework that provides useful guidelines to disclose this type of information and reduce the required effort by the companies (Guthrie & Petty, 2000; Striukova et al., 2008). On the contrary, other studies supported the presence of an increasing trend in the amount of information disclosed on intangible assets (Abdifatah & Mubaraq, 2012; Abeysekera, 2008; Abeysekera & Guthrie, 2005; Bergamini and Zambon, 2002; Bukh et al., 2005; De Silva et al., 2014; Oliveras et al., 2004, 2008; Sonnier et al., 2008; Striukova et al., 2008; Sujan & Abeysekera, 2007; Vamdemaele et al., 2005; Williams, 2001).

Moreover, in their study, Schaper et al. (2017) wanted to demonstrate the presence of a shift from Intellectual Capital reporting, which is characterized by an accounting perspective, to Intellectual Capital Disclosure, which is a more value relevant type of communication. They showed that there is a continuous process of development of new forms of reporting to solve the main critical issues of the previous one.

Over time, this aspect generated different lines of research.

A first stream of research is focused on the explanatory factors behind the decision to disclose information about Intellectual Capital. A higher level of ICD could produce a series of advantages for the organizations, especially if we consider the case of a firm with a high level of intangibles (Gelb, 2002). First, it increases the level of communication transparency and reduces, as a consequence, the level of information asymmetries between companies and stakeholders (such as shareholders, creditors, customers, employees and so on) by providing a description of the actual and future plan for company value creation and by increasing understanding of the business for all stakeholders (Branswijck & Everaert, 2012; Cañibano Calvo et al., 2002; Eccles & Mavrinac, 1995; Eccles et al., 2001; Holmen, 2005; Johanson, 2003; Lerro & Schiuma, 2013; Nielsen & Madsen, 2008; Zéghal & Maaloul, 2011). This effect is also consistent with the result showed by Lev (1992) on the reduction of the information gap between a company and its stakeholders due to the adoption of a transparent voluntary disclosure strategy. A higher level of information on Intellectual Capital can help companies in reaching stakeholders' needs (Brüggen et al., 2009) and in creating a more stable relationship with them (Guthrie et al., 2004). Second, as suggested by Vergauwen and van Alem (2005), it directly influences the assessment of the company's actual value and future wealth creation capabilities (Holmen, 2005; Williams, 2001). Third, it supports a more efficient process of decision-making, not only for companies, but also for investors (Bismuth & Tojo, 2008; García-Ayuso, 2003; García-Meca & Martinez, 2007). Fourth, previous studies showed that it reduces the company's cost of capital (Bismuth & Tojo, 2008; Dumay, 2016; Mangena et al., 2010; Nielsen et al., 2015) and improves the firm's performance (Dumay & Tull, 2007). Finally, a recent part of the literature focused on the improvement of the corporate image and reputation related to a higher level of voluntary disclosure on IC issues (Fombrun, 1996; Holmen, 2005; Van der Meer-Kooistra & Zijlstra, 2001). Certainly, disclosing information on intangible assets allows companies to draw a complete picture of themselves because they include information that is not necessary and already considered in the financial statements (Zambon, 2002). ICD is also useful for making financing decisions (Catasús & Gröjer, 2003; Hazianti & Jaafar, 2013) and attracts actors with higher skills (Bukh et al., 2005; Petty & Cuganesan, 2005). These advantages also produce a series of benefits for company stakeholders (Vergauwen & van Alem, 2005).

However, there could be a series of disadvantages when information is disclosed: providing relevant information could lead to a loss of company competitiveness (Cañibano Calvo et al., 2000; Vergauwen & van Alem, 2005; Williams, 2001), create problems in the allocation and use of resources (Van der Meer-Kooistra & Zijlstra, 2001), and add costs related to the process of disclosure due to the peculiarities of intangible assets

(Vergauwen & van Alem, 2005). Other issues concern the absence of a market as a reference point to obtain the right value to assign to intangibles (Jarboe, 2007; Upton, 2001). Also, there may be a high price to pay in terms of both money and time to fund process of measurement (Van der Meer-Kooistra & Zijlstra, 2001). There also may arise the risk of legal costs related to the disclosure of false information (Elliot & Jacobson, 1994; Lev, 1995; Tracy-Anne et al., 2014). Moreover, authors of these reports may influence or, worse, manipulate the information they present (Dumay, 2012; Dumay & Cai, 2014, 2015).

So, we can conclude that, in general, organizations disclose information only if the advantages are more than the disadvantages (Depoers, 2000; Guthrie et al., 2006), and this occurs also in the case of ICD.

A second stream of previous research studied the impact of some variables on the decision to disclose information regarding intangible assets.

Some companies' characteristics could determine differences in the disclosure of information. For instance, industry and firm size were identified as key determinants of the disclosure of information concerning Intellectual Capital (Bozzolan et al., 2003; Brüggen et al., 2009). Some authors showed the existence of a positive relationship between firm size and this type of disclosure (Brüggen et al., 2009; Castelo et al., 2010; Guthrie et al., 2006; Kateb, 2012; Nurunnabi et al., 2011; Santos & Venancio, 2013). Regarding the industry effect, Abdolmohammadi (2005) found that companies in new sectors are more interested in technological information with respect to companies in traditional sectors, which are more interested in issues related to intellectual property. Moreover, Sonnier (2008) studied a sample of publicly traded US companies and suggested that high technology companies disclose more information than the traditional ones. This result is also confirmed by other studies (Boesso & Kumar, 2007; Guthrie et al., 2004; Sonnier, 2008; Whiting & Miller, 2008). Sujan and Abeysekera (2007) suggested that materials and energy industries disclose less information on intangible assets when compared with other industries (such as services industry) because their market value depends more on physical assets. Prakash (2015) found differences in the content of the disclosure in different sectors. Other studies in this line of research are the following: Archambault and Archambault (2003), Bozzolan et al. (2003), Gandía (2003), Bukh et al. (2005), Guthrie et al. (2006), Shareef and Davey (2006), Sujan and Abeysekera (2007), Li et al. (2008), Schneider and Samkin (2008), Joshi et al. (2011), Bellora and Guenther (2013). However, it is also necessary to consider that it is difficult to compare disclosure originated by companies from different sectors, because they have different features, have to cope with different issues and apply different kind of measures.

With reference to the type of organization, some authors observed that only a small part of these studies addressed the area of the public sector, even if within this section we can find important actors in the process of creating and sharing knowledge, such as in the case with universities (Guthrie & Dumay, 2015; Low et al., 2015; Secundo et al., 2015; Veltri & Silvestri, 2015).

Some studies provided different useful insights by analyzing the country factor: Guthrie and Petty (2000) for Australia; Bontis (2002, 2003) for Canada; Bozzolan et al. (2003) for Italy; Goh and Lim (2004) for Malaysia; Shareef and Davey (2006) for UK; Kamath (2007, 2008) and Vishnu and Gupta (2014) for India; Whiting and Miller (2008) for New Zealand; Oliveras et al. (2008) for Spain; An and Davey (2010) and Liao et al. (2013) for China; Razak et al. (2016) for Saudi Arabia. However, few studies compared information on the Intellectual Capital Disclosure of two or more different countries: Abeysekera and Guthrie (2005) for companies in developed countries compared with non-developed countries; Guthrie et al. (2006) concentrated on Hong Kong and Australia; Abeysekera (2008) found some differences in this kind of disclosure for Sri Lanka and Singapore; Joshi et al. (2012) studied ICD of Indian and Australian IT companies; Ramanauskakité and Laginauskaité (2014) analyzed Lithuania and Estonia; Bianchi et al. (2016) conducted a study for France, Germany, Italy and the UK; Catalfo and Wulf (2016) did the same for Italy and Germany and Pisano et al. (2017) for European non-financial firms listed on the Italian, French and German stock exchanges. Finally, Wang et al. (2016) compared China and India for the IT sector, finding that Indian IT companies disclose more IC (and also with a higher quality) than Chinese IT companies do. Also of note, Abeysekera (2008) found that there is typically a higher level of disclosure in developed countries.

Finally, a group of contributions (Bianchi et al., 2016; Ferchichi & Paturel, 2013; Uyar & Kilic, 2012; Vafei et al., 2011; Whiting & Miller, 2008) showed that there is a positive relationship between ICD and the value of a company (for instance, in terms of operating cash flow), while Pisano et al. (2017) observed a negative effect of a concentrated ownership on the human capital disclosure.

3.11.3 Intellectual Capital Disclosure (ICD) Within Integrated Reporting and the Determinants of Its Quality

Earlier we described the main advantages related to the adoption of the Intellectual Capital Disclosure (ICD) that are related to the companies' process of value creation. However, previous form of ICD, such as sustainability reporting, usually failed in reporting information on intangibles (Bontis, 2003; Guthrie et al., 2006). Nowadays, there is a more recent form of disclosure (adopted especially by large companies) that maintains the same focus on the process of value creation as primary purpose and that is called Integrated Reporting (IR). One big difference between traditional disclosure on IC and IR is that the IR is not only concentrated to report information on intangible assets, but that its purpose is to provide a holistic picture of the company's value creation by describing the entire business (Abhayawansa, 2013; Beattie & Smith, 2013; Dumay et al., 2016). The concept of integration characterized the Integrated Report in the sense that it should highlight the relationship between the company's strategy and performance and the integration between different kinds of company's capitals. Moreover, the process of value creation must not only be internal, but it should also depend on the relationships with actors and factors external to the company. For this reason, the Integrated Report provides financial and non-financial information in the same report (International Integrated Reporting Council—IIRC, 2013).

The Integrated Report considers the Intellectual Capital within the fundamental concepts (IIIRC, 2013) as a part of the six capitals included in the International Integrated Reporting Framework (IIRF). More in detail, the framework suggests the existence of six capitals in the process of value creation: three physical capitals (financial, manufactured and natural) and three intangible capitals (human, social and relational and intellectual or organizational). The three intangible capitals combined identify the broader concept of Intellectual Capital. Human capital refers to the employees' competencies, experiences and propensity to innovate. Social and relational capital includes the relationships and the construction of networks with different stakeholders by considering the ability to share information, the presence of common norms and values and trust in the company's reputation. Finally, intellectual or organizational capital comprises the intellectual property (patents, copyrights, software, rights and licenses) and the firm's tacit knowledge, systems, procedures and protocols.

Notwithstanding the relevance of the six capitals in the International Integrated Reporting Framework, only a few studies considered the Intellectual Capital Disclosure within the Integrated Reporting (Busco et al., 2013; Dumay & Cai, 2014; Melloni, 2015). This stream of research is generally an evolution of previous contributions focused on studying the major determinants of the Intellectual Capital Disclosure in the sustainability reports (Cordazzo, 2005; Del Bello, 2006; Oliveira et al., 2010; Pedrini, 2007; Striukova et al., 2008). Moreover, the study of the quality of ICD in IR is limited to a small number of contributions (Melloni, 2015), while we identified other studies on the quality of the ICD within sustainability reports (Beattie et al., 2004; Bozzolan et al., 2003; Bukh et al., 2005; Campbell and Ridhuan Abdul Rahman, 2010; Cinquini et al., 2012).

For instance, Melloni (2015) analyzed the quality of the ICD provided in the IR and the possibility that this kind of disclosure is used by companies more with the purpose to manage their image and reputation than to provide useful information to stakeholder.

Regarding the literature on the determinants of the ICD within the IR, this stream of research is very scarce (Melloni, 2015).

Instead, the literature on the determinants of voluntary disclosure quality is wide. In general, these studies identified the following determinants of the quality of the disclosure: firm size (Cooke, 1989; Hossain et al., 1995; Meek et al., 1995; Watson et al., 2002), audit size or audit quality (DeAngelo, 1981), types of industry (Adams & Hossain, 1998; Cooke, 1989; Meek et al., 1995; Watson et al., 2002), leverage (Hossain et al., 1995), profitability (Haniffa & Cooke, 2002) and ownership concentration (Chau & Gray, 2002; Ghazali & Weetman, 2006; Haniffa & Cooke, 2002).

If we focused only on previous literature on Integrated Reporting, we would notice that authors concentrated more on studying the determinants of its adoption by companies (Frias-Aceituno et al., 2013, 2014; Jensen & Berg, 2012; Lai et al., 2014; Sierra-García et al., 2015), while few studies considered the issue of the quality of this kind of report. They analyzed the following main determinants: firm size, industry, country, firm performance (profitability, leverage), assurance, corporate governance and ownership structure of the company (Frías-Aceituno et al., 2012, 2014; Mahoney et al., 2013; Qu et al., 2015; Sierra-García et al., 2015).

3.11.4 Introduction to the Empirical Analysis

This section will be dedicated to an empirical analysis based on the main theories and concepts discussed in the previous sections.

The analysis refers to a sample of 53 firms, with the purpose to determine what is the extent to which Intellectual Capital is included within their organizations and identify possible determinants of this type of disclosure.

The sample was randomly selected, so it is composed of firms of different regions around the world and different industries. All of them can be classified as large enterprises, mainly due to their level of employees and their total assets. The main reasons behind this choice is that, since most of them are multinational companies, it was easier to find public data and to have the availability of well-detailed reports with useful evidence to support the study and the review.

The reference year for the analysis is 2020 (Table 3.1).

The main sources of information used to conduct the study were the integrated reports published by the selected companies on their websites and the Bloomberg platform, mainly used for financial data.

The following analysis is divided into two steps:

1. Map the level of IC disclosure of those companies;
2. Perform a regression analysis with qualitative and quantitative variables that may represent factors that influence IC disclosure.

For what concerns the first point, the aim was to understand the degree to which IC is included in the corporate disclosure of those companies. As seen in the previous paragraph, IC is the sum of different types of capital, which are organizational capital, relational capital and human capital. Starting from this basis, a score of between 1 and 5 for each type of capital (organizational, relational and human) was assigned to the integrated report of those companies. A score of 15 represented the maximum value achievable and values were given as follows:

Table 3.1 The sample

Sample			
Industry type			
Financial Services	15	**Region**	
Healtcare	3	Anglosaxon	17
Oil & Gas	10	Australia	1
Utilities	7	Brazil	2
Basic Materials	3	Canada	1
Consumer goods	6	Chile	1
Real estate	2	Europe	12
Industrials	3	Hong-Kong	1
Professional services	2	Japan	4
Telecommunications	2	New Zeland	1
	53	Russia	3
		Singapore	1
Ownership structure		South Africa	7
Private company	10	South Korea	1
Public sector	5	Sri Lanka	1
Publicly listed companies	38		53
	53		

- Any information on Intellectual Capital is present: Score = 0;
- Intellectual Capital present but poor narrative description, with only historical information: Score = 1;
- Intellectual Capital present and enough described based mainly on quantitative and historical and/or non-time-specific information: Score = 2;
- Sufficient description (quantitative and qualitative information) and some information referring to IR guiding principles, presence of historical and/or non-time-specific information: Score = 3;
- Quite detailed description (quantitative and qualitative information) and much information referring to IR guiding principles, presence of forward-looking information: Score = 4;
- Excellent description (quantitative and qualitative information) and most IR guiding principles used, presence of forward-looking information: Score = 5.

Then, for what concerns the second part of the analysis, the qualitative variables identified are:

- Industry type, which, in turn, can be divided into high impact industries (Industrials, Basic Materials, Healthcare, Oil & Gas), social sensitive industries (Financial Services), and other services (Consumer Services, Professional Services, Utilities, Consumer Goods, Telecommunications, Real Estate);
- Region, by dividing them into Anglosaxon (UK, US, Australia, New Zealand, Canada, South Africa), Europe (Netherlands, Italy, Switzerland, Germany, Denmark) and other countries (China, Singapore, Japan, Sri Lanka, Russia, South Korea, Brazil);
- Ownership structure, by identifying if they were private companies, publicly listed companies or companies or companies belonging to the public sector.

On the other hand, the quantitative variables included are:

- Firm size, represented by the number of employees for the period analyzed;

- Leverage, calculated as net financial debt scaled by equity. In this case, the numbers are in absolute values as found in the Bloomberg platform;
- Profitability, represented by the Return on Equity;
- Total assets, represented by the total level of assets of the period analyzed;
- Age, which was calculated as the number of years since the establishment of the company up to the end of 2020;
- IR Seniority, calculated as the number of years since the adoption of integrated reporting.

Next, a linear regression model is set up in order to investigate the impact that those variables have on ICD quality.

After having introduced the whole structure of the analysis, it is now important to explain the results found.

3.11.5 ICD Quality Analysis

As mentioned above, the first step was to review the integrated reports of the 53 companies selected as a sample and give a score for each capital component that, summed together, gave the total score for intellectual capital disclosure quality.

Five companies reached a score of just 7 out of 15, while the average of the values for IC is 9.81. The ICD quality of the sample selected is not as high as expected and, other than two companies, all the others reached a value equal to or below 12, with more than a half reaching a score of 9, 10 or 11.

Since the total value is given by the sum of three different components, it is important to investigate if there are any differences among those components or not. If not, it can be possible to conclude that the way and the degree of information that companies disclose is quite similar, at least for the majority of them. If so, it will be interesting to understand what the drivers of those differences are.

According to that, the sum and the mean for Organizational Capital, Relational Capital and Human Capital are calculated to verify their scores. The result shows significant differences between them: for Organizational Capital, the mean of the 53 scores given to each company was 2.94, while the sum was 156; for Relational Capital, the mean was 3.60, while the sum was 191; and finally, for Human Capital the mean was 3.26, while the sum was 173.

Some important considerations can be made around this point. The first one is that companies are more inclined to disclose relevant information about their relationship with stakeholders and communities, probably to improve their reputation. It is easier to understand why, on the other hand, organizational capital had the lowest score: enterprises are pheraps less inclined to publicly disclose, at least to the extent for which they are not obligated by law, their tacit in-house knowledge, systems and procedures. If it is true that it could be more difficult to disclose such things, it is also undeniable that they are related to the competitiveness of firms, and by disclosing them the risk is that competitors gain more information that would bring them to better understand the business of those companies. The total value of human capital fits almost perfectly between the other two, meaning that it is not the priority for firms to disclose employee's competencies, motivations, etc., but they are willing to publish that information since they do not represent such a competitive advantage as the information related to organizational capital.

These considerations are suitable and underlie what many theories already assessed; in the author's opinion, it may take a few more years for companies to completely go beyond seeing profitability from only a financial point of view. For certain, it will be fundamental to find a new equilibrium between the traditional purpose of companies—to be profitable—and the new requests for higher concern for environmental and social responsibility and a renewed concept of competitiveness.

3.11.6 Empirical Analysis

As introduced above, after having mapped the ICD quality for all the companies that composed the sample of the study, an empirical analysis through a multiple linear regression model is conducted.

The aim of the analysis was to test and understand if the ICD quality was significantly affected by qualitative and quantitative variables listed before or, in other terms, if changes in the ICD were explainable by those variables. So, the dependent variable selected to set up the model was the ICD quality.

Here Table 3.2, the model and its results.

Before entering the analysis, it is important to make a specification: in this model some variables were excluded—mainly the financial ones—solely because most of them had a negative impact on the robustness of the model. The main reason for that were some huge differences that many financial values had within the enterprises selected, which had the consequence to lower the capability of the model to explain the variations of the dependent variable.

As for the regression model, some interesting considerations can be made. First of all, the correlation coefficient—represented by "R"—has a value of 0.57, meaning that there is a positive, even if not so strong, relationship between the variables of the model. The robustness of the model is underlined by the value of the "F significance", which, by having a value very close to 0.05, allows for assessing that the selected dependent variable can be considered as having been properly selected for the analysis made.

The most interesting results arise if we go deeper to analyze output for the independent variables of the model, especially by using the p-value test. At a level of confidence 0.05, selected mainly for coherence with the values that the model gives as output, if we set as the Null Hypothesis H0 that the regressor does not relevantly contribute to explain the dependent variable and as Alternative Hypothesis H1 that the regressor significantly contributes to explain it, we can easily perform the p value test. At a level of confidence equal to 0.05, it is possible to accept the hypothesis that the regressor does not relevantly contribute to explain variances of ICD quality. On the other hand, the three variables highlighted in Table 3.2 have a contribute to explain the dependent variable. For those variables, since they have positive values, it means that if they increase they positively impact the dependent variable. It is truly interesting that, for each qualitative variable considered, there is one that has an impact on ICD

Table 3.2 Multiple linear regression model

Model summary								
R	0.526159236							
R squared	0.276843541							
Adjusted *R* squared	0.145360549							
std. error of the estimate	1.528294384							
observations	53							
	gdl	*SQ*	*MQ*	*F*	*F Significance*			
Regression	8	39.34312362	4.917890453	2.105546397	0.055543494			
Residues	44	102.7700839	2.335683726					
Total	52	142.1132075						
	Coefficients	*Standard error*	*T Stat*	*Significance value*	*Lower 95%*	*Upper 95%*	*Lower 95,0%*	*Upper 95,0%*
Intercept	6.370284506	1.047293678	6.082615257	2.55144E-07	4.259602786	8.480966227	4.259602786	8.480966227
High impact industries	0.724761926	0.526227988	1.377277422	0.175392938	−0.335780897	1.78530475	−0.335780897	1.78530475
Social sensitive industries	1.2507309	0.607604412	2.058462507	0.045497418	0.026184671	2.47527713	0.026184671	2.47527713
Anglosaxon	0.319604716	0.504578956	0.633408731	0.529745616	−0.69730735	1.336516783	−0.69730735	1.336516783
Europe	1.553801971	0.617047689	2.51812299	0.015510746	0.310224067	2.797379874	0.310224067	2.797379874

(continued)

Table 3.2 (continued)

Model summary								
Publicly listed	1.714673765	0.798409772	2.147611197	0.037292065	0.1055846	3.32376293	0.1055846	3.32376293
Private companies	0.993965698	0.877680033	1.132492093	0.263561509	−0.774882182	2.762813578	−0.774882182	2.762813578
Age	0.005322838	0.003871209	1.374980702	0.176098955	−0.002479072	0.013124748	−0.002479072	0.013124748
IR seniority	0.090656606	0.046569394	1.946699276	0.057972562	−0.003197841	0.184511053	−0.003197841	0.184511053

quality, as well as the importance of IR seniority in explaining the IDC quality too.

3.12 Conclusions

After having reported the evidence of the empirical analysis, it is important to make a summary of the main findings, and the critical matters and areas that could be subject to further research in the near future.

First of all, the ICD quality mapping clearly showed that the weight of the different components of capital have on ICD itself is very different between firms but, at the same time, very homogeneous within the categories themselves. If firms want to increase their level of transparency on every area considered by the integrated reporting, they will be more willing to disclose even matters that are more strategic.

Since it was verified that there was a positive relationship between quantitative variables, including the return of equity and ICD quality, they will be benefit from it.

Then, IR Seniority will positively contribute to the quality of IR disclosure: it is possible to assess that in the coming years firms will be able to better understand the benefits of more transparency regarding non-financial matters and so learn as well how to do it in the best way possible.

It is quite evident that publicly listed firms are at the forefront of this type of reporting, firstly because, by being obligated to do it, they have adopted it for a longer time, and, secondly, because they know it will have a positive impact, even on their finances. Basically, both of the just reviewed previous results contribute to certifying this statement.

An improvement of the model should consist in the integration of all variables in it: in this case it was necessary in order to increase the overall robustness of the model and, since all the data used were collected from reliable sources, it is likely that most of the quantitative variables were not able to help to explain the variations of the dependent variable. However, it is not something that should surprise us: for many multinational corporations it is difficult to relate certain quantitative values—such as total assets of their profitability in one year—with ICD quality, especially if they have adopted IR only recently.

References

Abdifatah, A. H., & Mubaraq, S. (2012). The trends of intellectual capital disclosures: Evidences from the Nigerian banking sector. *Journal of Human Resource Costing and Accounting, 16*(3), 184–209. https://doi.org/10.1108/14013381211286360

Abdolmohammadi, M. J. (2005). Intellectual capital disclosure and market capitalization. *Journal of Intellectual Capital, 6*(3), 397–416. https://doi.org/10.1108/14691930510611139

Abeysekera, I. (2008). Intellectual capital disclosure trends: Singapore and Sri Lanka. *Journal of Intellectual Capital, 9*(4), 723–737. https://doi.org/10.1108/14691930810913249

Abeysekera, I., & Guthrie, J. (2005). Annual reporting trends of intellectual capital in Sri Lanka. *Critical Perspectives on Accounting, 16*(3), 151–163.

Abhayawansa, S. A. (2013). A review of guidelines and frameworks on external reporting of intellectual capital. *Journal of Intellectual Capital, 15*(1), 100–141. https://doi.org/10.1108/JIC-04-2013-0046

Abhayawansa, S., & Guthrie, J. (2010). Intellectual capital and the capital market: A review and synthesis. *Journal of Human Resource Costing & Accounting, 14*(3), 196–226. https://doi.org/10.1108/14013381011095472

Abhayawansa, S., & Guthrie, J. (2014). Importance of intellectual capital information: A study of Australian analyst reports. *Australian Accounting Review, 68*(24), 66–83. https://doi.org/10.1111/auar.12012

AccountAbility (2006). The materiality Report. Aligning strategy performance and reporting.

Adams, M., & Hossain, M. (1998). Managerial discretion and voluntary disclosure: Empirical evidence from the New Zealand life insurance industry. *Journal of Accounting and Public Policy, 17*(3), 245–281.

Adams, S., & Simnett, R. (2011). Integrated reporting: An opportunity for Australia's not-for-profit sector. *Australian Accounting Review, 21*(3), 292–301. https://doi.org/10.1111/j.1835-2561.2011.00143.x

An, Y., & Davey, H. (2010). Intellectual capital disclosure in China (mainland) companies. *Journal of Intellectual Capital, 11*(3), 326–347. https://doi.org/10.1108/14691931011064572

An, Y., Sharma, U., & Wang, Z. (2015). Towards a conceptual template for intellectual capital measurement and reporting. *International Journal of Business and Management, 10*(7), 236–245.

Archambault, J. J., & Archambault, M. E. (2003). A multinational test of determinants of corporate disclosure. *International Journal of Accounting, 38*(2), 173–194. https://doi.org/10.1016/S0020-7063(03)00021-9

Ariff, A. M., Cahan, S. F., & Emanuel, D. M. (2014). Institutional environment, ownership, and disclosure of intangibles: Evidence from East Asia. *Journal of International Accounting Research, 13*(1), 33–59. https://doi.org/10.2308/jiar-50655

Augier, M., & Teece, D. J. (2005). An economics perspective on intellectual capital. In B. Marr (Ed.), *Perspectives on intellectual capital* (pp. 3–28). Elsevier Butterworth Heinemann.

Beattie, V., & Thomson, S. (2010). *Intellectual capital reporting: Academic Utopia or corporate reality in a brave new world?* The Institute of Chartered Accountants of Scotland.

Beattie, V., McInnes, B., & Fearnley, S. (2004). A methodology for analysing and evaluating narratives in annual reports: A comprehensive descriptive profile and metrics for disclosure quality attributes. *Accounting Forum, 28*(3), 205–236. https://doi.org/10.1016/j.accfor.2004.07.001

Beattie, V., & Smith, S. J. (2013). Value creation and business models: Refocusing the intellectual capital debate. *The British Accounting Review, 45*(4), 243–254. https://doi.org/10.1016/j.bar.2013.06.001

Beattie, V., & Thomson, S. J. (2007). Lifting the lid on the use of content analysis to investigate intellectual capital disclosure. *Accounting Forum, 31*(2), 129–163. https://doi.org/10.1016/j.accfor.2007.02.001

Bellora, L., & Guenther, T. W. (2013). Drivers of innovation capital disclosure in intellectual capital statements: Evidence from Europe. *The British Accounting Review, 45*, 225–270. https://doi.org/10.1016/j.bar.2013.06.002

Bianchi, S., Corvino, S., & Rigolini, D. (2016). Relational capital disclosure, corporate reporting and company performance evidence from Europe. *Journal of Intellectual Capital, 17*(2), 186–217. https://doi.org/10.1108/JIC-07-2015-0065

Bismuth, A., & Tojo, Y. (2008). Creating value from intellectual assets. *Journal of Intellectual Capital, 9*(2), 228–245.

Boesso, G., & Kumar, K. (2007). Drivers of corporate voluntary disclosure: A framework and empirical evidence from Italy and the United States. *Accounting, Auditing and Accountability Journal, 20*(2), 269–296. https://doi.org/10.1108/09513570710741028

Bontis, N. (1998). Intellectual capital: An exploratory study that develops measures and models. *Management Decision, 36*(2), 63–76. https://doi.org/10.1108/00251749810204142

Bontis, N. (2002). Intellectual capital disclosure in Canadian corporations. *Journal of Human Costing and Accounting, 3*(3), 9–20.

Bontis, N. (2003). Intellectual capital disclosure in Canadian corporations. *Journal of Human Resource Costing & Accounting, 7*(1), 9–20. https://doi.org/10.1108/eb029076

Bozzolan, S., Favotto, F., & Ricceri, F. (2003). Italian annual intellectual capital disclosure: An empirical analysis. *Journal of Intellectual Capital, 4*(4), 543–558. https://doi.org/10.1108/14691930310504554

Branswijck, D., & Everaert, P. (2012). Intellectual capital disclosure commitment: Myth or reality? *Journal of Intellectual Capital, 13*(1), 39–56. https://doi.org/10.1108/14691931211196204

Brennan, N. (2001). Reporting intellectual capital in annual reports: Evidence from Ireland. *Accounting, Auditing & Accountability Journal, 14*(4), 423–436. https://doi.org/10.1108/09513570110403443

Brüggen, A., Vergauwen, P., & Dao, M. (2009). Determinants of intellectual capital disclosure: Evidence from Australia. *Management Decision, 47*(2), 233–245. https://doi.org/10.1108/00251740910938894

Bukh, P. N., Larsen, H. T., & Mouritsen, J. (2001). Constructing intellectual capital statements. *Scandinavian Journal of Management, 17*(1), 87–108. https://doi.org/10.1016/S0956-5221(00)00034-8

Bukh, P. N., Nielsen, C. H., Gormsen, P. U., & Mouritsen, J. (2005). Disclosure of intellectual capital indicators in Danish IPO prospectuses. *Accounting Auditing and Accountability Journal, 18*(6), 731–732.

Busco, C., Frigo, M. L., Riccaboni, A., & Quattrone, P. (2013). *Integrated reporting: Concepts and cases that redefine corporate accountability*. Springer.

Campbell, D., Rahman, R. A., & M. (2010). A longitudinal examination of intellectual capital reporting in Marks & Spencer annual reports, 1978–2008. *British Accounting Review, 42*(1), 56–70. https://doi.org/10.1016/j.bar.2009.11.001

Cañibano Calvo, L., García-Ayuso Covarsí, M., & Sánchez Muñoz, P. (2000). Accounting for intangibles: A literature review. *Journal of Accounting Literature, 19*, 102–130.

Cañibano Calvo, L., Sánchez Muñoz, P., García-Ayuso Covarsí, M., & Chaminade Olea, C. (2002). *Meritum: Guidelines for managing and reporting on intangibles*. Fundación Airtel Móvil.

Castelo, M., Delgado, C., Sá, M., & Sousa, C. (2010). An analysis of intellectual capital disclosure by Portuguese companies. *EuroMed Journal of Business, 5*(3), 258–278. https://doi.org/10.1108/14502191011080809

Castilla-Polo, F., & Gallardo-Vázquez, D. (2016). The main topics of research on disclosures of intangible assets. A critical review. *Accounting, Auditing & Accountability Journal, 29*(2), 323–356. https://doi.org/10.1108/AAAJ-11-2014-1864

Castilla-Polo, F., & Ruiz-Rodríguez, C. (2017). Content analysis within intangible assets disclosure. A structured literature review. *Journal of Intellectual Capital, 18*(3), 506–543. https://doi.org/10.1108/JIC-11-2016-0123

Catalfo, P., & Wulf, I. (2016). Intangibles disclosure in management commentary regulation in Germany and Italy: A semantic approach. *Journal of Intellectual Capital, 17*(1), 103–119. https://doi.org/10.1108/JIC-09-2015-0083

Catasús, B., & Gröjer, J. E. (2003). Intangibles and credit decisions—Results from an experiment. *European Accounting Review, 12*(2), 327–357. https://doi.org/10.1080/0963818032000089418

Chau, G. K., & Gray, S. J. (2002). Ownership structure and corporate voluntary disclosure in Hong Kong and Singapore. *The International Journal of Accounting, 37*(2), 247–265. https://doi.org/10.1016/S0020-7063(02)00153-X

Chiucchi, M. S., & Dumay, J. (2015). Unlocking intellectual capital. *Journal of Intellectual Capital, 16*(2), 305–330. https://doi.org/10.1108/JIC-01-2015-0004

Cinquini, L., Passetti, E., Tenucci, A., & Frey, M. (2012). Analyzing intellectual capital information in sustainability reports. Some empirical evidence. *Journal of Intellectual Capital, 13*(4), 531–561. https://doi.org/10.1108/14691931211276124

Cohen, J. A. (2005). *Intangible assets. Valuation and economic benefit*. Wiley Finance.

Cooke, T. E. (1989). Voluntary corporate disclosure by Swedish companies. *Journal of International Financial Management & Accounting, 1*(2), 171–195. https://doi.org/10.1111/j.1467-646X.1989.tb00009.x

Cordazzo, M. (2005). IC statement vs. environmental and social reports: An empirical analysis of their convergences in the Italian context. *Journal of Intellectual Capital, 6*(3), 441–464.

Cuozzo, B., Dumay, J., Palmaccio, M., & Lombardi, R. (2017). Intellectual capital disclosure: A structured literature review. *Journal of Intellectual Capital, 18*(1), 9–28. https://doi.org/10.1108/JIC-10-2016-0104

Curado, C., Henriques, L., & Bontis, N. (2011). Intellectual capital disclosure payback. *Management Decision, 49*(7), 1080–1098. https://doi.org/10.1108/00251741111151154

De Silva, T., Stratford, M., & Clark, M. (2014). Intellectual capital reporting: A longitudinal study of New Zealand companies. *Journal of Intellectual Capital, 15*(1), 157–172. https://doi.org/10.1108/JIC-03-2013-0034

DeAngelo, L. E. (1981). Auditor size and audit quality. *Journal of Accounting and Economics, 3*(3), 183–199.

Del Bello, A. (2006). Intangibles and sustainability in local government reports: An analysis into an uneasy relationship. *Journal of Intellectual Capital, 7*(4), 440–456. https://doi.org/10.1108/14691930610709103

Depoers, F. (2000). A cost benefit study of voluntary disclosure: Some empirical evidence from French listed companies. *European Accounting Review, 9*(2), 245–263. https://doi.org/10.1080/09638180050129891

Dierickx, I., & Cool, K. (1989). Asset stock accumulation and sustainability of competitive advantage. *Management Science, 35*(12), 1504–1511. https://doi.org/10.1287/mnsc.35.12.1504

Dumay, J. (2012). Grand theories as barriers to using IC concepts. *Journal of Intellectual Capital, 3*(1), 4–15. https://doi.org/10.1108/14691931211196187

Dumay, J. (2014). 15 years of the journal of intellectual capital and counting: A manifesto for transformational IC research. *Journal of Intellectual Capital, 15*(1), 2–37. https://doi.org/10.1108/JIC-09-2013-0098

Dumay, J. (2016). A critical reflection on the future of intellectual capital from reporting to disclosure. *Journal of Intellectual Capital, 17*(1), 168–184. https://doi.org/10.1108/JIC-08-2015-0072

Dumay, J., Bernardi, C., Guthrie, J., & Dermatini, P. (2016). Integrated reporting: A structured literature review. *Accounting Forum, 40*(3), 166–185. https://doi.org/10.1016/j.accfor.2016.06.001

Dumay, J., & Cai, L. (2014). A review and critique of content analysis as a methodology for inquiring into IC disclosure. *Journal of Intellectual Capital, 15*(2), 264–290. https://doi.org/10.1108/JIC-01-2014-0010

Dumay, J., & Cai, L. (2015). Using content analysis as a research methodology for investigating intellectual capital disclosure: A critique. *Journal of Intellectual Capital, 16*(1), 1–36. https://doi.org/10.1108/JIC-04-2014-0043

Dumay, J., & Lu, J. (2010). Disclosing improvements in human capital: Comparing results to the rhetoric. *Journal of Human Resource Costing & Accounting, 14*(1), 70–97. https://doi.org/10.1108/14013381011039807

Dumay, J. C., & Tull, J. A. (2007). Intellectual capital disclosure and price-sensitive Australian stock exchange announcements. *Journal of Intellectual Capital, 8*(2), 236–255. https://doi.org/10.1108/14691930710742826

Eccles, R. G., & Krzus, M. P. (2010). *One report: Integrated reporting for a sustainable strategy*. John Wiley & Sons.

Eccles, R. G., Herz, R. H., Keegan, E. M., & Phillips, D. M. (2001). *The value reporting revolution: Moving beyond the earnings game*. John Wiley & Sons.

Eccles, R. G., & Krzus, M. P. (2014). *The integrated reporting movement: Meaning, momentum, motives, and materiality*. John Wiley & Sons.

Eccles, R. G., & Mavrinac, S. C. (1995). Improving the corporate disclosure process. *Sloan Management Review, 36*(4), 11–25.

Edvinsson, D. (2002). *Corporate longitude: What you need to know to navigate the knowledge economy* (p. 8). Financial Times Prentice Hall, Pearson Education, Inc., Upper Saddle River, N.J.

Edvinsson, L., & Malone, M. S. (1997). *Intellectual capital: The proven way to establish your company's real value by measuring its hidden values*. Piatkus.

Elliot, R. K., & Jacobson, P. D. (1994). Cost and benefits of business information disclosure. *Accounting Horizons, 8*(4), 80–96.

EY Climate Change and Sustainability Services (2014). *Integrated reporting tips for organizations on elevating value*. http://www.ey.com/Publication/vwLUAssets/EY-integrated-reporting-tips-for-organizations-onelevating-value/$FILE/EY-integrated-reporting-tips-for-organizations-on-elevating-value.pdf

Faux, J. (2012). Environmental event materiality and decision making. *Managerial Auditing Journal, 27*(3), 284–298. https://doi.org/10.1108/02686901211207500

Ferchichi, J., & Paturel, R. (2013). The effect of intellectual capital disclosure on the value creation: An empirical study using Tunisian annual reports. *International Journal of Accounting and Financial Reporting, 3*(1), 81–107.

Financial Accounting Standards Board (FASB) (2001). *Improving business reporting: Insights into enhancing voluntary disclosures*. Available at www.fasb.org

Firer, S., & Williams, S. M. (2005). Firm ownership structure and intellectual capital disclosures. *Journal of Accounting Research, 19*(1), 1–18. https://doi.org/10.1080/10291954.2005.11435116

Fombrun, C. J. (1996). *Reputation: Realizing value from corporate image.* Harvard Business School Press.

Frias-Aceituno, J. V., Rodriguez-Ariza, L., & Garcia-Sanchez, I. M. (2012). The role of the board in the dissemination of integrated corporate social reporting. *Corporate Social Responsibility and Environmental Management, 20*(4), 219–233. https://doi.org/10.1002/csr.1294

Frias-Aceituno, J. V., Rodriguez-Ariza, L., & Garcia-Sanchez, I. M. (2014). Explanatory factors of integrated sustainability and financial reporting. *Business Strategy and the Environment, 23*(1), 56–72. https://doi.org/10.1002/bse.1765

Gamerschlag, R. (2013). Value relevance of human capital information. *Journal of Intellectual Capital, 14*(2), 325–345. https://doi.org/10.1108/14691931311323913

Gandía, J. L. (2003). Intangibles disclosure information on internet by multinational corporations. *The International Journal of Digital Accounting Research, 3*(5), 61–99.

Gao, S. S., & Zhang, J. J. (2006). Stakeholder engagement, social auditing and corporate sustainability. *Business Process Management Journal, 12*(6), 722–740. https://doi.org/10.1108/14637150610710891

García-Ayuso, M. (2003). Factors explaining the inefficient valuation of intangibles. *Accounting, Auditing & Accountability Journal, 16*(1), 57–69. https://doi.org/10.1108/09513570310464282

García-Meca, E., & Martinez, I. (2007). The use of intellectual capital information in investment decisions. An empirical study using analyst report. *International Journal of Accounting, 42*(1), 57–81. https://doi.org/10.1016/j.intacc.2006.12.003

Gelb, D. S. (2002). Intangible assets and firms' disclosures: An empirical investigation. *Journal of Business Finance & Accounting, 29*(3–4), 457–476. https://doi.org/10.1111/1468-5957.00438

Gerpott, T. J., Thomas, S. E., & Hoffmann, A. P. (2008). Intangible asset disclosure in the telecommunications industry. *Journal of Intellectual Capital, 9*(1), 37–61. https://doi.org/10.1108/14691930810845795

Ghazali, N. A. M., & Weetman, P. (2006). Perpetuating traditional influences: Voluntary disclosure in Malaysia following the economic crisis. *Journal of International Accounting, Auditing and Taxation, 15*(2), 226–248. https://doi.org/10.1016/j.intaccaudtax.2006.08.001

Giustina, S., Alessandro, M., Gianluca, E., & Passiante, G. (2010). Intangible assets in higher education and research: Mission, performance or both.

Journal of Intellectual Capital, 11(2), 140–157. https://doi.org/10.1108/14691931011039651

Goh, P. C., & Lim, K. P. (2004). Disclosing intellectual capital in company annual reports: Evidence from Malaysia. *Journal of Intellectual Capital, 5*(3), 500–510. https://doi.org/10.1108/14691930410550426

Guthrie, J., & Ricceri, F. (2004). *External intellectual capital reporting. Contemporary evidence from Hong Kong and Australia*. Paper presented at IC Congress, Helsinki.

Guthrie, J., & Dumay, J. (2015). Guest editorial: New frontiers in the use of intellectual capital in the public sector. *Journal of Intellectual Capital, 16*(2), 258–266. https://doi.org/10.1108/JIC-02-2015-0017

Guthrie, J., & Petty, R. (2000). Intellectual capital: Australian annual reporting practices. *Journal of Intellectual Capital, 1*(3), 241–251. https://doi.org/10.1108/14691930010350800

Guthrie, J., Petty, R., & Ricceri, F. (2006). The voluntary reporting of intellectual capital: Comparing evidence from Hong Kong and Australia. *Journal of Intellectual Capital, 7*(2), 254–271. https://doi.org/10.1108/14691930610661890

Guthrie, J., Petty, R., Yongvanich, P., & Ricceri, F. (2004). Using content analysis as a research method to inquire into intellectual capital reporting. *Journal of Intellectual Capital, 5*(2), 282–293.

Hampton, R. (2012). Brace yourself: More regulatory changes. Accountancy SA, 22–23.

Haniffa, R. M., & Cooke, T. E. (2002). Culture, corporate governance and disclosure in Malaysian corporations. *Abacus, 38*(3), 317–349. https://doi.org/10.1111/1467-6281.00112

Hazianti, A., & Jaafar, H. (2013). The influence of capital-raising activity on intangible reporting: Evidence from Malaysia. *International Journal of Trade, Economics and Finance, 6*(4), 376–379.

Holmen, J. (2005). Intellectual capital reporting. *Management Accounting Quarterly, 6*(4), 1.

Hossain, M., Perera, M. H. B., & Rahman, A. R. (1995). Voluntary disclosure in the annual reports of New Zealand companies. *Journal of International Financial Management & Accounting, 6*(1), 69–87. https://doi.org/10.1111/j.1467-646X.1995.tb00050.x

Hsu, Y., & Fang, W. (2009). Intellectual capital and new product development performance: The mediating role of organizational learning capability. *Technological Forecasting and Social Change, 76*(5), 664–677. https://doi.org/10.1016/j.techfore.2008.03.012

IIRC Pilot Programme Business Network (2013). Available at https://www.integratedreporting.org/wp-content/uploads/2013/11/IIRC-Pilot-Programme-Business-Network-backgrounder-October-2013.pdf

Itami, R. (1987). *Mobilizing invisible assets.* Harvard University Press Cambridge.

Jarboe, K. P. (2007). *Measuring intangibles. A summary of recent activity, alliance for science and technology research in America.* Washington, DC.

Jensen, J. C., & Berg, N. (2012). Determinants of traditional sustainability reporting versus integrated reporting: An institutionalist approach. *Business Strategy and the Environment, 21*(5), 299–316. https://doi.org/10.1002/bse.740

Johanson, U. (2003). Why are capital market actors ambivalent to information about certain indicators on intellectual capital? *Accounting, Auditing & Accountability Journal, 16*(1), 31–38. https://doi.org/10.1108/09513570310464255

Joshi, M., Singh Ubha, D., & Sidhu, J. (2012). Intellectual capital disclosures by Indian and Australian information technology companies: A comparative analysis. *Journal of Intellectual Capital, 13*(4), 582–598. https://doi.org/10.1108/14691931211276142

Joshi, M., Ubha, D. S., & Sidhu, J. (2011). Intellectual capital disclosure in Indian: A case study of information technology sector. *Global Business Review, 12*(1), 37–49. https://doi.org/10.1177/097215091001200103

Kamath, B. (2008). Intellectual capital disclosure in India: Content analysis of 'TecK' firms. *Journal of Human Resource Costing & Accounting, 12*(3), 213–224. https://doi.org/10.1108/14013380810919859

Kamath, G. B. (2007). The intellectual capital performance of the Indian banking sector. *Journal of Intellectual Capital, 8*(1), 96–123. https://doi.org/10.1108/14691930710715088

Kaplan R., & Norton, D. (1996). Balanced scorecard. Tradurre la strategia in azione. Isedi.

Kateb, I. (2012). An analysis of the determinants of voluntary structural capital disclosure by listed French companies. *International Journal of Financial Management, 7*(11), 95–110.

Kaufmann, L., & Schneider, L. (2004). Intangibles. A synthesis of current research. *Journal of Intellectual Capital, 5*(3), 366–388. https://doi.org/10.1108/14691930410550354

Keong, K. (2008). Intellectual capital: Definitions, categorization and reporting models. *Journal of Intellectual Capital, 9*(4), 609–638.

Kong, E. (2010). Intellectual capital management enablers: A structural equation modeling analysis. *Journal of Business Ethics, 93*(3), 373–391.
Kujansivu, P. (2008). *Intellectual capital management. Understanding why Finnish companies do not apply intellectual capital management models*. PhD dissertation thesis, Tampere University of Technology, Tampere.
Kwee, K. C. (2008). Intellectual capital: Definitions, categorization and reporting models. *Journal of Intellectual Capital, 9*(4), 609–638.
Larrinaga-Gonzalez, C., & Bebbington, J. (2001). Accounting change or institutional appropriation? – A case study of the implementation of environmental accounting. *Critical Perspectives on Accounting, 12*(3), 269–292. https://doi.org/10.1006/cpac.2000.0433
Lerro, A., & Schiuma, G. (2013). Intellectual capital assessment practices: Overview and managerial implications. *Journal of Intellectual Capital, 14*(3), 352–359. https://doi.org/10.1108/JIC-03-2013-0041
Lev, B. (2001). *Intangibles: Management, measurement and reporting*. Brooking Institution Press.
Lev, B., Cañibano, L., & Marr, B. (2005). An accounting perspective on intellectual capital. In B. Marr (Ed.), *Perspectives on intellectual capital* (pp. 42–56). Elsevier Butterworth Heinemann.
Lev, B. (1992). Information disclosure strategy. *California Management Review, 34*(4), 9–32. https://doi.org/10.2307/41166701
Lev, B. (1995). Disclosure and litigation. *California Management Review, 37*(3), 8–28.
Li, J., Pike, R., & Haniffa, R. (2008). Intellectual capital disclosure and corporate governance structure in UK firms. *Accounting Business Research, 38*(2), 137–159. https://doi.org/10.1080/00014788.2008.9663326
Li, S. T., Tsa, M. H., & Lin, C. (2010). Building a taxonomy of a firm's knowledge assets: A perspective of durability and profitability. *Journal of Information Science, 36*(1), 36–56. https://doi.org/10.1177/0165551509347955
Liao, L., Low, M., & Davey, H. (2013). Chinese and English language version: Intellectual capital disclosure. *Journal of Intellectual Capital, 14*(4), 661–686. https://doi.org/10.1108/JIC-03-2013-0030
Lin, C. S., & Huang, C. P. (2011). Measuring competitive advantage with an asset-light valuation model. *African Journal of Business Management, 5*(1), 5100–5108.
Low, M., Samkin, G., & Li, Y. (2015). Voluntary reporting of intellectual capital. *Journal of Intellectual Capital, 16*(4), 779–808.

Mahesh, J., Dharminder, S. U., & Jasvinder, S. (2012). Intellectual capital disclosures by Indian and Australian information technology companies. *Journal of Intellectual Capital, 13*(4), 582–598. https://doi.org/10.1108/14691931211276142

Mahoney, L.s., Thorne, L., Cecil, L., & LaGore, V. (2013). A research note on standalone corporate social responsibility reports: Signaling or greenwashing? *Critical Perspectives on Accounting, 24* (4/5), 350–359. https://doi.org/10.1016/j.cpa.2012.09.008

Mangena, M., Pike, R., & Li, J. (2010). *Intellectual capital disclosure practices and effects on the cost of equity capital: UK evidence*. The Institute of Chartered Accountants of Scotland.

Marshall, A. (1920). *Principles of Economics: An Introductory Volume*. Macmillan.

Martín, G., Delgado, M., López, P., & Navas, J. E. (2011). Towards 'an intellectual capital-based view of the firm': Origins and nature. *Journal of Business Ethics, 98*(4), 649–662.

Mat, N., Hooper, K., & Olesen, K. (2012). Analysis of intellectual capital disclosure: An illustrative example. *Journal of Intellectual Capital, 13*(2), 196–220. https://doi.org/10.1108/14691931211225030

Mathur, V. N., Price, A. D. F., & Austin, S. (2008). Conceptualizing stakeholder engagement in the context of sustainability and its assessment. *Construction Management and Economics, 26*, 601–609. https://doi.org/10.1080/01446190802061233

Meek, G. K., Roberts, C. B., & Gray, S. J. (1995). Factors influencing voluntary annual report disclosures by US, UK and continental European multinational corporations. *Journal of International Business Studies, 26*, 555–572.

Melloni, G. (2015). Intellectual capital disclosure in integrated reporting An impression management analysis. *Journal of Intellectual Capital, 16*(3), 661–680. https://doi.org/10.1108/JIC-11-2014-0121

Meritum. (2002). *Measuring intangibles to understand and improve innovation management*. European Commission, Brussels.

Milne, M. J., & Gray, R. (2013). W(h)ither ecology? The triple bottom line, the Global Reporting Initiative and corporate sustainability reporting. *Journal of Business Ethics, 118*(1), 13–29.

Mio, C. (2013). *Materiality and assurance: building the link. Integrated Reporting* (pp. 79–94). Springer International Publishing.

Nahapiet, J., & Ghosal, S. (1998). Social capital, intellectual capital and the organisational advantage. *Academy of Management Review, 23*(2), 242–266.

Nielsen, C., & Madsen, M. T. (2008). Discourses of transparency in the intellectual capital reporting debate: Moving from generic reporting models to management defined information. *Critical Perspectives on Accounting, 20*(7), 847–854. https://doi.org/10.1016/j.cpa.2008.09.007

Nielsen, C., Rimmel, G., & Yosano, T. (2015). Outperforming markets: IC and the long-term performance of Japanese IPOs. *Accounting Forum, 39*(2), 83–96. https://doi.org/10.1016/j.accfor.2015.04.001

Nurunnabi, M., Hossain, M., & Hossain, M. D. (2011). Intellectual capital reporting in a South Asian country: Evidence from Bangladesh. *Journal of Human Resource Costing and Accounting, 15*(3), 196–223. https://doi.org/10.1108/14013381111178587

Oliveira, L., Rodrigues, L., & Russell, C. (2010). Intellectual capital reporting in sustainability reports. *Journal of Intellectual Capital, 11*(4), 575–594. https://doi.org/10.1108/14691931011085696

Oliveras, E., Gowthorpe, C., Perramon, J., & Kasperskaya, Y. (2004). *Reporting intellectual capital in Spain 2000–2002.* Paper presented at IC Congress, Helsinki.

Oliveras, E., Gowthorpe, C., Kasperskaya, Y., & Perramon, J. (2008). Reporting intellectual capital in Spain. *Corporate Communications: An International Journal, 13*(2), 161–181. https://doi.org/10.1108/13563280810869596

Pedrini, M. (2007). Human capital convergences in intellectual capital and sustainability reports. *Journal of Intellectual Capital, 8*(2), 346–366. https://doi.org/10.1108/14691930710742880

Petty, R., & Cuganesan, S. (2005). Voluntary disclosure of intellectual capital by Hong Kong companies: Examining size, industry and growth effects over time. *Australian Accounting Review, 15*(36), 40–50. https://doi.org/10.1111/j.1835-2561.2005.tb00291.x

Pisano, S., Lepore, L., & Lamboglia, R. (2017). Corporate disclosure of human capital via LinkedIn and ownership structure: An empirical analysis of European companies. *Journal of Intellectual Capital, 18*(1), 102–127. https://doi.org/10.1108/JIC-01-2016-0016

Powell, S. (2003). Accounting for intangible assets: Current requirements, key players and future directions. *European Accounting Review, 12*(4), 797–813. https://doi.org/10.1080/0963818031000162847 3

Prakash, S. (2015). *Report on the scope and quality of CSR reports from the world largest companies.* CSR-Sustainability Monitor Weissman Center for International Business Baruch College, New York, NY.

Qu, W., Ee, M. S., Liu, L., Wise, V., & Carey, P. (2015). Corporate governance and quality of forward- looking information: Evidence from the Chinese stock market. *Asian Review of Accounting, 23*(1), 39–67. https://doi.org/10.1108/ARA-03-2014-0029

Ramanauskakitė, A., & Laginauskaitė, M. R. (2014). Disclosure on intellectual capital in annual reports of Nasdaq OMX Baltic-listed companies. *Ekonomika, 93*(4), 135–156.

Razak, R. A., Mohammad, J., & Tobiagi, S. M. (2016). Intellectual capital disclosures practices and intellectual capital performance in Saudi Arabia Financial Institution. *Journal of Business Studies Quarterly, 7*(4), 1–14.

Roberts, R. W. (1992). Determinants of corporate social responsibility disclosure. *Accounting, Organizations and Society, 17*(6), 595–612. https://doi.org/10.1016/0361-3682(92)90015-K

Roulstone, D. T. (2011). Discussion of intangible investment and the importance of firm-specific factors in the determination of earnings. *Review of Accounting Studies, 16*(3), 574–586.

Santos, J. C., & Venancio, M. T. (2013). Intellectual capital: Information disclosure practices by Portuguese companies. *Revista Universo Contábil, 9*(2), 174–194.

Schaper, S., Nielsen, C., & Roslender, R. (2017). Moving from irrelevant intellectual capital (IC) reporting to value-relevant IC disclosures. *Journal of Intellectual Capital, 18*(1), 81–101.

Schiuma, G., Lerro, A., & Sanitate, D. (2008). Intellectual capital dimensions of Ducati's turnaround—Exploring knowledge assets grounding a change management program. *International Journal of Innovation Management, 12*(2), 161–193.

Schneider, A., & Samkin, G. (2008). Intellectual capital reporting by the New Zealand local government sector. *Journal of Intellectual Capital, 9*(3), 456–486. https://doi.org/10.1108/14691930810892036

Secundo, G., Elena-Perez, S., Martinaitis, Z., & Leitner, K. (2015). An intellectual capital maturity model (ICMM) to improve strategic management in European universities: A dynamic approach. *Journal of Intellectual Capital, 16*(2), 419–442. https://doi.org/10.1108/JIC-06-2014-0072

Shareef, F., & Davey, H. (2006). Accounting for intellectual capital: Evidence from listed English football clubs. *Journal of Applied Accounting Research, 7*(3), 78–116. https://doi.org/10.1108/96754260580001042

Sharma, K., & Kaur, M. (2016). Web based disclosure practices of intangible assets of selected Indian companies-an empirical study. *Imperial Journal of Interdisciplinary Research, 2*(3), 521–528.

Sierra-García, L., Zorio-Grima, A., & García-Benau, M. A. (2015). Stakeholder engagement, corporate social responsibility and integrated reporting: An exploratory study. *Corporate Social Responsibility and Environmental Management, 22*(5), 286–304. https://doi.org/10.1002/csr.1345

Singh, R. D., & Narwal, K. P. (2015). Intellectual capital and its consequences on company performance: A study of Indian sectors. *International Journal of Learning and Intellectual Capital, 12*(3), 300–322. https://doi.org/10.1504/IJLIC.2015.070169

Singh, S., & Kansal, M. (2011). Voluntary disclosures of intellectual capital. *Journal of Intellectual Capital, 12*(2), 301–318. https://doi.org/10.1108/14691931111123430

Skoog, M. (2003). Visualizing value creation through the management control of intangibles. *Journal of Intellectual Capital, 4*(4), 487–504. https://doi.org/10.1108/14691930310504527

Solomon, J. F., Solomon, A., Joseph, N. L., & Norton, S. D. (2013). Impression management, myth creation and fabrication in private social and environmental reporting: Insights from Erving Goffman. *Accounting, Organizations and Society, 38*(3), 195–213. https://doi.org/10.1016/j.aos.2013.01.001

Sonnier, B. M. (2008). Intellectual capital disclosures: High tech versus traditional sector companies. *Journal of Intellectual Capital, 9*(4), 705–722. https://doi.org/10.1108/14691930810913230

Stewart, T. A. (2001). *The wealth of knowledge: Intellectual capital and the twenty-first century organization* (p. 13). Currency Doubleday, New York, N.Y.

Stewart, T. A. (1997). *Intellectual capital: The new wealth of organisations.* Doubleday-Currency.

Striukova, L., Uneman, J., & Guthrie, J. (2008). Corporate reporting of intellectual capital: Evidence from UK companies. *The British Accounting Review, 40*(4), 297–313. https://doi.org/10.1016/j.bar.2008.06.001

Stubbs, W., & Higgins, C. (2014). Integrated reporting and internal mechanisms of change. *Accounting, Auditing & Accountability Journal, 27*(7), 1068–1089. https://doi.org/10.1108/AAAJ-03-2013-1279

Suchman, M. C. (1995). Managing legitimacy: Strategic and institutional approaches. *Academy of Management Review, 20*(3), 571–610. https://doi.org/10.5465/amr.1995.9508080331

Sujan, A., & Abeysekera, I. (2007). Intellectual capital reporting practices of the top Australian firms. *Australian Accounting Review, 17*(24), 62–74. https://doi.org/10.1111/j.1835-2561.2007.tb00445.x

Sveiby, K. (2001). *Methods for measuring intangible assets*. Available at www.sveiby.com/articles/IntangibleMethods.htm

Sveiby, K. (2010). *Methods for measuring intangible assets*. Available at www.sveiby.com/articles/IntangibleMetods.html

Sveiby, K. E. (1997). *The new organisationalwealth: Managing and measuring knowledge based assets*. Berrett-Koehler Publisher.

Teece, D. J. (2000). *Managing intellectual capital: Organizational, strategic, and policy dimensions*. Oxford University Press.

Tracy-Anne, D. S., Stratford, M., & Clark, M. (2014). Intellectual capital reporting: A longitudinal study of New Zealand companies. *Journal of Intellectual Capital, 15*(1), 157–172. https://doi.org/10.1108/JIC-03-2013-0034

Upton, W. S. (2001). *Business and financial reporting, challenges from the new economy, financial accounting series*. Special report, Financial Accounting Series, CT.

Uyar, A., & Kilic, M. (2012). Value relevance of voluntary disclosure: Evidence from Turkish firms. *Journal of Intellectual Capital, 13*(3), 363–376. https://doi.org/10.1108/14691931211248891

Vafei, A., Taylor, D., & Ahmed, K. (2011). The value relevance of intellectual capital disclosures. *Journal of Intellectual Capital, 12*(3), 407–429. https://doi.org/10.1108/14691931111154715

Vamdemaele, S. N., Vergauwen, P. G., & Smith, A. J. (2005). Intellectual capital disclosure in The Netherlands, Sweden and the UK: A longitudinal and corporative study. *Journal of Intellectual Capital, 6*(3), 417–426. https://doi.org/10.1108/14691930510611148

Van der Meer-Kooistra, J., & Zijlstra, S. M. (2001). Reporting on intellectual capital. *Accounting, Auditing & Accountability Journal, 14*(4), 456–476. https://doi.org/10.1108/09513570110403461

Veltri, S., & Silvestri, A. (2015). The free state university integrated reporting: A critical consideration. *Journal of Intellectual Capital, 16*(2), 443–462. https://doi.org/10.1108/JIC-06-2014-0077

Vergauwen, P., & Van Alem, F. (2005). Annual report IC disclosures in the Netherlands, Franceand Germany. *Journal of Intellectual Capital, 6*(1), 89–104. https://doi.org/10.1108/14691930510574681

Vishnu, S., & Gupta, V. K. (2014). Intellectual capital and performance of pharmaceutical firms in India. *Journal of Intellectual Capital, 15*(1), 83–99. https://doi.org/10.1108/JIC-04-2013-0049

Wallman, S. M. H. (1996). The future of accounting and financial reporting. Part II: The colorized approach. *Accounting Horizons, 10*(2), 138–148.

Wang, Q., Sharma, U., & Davey, H. (2016). Intellectual capital disclosure by Chinese and Indian information technology companies: A comparative analysis. *Journal of Intellectual Capital, 17*(3), 507–529. https://doi.org/10.1108/JIC-02-2016-0026

Watson, A. (2011). Financial information in an integrated report: a forward looking approach. Accountancy SA, 14–17.

Whiting, R., & Miller, J. (2008). Voluntary disclosure of intellectual capital in New Zealand annual reports and the hidden value. *Journal of Human Resource Costing and Accounting, 12*(1), 26–50. https://doi.org/10.1108/14013380810872725

Williams, S. M. (2001). Is intellectual capital performance and disclosure practices related? *Journal of Intellectual Capital, 2*(3), 192–203.

Xiao, H. (2008). Corporate reporting of intellectual capital: Evidence from China. *The Business Review, 11*(1), 124–129.

Yi, A., & Davey, H. (2010). Intellectual capital disclosure in Chinese (mainland) companies. *Journal of Intellectual Capital, 11*(3), 326–347. https://doi.org/10.1108/14691931011064572

Zambon, S. (2002, April). Accounting, intangibles and intellectual capital: an overview of the issues and some considerations. First report, University of Ferrara. Available at www.euintangibles.net/conferences/

Zambon, S., & Marzo, G. (2007). Visualising the invisible: Measuring and reporting on intangibles and intellectual capital. In *Visualising intangibles: measuring and reporting in the knowledge economy* (pp. 1–6). Ashgate.

Zéghal, D., & Maaloul, A. (2011). The accounting treatment of intangibles—A critical review of the literature. *Accounting Forum, 35*(4), 262–274. https://doi.org/10.1016/j.accfor.2011.04.003

4

The Assurance of Non-financial Reporting

The chapter deals with the assurance of non-financial reporting and refers exclusively to the external audit process carried out by individual consultants and/or audit firms.

The auditing process includes all those activities that lead the auditor to issue an opinion on the financial or consolidated financial statements.

Recently, this process has undergone an evolution following the introduction of new reporting models for environmental and social information. In fact, given the growing importance of the sustainability issue, it has become appropriate to extend the assurance process to non-financial reports. As for traditional financial statements, the purpose is to increase the reliability and transparency of the information reported.

After a brief introduction on the topic, this chapter will conduct a literature review of the main academic contributions on the assurance of non-financial reporting, with the aim of describing the main issues addressed, highlighting any critical issues and providing ideas for future research.

V. Minutiello, *The Fusion of Accounting and Accountability*,
https://doi.org/10.1007/978-3-031-81385-6_4

4.1 Why Non-financial Reporting Auditing?[1]

Since the 1970s, companies have increased interest in reporting on Corporate Social Responsibility issues (Kolk, 2008). Following this, consumer attention towards sustainability has also gradually increased over the years. This process towards sustainability is not limited only to companies, but extends to all corporate stakeholders (Costa, 2021).

As explained in the previous chapters, this scenario has also led to a revolution in terms of communication by companies, which have found themselves having to account for their environmental and social impacts. They have been pushed to undertake non-financial reporting paths.

Communication has always allowed organizations to establish and maintain their relationships with stakeholders, but, at the same time, it has been able to impact their reputation and image. With specific reference to sustainability, this has meant that reporting is often used solely and opportunistically as a tool to improve a company's reputation.[2] Furthermore, non-financial communication implies a constant commitment to finding results and data on environmental and social performance, to which is added continuous monitoring and adequate representation of the performance. The company must select objectives and key performance indicators (KPIs) and comply with the selected reporting framework[3] (Dienes et al., 2016). It must declare what it is doing, and how and where it wants to arrive at in order to become sustainable (Cobianchi, 2022).

For these reasons, the assurance activity of non-financial reports has become fundamental in certifying with absolute **transparency** the data communicated to third parties. In fact, it constitutes an evaluation method that follows for having precise principles and standards to evaluate the credibility and quality of elements relating to the organization

[1] Throughout the chapter, reference will be made several times to "*non-financial reporting*", as a synonym for "*sustainability report*", "*integrated report*", "*ESG report*" and including, more generally, all those documents intended for the communication of information on not only economic, but also social and environmental performance.

[2] See the aforementioned phenomenon of "*greenwashing*".

[3] For example, GRI Standards vs International Integrated Reporting Framework.

being analyzed and the content within the reports (AccountAbility, 2005).

In this sense, the main tasks of the **auditor** will be to carefully analyze the company processes, in order to check compliance with the procedures adopted and in terms of sustainability, propose suggestions to guarantee the continuous improvement of the company processes (Costa, 2021).

To carry out this activity, there are two main reference standards. The first is the revised **ISAE 3000** ("*Assurance engagements other than audits or reviews of historical financial information*") issued by the IAASB. It deals in detail with the objectives and definitions of an assurance engagement, the ethical principles, the methods of accepting and maintaining the engagement, quality control, professional skepticism and the assurance techniques to be used, the planning and performance of the engagement, the acquisition of evidence and the drafting of the conclusion of the work with the issuing of the report. The second, instead, constitutes the first sustainability assurance standard in the world and is the **AA1000AS (2003)** by AccountAbility. This standard was updated in 2008 and 2020 and includes the following topics: purpose and scope of the standard, the preconditions for accepting an assurance engagement assignment, the methods of conducting the work and issuing the report and the documentation released to the company's management.

In addition to the frameworks used to conduct assurance activities, it is appropriate to identify the main **motivations** that push companies to undertake this path:

- To increase the credibility of reporting;
- To belong to a sector sensitive to ESG issues;
- To use internationally recognized ESG reporting standards;
- To establish the presence of virtuous corporate governance mechanisms, such as a Sustainability Committee and/or a Chief Sustainability Officer (CSO) and/or the presence of expert figures within risk management systems on ESG issues (Venturini, 2023).

However, to date, practice has highlighted some critical issues in the assurance process, consisting of the absence of key findings to reach a conclusion on the reliability of the ESG report, the lack of an adequate stakeholder engagement process in the definition phase of the assurance scope, the presence of managerial capture and/or managerial control in the definition of the reporting areas, the lack of audit by the assurance provider regarding the completeness of the report information, variability in the formulation of the conclusions and a very "*formal*" approach to reporting, which is poorly integrated with financial data and not relevant on a strategic level (Venturini, 2023).

In light of these critical issues, the academic world is mobilizing to propose possible solutions that can improve the assurance process of non-financial reports. Hence the idea of conducting the following literature review, with the aim of illustrating, without claiming to be exhaustive, the main contributions of research on the topic.

4.2 A Review of the Literature

In light of the relevance of the topic, the focus of the following chapter is a review of the academic literature, with the aim of identifying whether and how the topic of assurance of non-financial reports has been addressed in the literature and what may be possible food for thought to improve the current auditing process.

Conducting a literature review involves implementing a structured process aimed at mapping the contributions of different authors within a research area, using specific selection criteria. According to Denyer and Tranfield (2009), a **systematic literature review** "*is a specific methodology that identifies existing studies, selects and evaluates contributions, analyses and summarises data and reports evidence in such a way as to allow reasonable clarity and reach conclusions about what is or is not known*".

4.2.1 Methodology

To conduct the literature review, a series of key steps was followed. First, the research objective was defined, i.e. to provide an overview of the topic of auditing of non-financial reporting, to highlight the presence of any critical issues, and to provide ideas for future research. Subsequently, the database used was selected and the search string was defined based on a series of selected keywords. Similarly, inclusion and exclusion criteria for the analyzed papers were defined. The next step included the evaluation of the selected documents, thanks to which it was possible to identify the most relevant topics and thus proceed with an interpretation of the results. Finally, some reflections for possible future research were developed.

4.2.2 Defining Search Criteria

The selection and extraction process for the papers was carried out through the Scopus database. All the years available in the database up to the time of the research (August 2024) were included in the analysis.

The literature review was carried out using keywords that could cover the research field as completely as possible. The first search was carried out using the following keywords: "*assurance*", "*auditing*", "*audit*" and "*sustainability report**". To further expand the analysis and obtain a more complete picture of the literature, a second search was performed by modifying the previous one: the word "*sustainability report**" was therefore replaced with "*integrated report**".

The selection criteria adopted subsequently were the following:

- Document type: article, literature review;
- Area: Business, Management and Accounting;
- Language: English.

The initial number of papers selected was 500.

Each paper was subjected to a screening of titles and abstracts in order to include only documents relevant to sustainable reporting. Papers that represented a duplication were also removed. Papers that deal with internal auditing of the company and, therefore, not independent, or wherein the topics of integrated reporting, sustainable development goals or environmental impacts had only marginal mentions regarding audit activity were excluded.

Consequently, the final sample included 224 papers (Fig. 4.1).

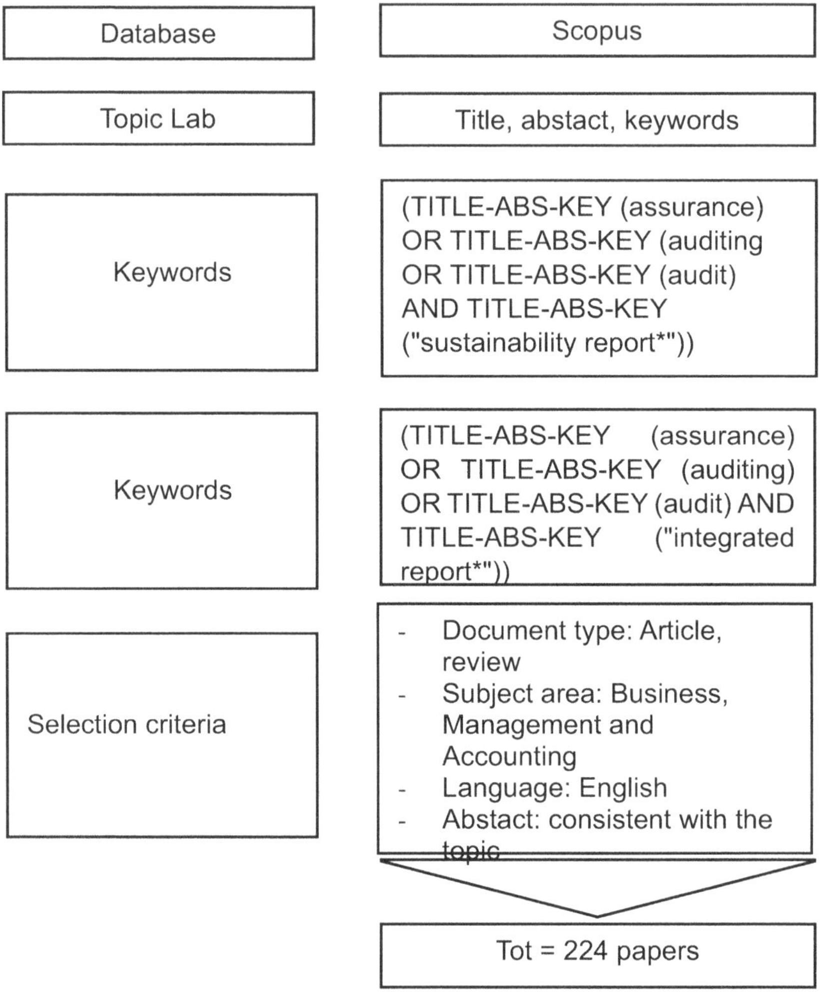

Fig. 4.1 The process of papers selection

4.2.3 Publishing Trends and Analysis by Country

The graph allows us to visualize the growing interest of authors in this field over the last few years (Fig. 4.2).

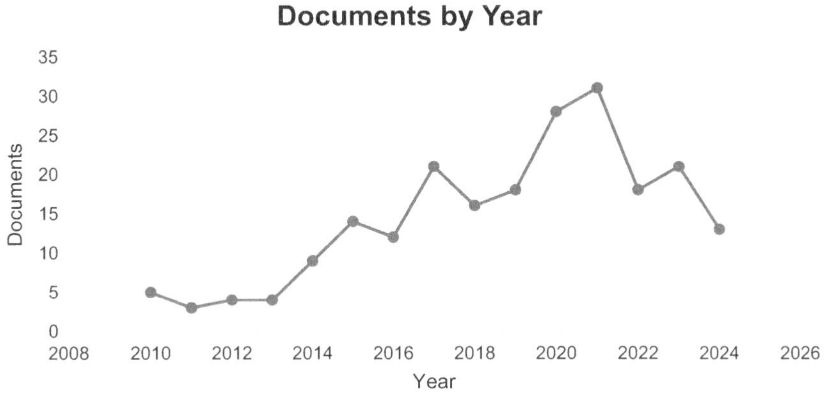

Fig. 4.2 N. of Documents by Year

From 2010 to 2014, it can be noted that there is a limited number of articles, while a significant peak is visible in 2015. The trend continues to grow, especially after 2021, with some dips occurring.

In addition to the interest in the topic, the increase can be justified by two factors: the entry into force of numerous regulatory interventions at the European level that have made non-financial communication mandatory for listed companies, banks and large insurance companies and the publication of the International Integrated Reporting Framework at the end of 2013. Due to these important innovations, the interest of authors in sustainability assurance methodologies increases and, consequently, the papers constantly increase over the years.

The apparent decrease in the current year is explained by the fact that the study was carried out until mid-2024.

If we consider a country analysis, approximately 50% of the studies considers the European scenario. This is justified by the strong regulation in EU countries. The world of audit at the European level was reformed by EU Regulation no. 537/2014 of the European Parliament and of the Council of the European Union of 16 April 2014, through which the law entrusts statutory auditors and audit firms with the task of carrying out statutory audits of the accounts of public-interest entities in order to increase public confidence in their financial statements and consolidated accounts. For this reason, most of the papers examine, for example, scenarios in countries such as Portugal, England (before it left the EU), Italy, Germany, Spain and Belgium.

It should not be underestimated that approximately 30% of the articles analyzes contexts in developing countries, a trend that has grown especially in recent years. The countries in question are: South Africa, Japan, Indonesia, Pakistan and Malaysia. Taking the African context as an example, Erin and Bamigboye (2021) studied that the assessment of sustainable information of African companies, with the exception of South African ones, still presents very low levels. The results of the studies show that voluntary disclosure, lack of commitment by company management, poor application of regulations and cost implications explain the lack of disclosure of sustainability objectives by the selected African companies.

At the same time, about 16% of the papers, instead, takes as a sample companies from different countries in the world, such as from the Fortune Global 250 list.

4.2.4 Most Cited Papers

Table 4.1 lists the articles with the highest number of citations in decreasing order. The first three contributions are discussed below.

The first paper (Kolk & Perego, 2010), with 365 citations, consists of a study that represents the key factors that are associated with the voluntary decision to audit social, environmental and sustainability reports. Firstly, the study provides insights into recent literature on auditing, accounting and sustainability. Secondly, the paper includes an empirical analysis that is carried out on a sample of an international group of 212 Fortune Global 250 companies that published reports in 1999, 2002 and 2005. The focus is on the variables that, according to the country, can hinder or facilitate a company's decision to conduct an assurance of its sustainability report. Some examples of such variables include legal systems and institutional arrangements. The results show that companies operating in more stakeholder-oriented countries are more likely to choose large companies as guarantee providers and to obtain sustainability guarantee

Table 4.1 Top cited papers

Authors	Title	Journal	N. of citations
Kolk, A. and Perego, P.	Determinants of the adoption of sustainability assurance statements: An international investigation	Business Strategy and the Environment	365
O'Dwyer, B. and Owen, D. L.	Assurance statement practice in environmental, social and sustainability reporting: A critical evaluation	British Accounting Review	340
O'Dwyer, B., Owen, D. and Uneman, J.	Seeking legitimacy for new assurance forms: The case of assurance on sustainability reporting	Accounting, Organizations and Society	324
Perego, P. and Kolk, A.	Multinationals' Accountability on Sustainability: The Evolution of Third-party Assurance of Sustainability Reports	Journal of Business Ethics	253
Turker, D. and Altuntas, C.	Sustainable supply chain management in the fast fashion industry: An analysis of corporate reports	European Management Journal	235
Hodge, K., Subramaniam, N., and Stewart, J.	Assurance of sustainability reports: Impact on report users' confidence and perceptions of information credibility	Australian Accounting Review	184
Persic, M., Jankovic, S., and Krivacic, D.	The association between sustainability governance characteristics and the assurance of corporate sustainability reports	Auditing	176
Junior, R. M., Best, P. J., and Cotter, J.	Sustainability Reporting and Assurance: A Historical Analysis on a Worldwide Phenomenon	Journal of Business Ethics	158

(continued)

Table 4.1 (continued)

Authors	Title	Journal	N. of citations
Simnett, R. and Huggins, A. L.	Integrated reporting and assurance: Where can research add value?	Sustainability Accounting, Management and Policy Journal	155
Dienes, D., Sassen, R. and Fischer, J.	What are the drivers of sustainability reporting? A systematic review	Sustainability Accounting, Management and Policy Journal	152

declarations. Furthermore, voluntary demand for sustainability assurance services is significantly influenced by the legal context in which a company operates.

The second paper (O'Dwyer & Owen, 2005) presents a detailed analysis of the assurance statements appearing in environmental, social and sustainability reports selected for the Association of Chartered Certified Accountants (ACCA) UK and European Sustainability Reporting Awards 2002. Based on the GRI guidelines, it is assessed to what extent the current assurance guarantee improves transparency and accountability towards stakeholders. The analysis raises questions about the independence of the audit practice, as well as revealing a high degree of management control over the process. The latter is highlighted by the fact that interested parties are almost absent from the audit processes. It also presents the differences between the work carried out by chartered accountants and that carried out by auditors. The former have a more limited approach and provide a relatively low level of assurance; the latter, on the other hand, adopt a rating system capable of providing a higher level of assurance, and a more comprehensive assessment. The paper concludes with recommendations for future research to explore in more depth the complexities and challenges involved in these assurance processes. In-depth case studies and interviews with assurance providers are recommended to gain their perspectives on the processes they undertake and the pressures they face. In particular, issues such as auditors' appointment process, perceived threats to their independence, their relationship with top management, potential for conflict and their commitment to accountability need to be explored. Given that assurance statements provide limited insights into the nature of the work undertaken, there is a need to also examine auditors' evolving relationships with management, how assurance statements are drafted and approved, auditors' perceptions of their core responsibilities and the added value of the credibility of the reporting process from the perspective of key stakeholder groups.

The third most cited paper (O'Dwyer et al., 2011) is a text written by the same authors as the previous paper. The study provides a more refined concept of legitimacy than has been used in previous assurance and sustainability research. It analyses how the legitimation processes adopted by sustainability auditors in a large professional services firm have influenced their attempts to develop this form of assurance practice. The analysis reveals a complex and interdependent interaction between attempts to secure moral and cognitive legitimacy with three key elements:

- Clients who commission sustainability assurance services;
- Non-client users of assurance statements; and
- The firm's internal risk department that approves the wording of assurance statements.

Developing pragmatic legitimacy with clients depends on establishing moral legitimacy with non-client users of assurance claims, while securing moral legitimacy with non-client users is contingent on gaining pragmatic legitimacy with the firm's internal risk department. Practitioners' legitimacy strategies are underpinned by a commitment to open dialogue within the assurance process, which is evident in their engagement with potential assurance users and their efforts to expand the content of the assurance claim and encourage user influence over what is assured. Future studies are also encouraged to delve deeper into the role that the internal risk department in the Big 4 professional services firms plays in the ongoing need for sustainability assurance.

Table 4.2 Journals with the highest number of publications

Journal	N. of papers
Sustainability Accounting, Management and Policy Journal	18
Corporate Social Responsibility and Environmental Management	15
Journal of Business Ethics	14
Journal of Cleaner Production	13
Business Strategy and the Environment	12
Auditing	6
Social Responsibility Journal	6

In conclusion, it can be said that these three themes have provided very important insights into sustainability auditing, and, for this reason, they have been widely cited in other studies.

4.2.5 Journals Analysis

Table 4.2 shows a list of Journals with the most publications.

As expected, the journals with the highest number of publications in the field of audit and sustainability are those that deal with Corporate social responsibility, environmental, ethics in companies and sustainability reporting.

4.2.6 Content Analysis of Papers

By analyzing the papers in the sample, it is possible to identify the following types of contributions:

- **Systematic Literature Reviews**, which consist of a structured procedure to evaluate all the contributions on a specific thematic area;
- **Systematic Literature Network Analysis (SLNA)**, a new approach to conducting a literature review that combines the Systematic Literature Review (SLR) with the Citation Network Analysis (CNA) and allows for identifying the most relevant contributions in a research field;

- **Theoretical studies**, which aim to improve the understanding of certain topics (such as the regulatory landscape on corporate reporting);
- **Empirical studies**, which can be characterized by the use of quantitative analysis methodologies (e.g., regressions) or qualitative analysis methodologies (case studies, interviews, etc.);
- **Mixed studies**, characterized by a preliminary part of theoretical study and subsequent empirical analysis;
- **Other types of studies** (e.g., market surveys).

In the sample analyzed, approximately 82% of the studies are empirical, while 18% are theoretical. This imbalance is explained by the highly practical nature of the topic covered in this chapter. Furthermore, in recent years the number of organizations that have undertaken sustainable activities has increased, while the auditing process of non-financial reports is a relatively new topic (De Simone et al., 2021). The authors of the contributions highlight the need to improve the guarantees relating to non-financial reports, the definition of international standards and sustainable metrics based on the accuracy, transparency and reliability of the information underlying environmental, social and governance results (Del Giudice & Rigamonti, 2020). Empirical studies allow the authors to validate their results and conclusions and can, therefore, make a greater contribution to improving the auditing process of non-financial reports.

By screening each article and reading the abstracts, it was possible to group some papers into categories based on the topics considered most interesting to explore further.

The first theme concerns the birth of the so-called ***combined assurance*** (CA). Since non-financial reporting practices can be subject to phenomena such as "*greenwashing*", the need to improve the credibility of the content of the reports has arisen (Zhou et al., 2018). From here comes the combined assurance, a model that is introduced in order to obtain an optimized integration between the assurance processes and between the internal and external assurance providers themselves, ensuring that the significant risks to which the company is exposed are adequately addressed. Unlike the single assurance model, the CA aims to address the increasingly complex nature of companies, including the various levels and actors in the sector (risk management, internal controls, quality of relationships, internal audit, etc.) by reducing issues, eliminating unnecessary guarantees for risk reduction at company level and improving the quality of the reports (Donkor et al., 2021). This assurance, in addition to being useful for improving the reliability of the information communicated, is a more effective mechanism in terms of credibility than independent assurance. The studies provide empirical evidence that the implementation and quality of CA communication are beneficial to the information environment by helping to reduce information asymmetry.

The second theme that emerged concerns the importance of having an assurance performed by one of the **Big Four**[4], one of the most discussed topics in the articles in the sample. Martínez-Ferrero and Sánchez (2018) study the reason why an audit by one of the Big Four, therefore by companies with more experience in the sector, has a positive effect on the detection of errors, omissions and false declarations, with the consequent issuance of a negative opinion on the dissemination of information on sustainability. Greater training, a high number of skills and greater experience in providing assurance services increase the propensity to provide more accurate and precise opinions on sustainability reports. The auditor's reputation is, therefore, a determinant in the reliability of the declaration. Mock et al. (2007) conducted bivariate and multivariate analyses to assess the association between the nature of the reports and the characteristics of the auditor. Both multivariate and correlation analyses show that the key factor associated with the level of assurance is the type of auditor. Furthermore, the use of symbols to indicate the nature of the assurance, the assurance of both qualitative and quantitative statements and the provision of recommendations regarding possible improvements to the sustainability report are all variables associated with the type of assurance provider and, therefore, the level of assurance. EU policy promotes the auditing of sustainability reports as a means to improve quality, but does not place restrictions on the choice of auditor. Fernandez-Feijoo et al. (2015) found that large companies are more likely

[4] It refers to the four largest accounting firms (Deloitte, PwC, KPMG, and EY).

to hire a Big 4 firm than small and medium-sized companies. Furthermore, this probability is higher in companies in the financial sector than in those in the primary and consumer goods sectors. In conclusion, characteristics such as size, type of company (public or private) and sector influence both the decision to have sustainability assurance performed and the choice of a Big 4 as auditor. This would be linked to the idea that large companies and those belonging to sectors with greater visibility and interest from stakeholders such as financial services have a greater need to demonstrate that they are socially responsible and legitimize their role in society (consistent with the legitimacy theory).

Another topic concerns the influence of the **role of women on Boards of Directors** (BoD) and the tendency to adopt sustainable development goals. More generally, we investigate how gender diversity in the board of directors influences the adoption of external sustainability reporting guarantees. Several studies have shown that the presence of women on boards of directors positively influences sustainable activities; in fact, the female gender is much more sensitive to ethical and social issues thanks to their greater awareness of environmental risks. Cicchiello et al. (2021) decided to address this topic differently from past studies, focusing on gender diversity in companies in developing countries (African and Asian). The reason for this decision lies in the historical gender inequality that has always characterized these countries, placing obstacles in the way of women's economic development. Increasing the number of women in companies would therefore improve the implementation of governance and sustainability policies in line with those adopted by already-developed economies. Investigating gender diversity in developing countries is very important to provide a broader understanding of the impact that gender diversity on the board has on sustainability reporting practices. Even the presence of a single female board member can make a difference, especially in companies where the male component dominates. Women have different communication and leadership styles compared to their male counterparts: they are more sensitive, empathetic and more socially responsible than men, who are generally more performance-oriented (Bravo, 2019).

Another interesting starting point concerns the articles that deal with the topic of sustainability assurance in **developing countries** such as

South Africa. The sampled companies are selected within the JSE, the largest stock exchange in Africa and the only capital market that requires the practice of integrated reporting (IR). The first phases of the papers involved a content analysis of the integrated reports of, for example, the first forty companies of the JSE and other companies that participated in the IIRC pilot programme ('IIRC Pilot Programme Business Network', 2013). Given the JSE listing requirements, it can be argued that larger companies are more likely to adopt sustainability reporting practices due to their visibility and legitimacy (Richard & Odendaal, 2021). The JSE amended its listing requirements to require listed companies to integrate their sustainability reporting into their annual reports, as investors and other stakeholders insisted on ensuring that corporate practices were transparent, accountable and fair to all stakeholders (Ridley et al., 2011).

The last issue discussed in several articles concerns **stakeholder engagement**. Some papers aim to highlight, first of all, the fact that reporting on sustainability policies, practices and measures, without independent assurance, has a reduced value for stakeholders (Ridley et al., 2011). In others, the role of stakeholders in assurance processes is the main focus of studies. It is investigated why assurance providers often address their statements to managers or CEOs rather than stakeholders, thus attributing to them a residual relevance (Manetti & Toccafondi, 2012). This situation is natural since assurance engagements are conferred by the above-mentioned categories rather than by the wider public composed of stakeholders. International standards should therefore be revised in this respect as they currently leave room for various interpretations. Literature has provided precise indications regarding the need to involve stakeholders more in SR processes, also observing how the quality of the report is strongly linked to the commitment of the interested parties in drafting them. Involving the interested parties in the decision-making processes through mutual dialogue and sharing information brings important benefits to the company thanks to a greater credibility of the reporting and the ability to interact, during the decision-making processes, with the external environment and the internal organizational structure (Gray, 2001). Stakeholder involvement is, therefore, a process that creates a dynamic context of interaction, mutual respect, dialogue and change and not a unilateral management of the stakeholders (Manetti & Toccafondi, 2012).

4.2.7 Keywords Analysis

An analysis that is considered particularly interesting concerns the keywords used in the papers. The aim is to investigate which are the most widespread and how they have evolved over the years. The keywords, in fact, can be considered as an approximation of the content of the paper.

Table 4.3 shows the keywords that are most used to deal with the topic of auditing of non-financial reports in the various papers. The term "*Quality*" refers to the quality of sustainable reports or the quality of the audit activity, while the term "*Non-financial*" is always followed by "*report*" or "*information*".

Keeping the focus on the analysis of keywords, it is also interesting to highlight the presence or absence of certain trends over the years and/or the birth of new keywords.

During the first few years, the most used keywords, which will then be repeated in almost all subsequent years, are "*assurance*", "*sustainability report*", "*stakeholders*", "*transparency*" and "*sustainability*".

In 2011, **neo-institutional** or **legitimacy theories** began to be used as the basis of studies. For example, neo-institutional theory tries to explain how institutional pressures influence environmental reports and

Table 4.3 Keywords analysis

Keywords	N. of repetitions
Sustainability	140
Assurance	135
Sustainability reporting	122
Reporting	109
Audit/auditing	71
Integrated reporting	59
Corporate social responsibility/CSR	54
Theory	25
Quality	20
Non-financial	16

lead to a process of adoption of innovative methods, systems and rules that are similar to each other. In essence, when organizations are subject to external pressures, they tend to undertake those actions considered legitimate by society (Smith et al., 2011).

Since 2012, topics related to the **International Auditing and Assurance Standards Boards**, the **International Standards Principles (ISA)** and the **Global Reporting Initiative (GRI**) have begun to spread. Although there are various guidelines for the preparation of non-financial reports, KPMG (2011) has estimated that approximately 80% of the Global Fortune 250 companies (a list of the 250 most powerful companies globally) follow the Global Reporting Initiative (GRI). For this reason, several papers take as a reference and sample of their studies only companies that follow these guidelines in their sustainability reports. Furthermore, people are starting to talk about the 4 most important companies in the auditing field, the so-called ***Big Four***. Some texts deal with the importance of the sustainable audit carried out by one of the Big Four, who are, in fact, considered to be of higher quality and are perceived as being more authentic and transparent by stakeholders (Mock et al., 2013).

Since 2016, papers have increasingly begun to focus on the study of companies in **emerging markets** and **developing countries**. For example, Yusoff et al. (2016) study the use of environmental auditing as a tool for achieving sustainable development, especially in the context of the public sector. Furthermore, the role of auditing in emerging country is still limited but of fundamental importance as development and productivity must not negatively affect society and the environment. Another topic that is addressed is **gender diversity**. Therefore, we begin to investigate how the presence of women can influence the disclosure of non-financial information. Studies by Gallén and Peraita (2017) demonstrate how countries with a greater propensity towards the female component provide a greater quantity of sustainability reports, even if not of higher quality. On the contrary, Bravo (2019) reveals a positive correlation between gender diversity within the Audit committee and the quality of ESG statements. Their findings strengthen the academic debate on the role of women in sustainability policies.

Analyzing the trend of keywords in recent years, it can be noted that there is a focus on the characteristics of the **Board of Directors**. In fact, there is an increasing presence of keywords such as: BoD characteristics, BoD committee attributes, BoD gender diversity, BoD attributes, etc. The relationship between the characteristics, composition and attributes of the Board of Directors of companies and their tendency to ensure their sustainability reports is starting to be investigated. The study by Aladwey et al. (2021) confirms that some characteristics of the Board of Directors significantly influence a company's decision to submit its CSR reports for assurance. The size of the board, the presence of female members and female executive directors or those with global work experience also contribute positively to this decision. Furthermore, the focus is on the characteristics of auditors and audit activity. In fact, there are key terms such as audit quality, auditor tenure, auditor behavior, auditor ethics, auditor specialization and audit committee characteristics. Some studies show that companies that present CSR reports have a higher quality of audit and audit committee, but also an increase in auditors' mandate and lower dismissal compared to those that do not present CSR reports (Donkor et al., 2021). Finally, it is particularly interesting, given the extreme topicality of the topic, to highlight the keywords related to the topic of climate change such as: "***Climate change disclosure***". Stakeholders are increasingly demanding and requiring companies to publicly disclose the impacts of their business practices on climate change (Dutta & Dutta, 2020). For example, the impact of external assurance on the level of information on climate change in countries such as Finland, where the climate is warming at a very rapid rate, is examined. The results of this study show that companies that have externally certified sustainability reports have superior environmental performance in terms of gas emissions, greenhouse effect and water consumption.

4.2.8 Limitations and Suggestions for Future Research

The analyzed papers present a series of limitations and suggestions for future research, which are set out below.

Regarding the countries studied, most of the papers focus their analysis on a single country (Spain, Italy, UK, Portugal, South Africa). This is a limitation as the results could not be generalized to other countries that do not have the same characteristics. The suggestions for future research, in fact, include extending the analysis sample to a greater number of countries in order to ascertain if generalization is possible, or not.

In terms of time, the papers used a certain time frame. Therefore, it would be interesting to repeat the analyses referring to a longer time frame to rely on a more significant number of observations and to achieve more reliable results.

The databases analyzed are made up of companies that present specific characteristics: for example, the companies within the GRI database that presented their reports in accordance with the GRI standards, large companies of the Global Fortune 500 and listed companies FTSE 350 were taken as a sample. The companies analyzed are generally listed companies whose results could have a limited explanatory capacity for unlisted companies or companies in a specific sector. Future research should consider more heterogeneous samples in order to expand the results to other sectors and consider small and medium-sized companies.

Other limitations are related to the analysis methodology. For example, the studies of the content of assurance statements have been carried out without more-in-dept investigating through interviews, case studies or observations or the use of qualitative approaches that imply the lack of reproducibility and generalizability. In purely theoretical analyses it is impossible to completely eliminate subjectivity. Other suggestions for future studies concern the combination of qualitative and quantitative approaches. Furthermore, some studies conduct interviews focused only on assurance providers, which could be biased, as they tend to promote only the benefits of the assurance practice. Some studies rely only on formalized GRI data, not taking into account companies that use different means of communication (e.g. social media) to inform stakeholders about their sustainability practices.

In terms of topics, further ideas for future studies concern the role of institutional pressures, which could push companies to seek higher levels of reliability and the presence of advantages deriving from more substantial checks.

In conclusion, wanting to provide some development perspectives of the assurance of non-financial reporting, it is believed that in the future the obligation of this activity will be expanded, due to the growing demand from stakeholders, for whom it is no longer sufficient that there only be the reporting of social and environmental performance, but that is also necessary to guarantee the reliability of the information reported. Furthermore, measures and interventions are needed that can improve the quality of the assurance process, also increasing its level. In this sense, it could be helpful to increase the standardization of the process, also thanks to the dissemination of precise principles to guide the activity.

References

AccountAbility (2005). *Assurance standard*. Available at https://www.unimc.it/it/sostenibilita/rilevazione-e-reporting/documenti/bs/08bsaa10002003assurancestandardita.pdf

Aladwey, L., Elgharbawy, A., & Ganna, M. A. (2021). Attributes of corporate boards and assurance of corporate social responsibility reporting: Evidence from the UK. *Corporate Governance: The International Journal of Business in Society, 22*(4), 748–780. https://doi.org/10.1108/CG-02-2021-0066

Bravo, F. (2019). Sustainable development disclosure: Environmental, social, and governance reporting and gender diversity in the audit committee. *Business Strategy and the Environment* [Preprint].

Cicchiello, A. F., et al. (2021). Gender diversity on corporate boards: How Asian and African women contribute on sustainability reporting activity. Gender in Management (pp. 801–820). Available at https://www.researchgate.net/publication/354128497_Gender_diversity_on_corporate_boards_How_Asian_and_African_women_contribute_on_sustainability_reporting_activity

Cobianchi, A. (2022). Comunicare la sostenibilità.

Costa, C. (2021, March 9). Il ruolo dell'Internal Auditor nella sostenibilità delle imprese. ESG360. Available at https://www.esg360.it/normative-e-compliance/il-ruolo-dellinternal-auditor-nella-sostenibilita-delle-imprese/

Del Giudice, A., & Rigamonti, S. (2020). Does audit improve the quality of ESG scores? Evidence from corporate misconduct. *Sustainability, 12*(14), 5670. https://doi.org/10.3390/su12145670

Denyer, D., & Tranfield, D. (2009). *Producing a systematic review*. Available at https://www.cebma.org/wp-content/uploads/Denyer-Tranfield-Producing-a-Systematic-Review.pdf

DeSimone, S., D'Onza, G., & Sarens, G. (2021). Correlates of internal audit function involvement in sustainability audits. *Journal of Management and Governance, 25*(2), 561–591. https://doi.org/10.1007/s10997-020-09511-3

Dienes, D., Sassen, R., & Fischer, J. (2016). What are the drivers of sustainability reporting? A systematic review. *Sustainability Accounting, Management and Policy Journal, 7*(2), 154–189. https://doi.org/10.1108/SAMPJ-08-2014-0050

Donkor, D., Djajadikerta, H. G., & Saiyidi, M. R. (2021). Impacts of combined assurance on integrated, sustainability and financial reporting qualities: Evidence from listed companies in South Africa. *International Journal of Auditing, 25*, 475–507. https://doi.org/10.1111/ijau.12229

Dutta, P., & Dutta, A. (2020). Impact of external assurance on corporate climate change disclosures: New evidence from Finland. *Journal of Applied Accounting Research, 22*(2), 252–285. https://doi.org/10.1108/JAAR-08-2020-0162

Erin, O. A., & Bamigboye, O. A. (2021). Evaluation and analysis of SDG reporting: Evidence from Africa. *Journal of Accounting & Organizational Change, 18*(3), 369–396. https://doi.org/10.1108/JAOC-02-2020-0025

Fernandez-Feijoo, B., Romero, S., & Ruiz Blanco, S. (2015). Multilevel approach to sustainability report assurance decisions. *Australian Accounting Review, 25*, 346–358. https://doi.org/10.1111/auar.12104

Gallén, M. L., & Peraita, C. (2017). The relationship between femininity and sustainability reporting. *Corporate Social Responsibility and Environmental Management, 24*(6), 496–508. https://doi.org/10.1002/csr.1423

Gray, R. (2001). Thirty years of social accounting, reporting and auditing: What (if anything) have we learnt? *Business Ethics: A European Review* [Preprint]. https://doi.org/10.1111/1467-8608.0020

IIRC Pilot Programme Business Network (2013). Available at https://www.integratedreporting.org/wp-content/uploads/2013/11/IIRC-Pilot-Programme-Business-Network-backgrounder-October-2013.pdf

Kolk, A. (2008). Sustainability, accountability and corporate governance: Exploring multinationals' reporting practices'. *Business Strategy and the Environment* (17), 1–15. https://doi.org/10.1002/bse.511

Kolk, A., & Perego, P. (2010). Determinants of the adoption of sustainability assurance statements: An international investigation. *Business Strategy and the Environment*, 182–198. https://doi.org/10.1002/bse.643

KPMG (2011). *International survey of corporate responsibility reporting*. https://www.open.edu/openlearn/pluginfile.php/387300/mod_resource/content/1/T219_1%20Reading%202%20KPMG%2C%202011.pdf
Manetti, G., & Toccafondi, S. (2012). The role of stakeholders in sustainability reporting assurance. *Journal of Business Ethics, 107*(3), 363–377. https://doi.org/10.1007/s10551-011-1044-1
Martínez-Ferrero, J., & Sánchez, I. (2018). The level of sustainability assurance: The effects of brand reputation and industry specialisation of assurance providers. *Journal of Business Ethics, 150*, 971–990. https://doi.org/10.1007/s10551-016-3159-x
Mock, T. J., Rao, S. S., & Srivastava, R. P. (2013). The development of worldwide sustainability reporting assurance: Worldwide Sustainability reporting assurance. *Australian Accounting Review, 23*(4), 280–294. https://doi.org/10.1111/auar.12013
Mock, T. J., Strohm, C., & Swartz, K. M. (2007). An examination of worldwide assured sustainability reporting. *Australian Accounting Review, 17*(41), 67–77. https://doi.org/10.1111/j.1835-2561.2007.tb00455.x
O'Dwyer, B., & Owen, D. L. (2005). Assurance statement practice in environmental, social and sustainability reporting: A critical evaluation. *The British Accounting Review*, 205–229. https://www.journals.elsevier.com/the-british-accounting-review-Assurance-of-sustainability-reports
O'Dwyer, B., Owen, D., & Uneman, J. (2011). *Seeking legitimacy for new assurance forms: The case of assurance on sustainability reporting*. Rochester, NY. https://papers.ssrn.com/abstract=1742822
Richard, G., & Odendaal, E. (2021). Credibility-enhancing mechanisms, other than external assurance, in integrated reporting. *Journal of Management and Governance, 25*, 61–93. https://doi.org/10.1007/s10997-020-09509-x
Ridley, J., D'Silva, K., & Szombathelyi, M. (2011). Sustainability assurance and internal auditing in emerging markets. *Corporate Governance: The International Journal of Business in Society, 11*(4), 475–488. Edited by G. Lenssen, Y. Blagov, and D. Bevan. https://doi.org/10.1108/14720701111159299
Smith, J., Haniffa, R., & Fairbrass, J. (2011). A conceptual framework for investigating "Capture" in corporate sustainability reporting assurance. *Journal of Business Ethics, 99*(3), 425–439. https://doi.org/10.1007/s10551-010-0661-4
Venturini, G. (2023). Prospettive future in tema di assurance dei report non finanziari: Il mondo dell'audit e i modelli di rendicontazione non finanziaria. In P. Tettamanzi & V. Minutiello (Eds.), *ESG: Bilancio di Sostenibilità e Integrated Reporting* (pp. 213–237). Ipsoa Wolters Kluwer.

Yusoff, Hadi, & Ahmad (2016). Sustainable development: What is the role of audit? *Journal of Sustainability Science and Management, 11*, 99–112. https://www.researchgate.net/publication/313720127_Sustainable_development_What_is_the_role_of_audit

Zhou, S., Simnett, R., & Hoang, H. (2018). Evaluating combined assurance as a new credibility enhancement technique. *AUDITING: A Journal of Practice & Theory, 38*(2), 235–259. https://doi.org/10.2308/ajpt-52175

5

Case Studies on the Adoption of Non-financial Reporting

This chapter reports three different case studies on the adoption of Sustainability or Integrated Reporting. The aim is to provide a practical point of view on the topic that has previously been treated only theoretically.

From a methodological point of view, the drafting of the case studies is based on a triangulation of data, which starts from the conduct of interviews and is integrated with the reading of the main documents drawn up by the companies regarding non-financial performance.

What emerges is the importance of establishing a strategy upstream that includes environmental and social sustainability objectives, with precise targets and a well-defined time horizon to achieve them. Thanks to the comparison it is possible to appreciate the diversity of approaches implemented, as well as the presence of alternative reporting solutions.

The element that remains common is the objective: to provide a truthful representation of the process of creating corporate value and the impacts (positive and/or negative) of the business on the economic-financial, social and environmental spheres. It is the author's opinion that the companies reported represent three virtuous examples of sustainable business development.

V. Minutiello, *The Fusion of Accounting and Accountability*,
https://doi.org/10.1007/978-3-031-81385-6_5

5.1 Despar Nord Aspiag Service S.R.L.

5.1.1 The Trend of the Modern Retail Trade

During 2023, retail sales grew by 2.8%, slowing down compared to + 4.6% in 2022. The main cause of this slowdown was due to inflation and its peak of 7.6% in March 2023, leading to an erosion of consumer purchasing power. The trends relating to the growth of e-commerce (increasing by 13%) and the affirmation of discounters (+5.5%) are confirmed.

Recently, great attention has also been paid to the issue of sustainability in this sector and consumers are increasingly making purchasing decisions based on the environmental impact their choices create. For manufacturers, this means figuring out how to establish a more sustainable development model, one that integrates economic, social and environmental dimensions and that is capable of seizing on the new business opportunities that are now emerging.

5.1.2 The Company History, Mission and Vision

Despar Nord (Aspiag Service S.r.l). is the concessionaire of the Despar brand in Triveneto, Emilia-Romagna and Lombardy, operating in the Modern Organized Distribution[1] sector and dealing in the wholesale and retail sale of food and non-food products, done through a large network of retail stores and shopping centers.

Aspiag Service is guided by four reference values that were identified together with management and shared with collaborators: **participation**, **inclusion**, **competence**, **proximity**.

[1] By company operating in the Modern Organized Distribution sector we mean a reality of modern food trade and not operating with the formulas of large-scale distribution, organized/associated distribution, chain stores, franchising, wholesale, cash and carry and online shopping, which carries out its business through shopping centers and self-service shops.

> Our task is to provide quality service to the customer through the management of our stores. The customer is our main interlocutor, and thanks to them we manage to create value.
> In this sense, **sustainability in recent years has become an opportunity**: the customer no longer pays attention only to quality, but also to the inclusion of sustainability elements within the products. We as a Company have for several years already invested in some of private label products lines that function as our main business card, showing the customers who frequent our stores who we are as a company. In some of these lines we have included sustainability elements, such as environmentally sustainable packaging due to the fact that is made from recycled materials or it pays greater attention to the selection of raw materials.

The story of the Despar brand started in 1932 in the Netherlands, the year Adriaan van Well founded SPAR International, a company that resulted from the union of traders and wholesalers and which still manages the brand internationally today. The original name "*Despar*" was an acronym for the Dutch phrase "*everyone benefits equally from harmonious cooperation*". From there comes the abbreviation "*Spar*", "*fir*" in Dutch.

The 60s were marked by the expansion of the brand in the Italian market: in 1962, after years of affiliation with local companies, Spar Centrale Italiana was born and later became the Despar Italia Consortium in 1968, which still manages the brand in Italy. Since then, Aspiag Service has had the concession for the corresponding territory.

In 1954, the first SPAR organization was born in Austria and in 1970 it became the current SPAR Austria, which founded Aspiag Service in 1989, following the takeover of branded companies from the Triveneto region, the latter becoming the current Regional Offices of Bolzano, Mestrino and Udine.

In the 1990s, expansions and acquisitions continued for Aspiag Service both nationally and internationally. Subsequently, the Company obtained two important certifications: OHSAS 18,001 in 2010 and ISO 14001 in 2013.

The health emergency of recent years and other external challenges, such as conflicts and climate change, have not blocked the development and innovation processes that had previously been undertaken. However, these events have brought on new challenges.

In 2023, Aspiag Service, with its 9285 collaborators, opened new retail stores, two of which are directly managed and 7 are franchisees. All of this growth is due also to the introduction of new processes in sales and purchasing, the construction of soon-to-be-opened stores, the renovations of existing retail stores, different management of logistics and the development of private label and local products. Furthermore, in 2023 the Company celebrated the tenth anniversary of its ISO 14001 environmental certification, confirming its commitment to sustainability.

The Company's retail stores (managed directly or in franchising) are located in the Veneto, Lombardy, Emilia-Romagna, Friuli-Venezia Giulia and Trentino-Alto Adige regions and are structured with three different brands (Despar, Eurospar and Interspar), depending on the size and product offering: the Despar format identifies small neighborhood supermarkets aimed at daily shopping; Eurospar identifies medium-sized sales points for weekly or fortnightly shopping; and Interspar is aimed at larger sales points with a wide range of services and products, including non-food items (e.g., electronics, household appliances and gardening). To date, there are 250 direct retail stores and 304 franchisees.

5.1.3 Integrated Reporting

Starting in 2011, Aspiag Service decided to equip itself with the **Integrated Reporting (IR)** tool to illustrate the process of creating value in the short, medium and long term for its stakeholders. Thanks to the report, it can evaluate and monitor the resources used and results attained, as well as ensure coordination of all internal units and the retrieval of useful information for an effective decision-making process. The Chief Financial Officer (CFO) led the process of preparing the report until 2020. In 2021, the drafting of the document was entrusted to the Public Relations department, supported by management control for data processing. Since October 2023, it has been managed by the ESG-Safety function.

For more than ten years we have been giving an account of what we do with IR. Previously we had activities managed by some Company functions, such as sponsorships or nutrition education programs with primary schools to create awareness on these issues. Then we undertook more important and structured projects for the Company: OHSAS 18,001 which concerns safety at work, Organizational Model 231/01[2] and the law on biodegradable shopping bags at the checkout (to be ready, we began preparing for the law a year before it came into effect). Over time, a **culture of sustainability** has gradually been created, project after project, allowing us to improve over time and work within the Company to create synergies and capture elements of sustainability in the work of each collaborator, both in the stores and in offices.
Thanks to IR we are able to be transparent about all these elements.
We have created a working group within the Company that collaborates with the various Company functions on specific projects. This spirit of collaboration has allowed us to create a culture and sharing that facilitates the Company's path toward sustainability. For us, sustainability also means guaranteeing the commercial success of the Company, since without this it is not possible to pursue environmental and social needs within and beyond our reality. In all these years we have always managed to be a growing company and to have a set of resources available to use for our environmental and social projects.

In terms of reporting, the Company was among the pioneers in the adoption of Integrated Reporting. The report brought with it a series of projects: in 2013 it was the first company in the sector to be certified according to the ISO 14001 standard; in 2014, its report was already essentially in line with the contents of the European Directive on Non-Financial Declarations (NFS).[3]

Our desire right from the start was to adopt IR because even if we already had a financial statement and a management report complete with all the necessary information, we wanted to increase transparency for the

[2] It concerns a set of protocols that regulate the company structure and the management of sensitive processes, thus reducing the risk of criminal offenses.

[3] This is EU Directive 2014/95, which introduces new minimum reporting standards on environmental and social matters for companies that exceed certain size limits. This Directive was implemented in Italy with Legislative Decree No. 254/2016.

market. When we saw the <IR> Framework of IIRC, it seemed to us to propose a reporting structure that was not easy, but in line with our needs: to show all the extras that our Company produces compared to its competitors and which derives from a series of capitals that we can bring back to the six of the Framework.[4] We needed a report that was completely aligned with our financial statements and the Company's costs and revenues, while at the same time bringing out all the non-financial aspects of our business. This also meant showing in some cases that the themes do not balance each other. With the financial statements we are used to having a perfect balance between all items, whereas in this case it does not occur: we can have positive externalities on one topic and negative externalities on another. Showing all these trade-offs is important for us and with the integrated report we can provide a disclosure on this.

To Develop the Report, the Company Follows the Following Phases:

1. Determining the Material Topics and Performance Indicators;
2. Assessment of the need to update the metrics;
3. Involvement of data owners within the Company;
4. Creation of a graphic structure to make the report more accessible;
5. Preparation of the draft document;
6. Certification through an external audit firm;
7. Publication and communication.

The structure of the Integrated Report follows that envisaged by the International Integrated Reporting Framework of the IIRC (currently part of the International Sustainability Standards Board) and reports a series of sustainability indicators consistent with the **GRI Standards**. In addition to the IIRC Framework, in fact, the whole topic of the GRI guidelines also emerges, since to date they represent the only certified metrics. However, these metrics are constantly evolving and this requires a process of constantly updating the reporting. Finally, a further point of reference is represented by the UN Agenda and the Sustainable Development Goals.

[4] These are the following capitals: financial capital, productive capital, intellectual capital, human capital, social and relational capital, and natural capital.

The document opens with the President's letter to the stakeholders and with some useful information to guide reading and continues with a division into three sections:

- "***About us***": this part is dedicated to the operational context and reports the history of the Company;
- "***What we do***": the description of the Company's business model and ESG strategy is envisaged, with particular attention paid to the description of the activities undertaken to actively involve its stakeholders and to the defining of the material topics. Furthermore, ample space is left in the part dedicated to the ESG strategy to the discussion of the commitments pursued towards sustainable development;
- "***What we have done***": this section is dedicated to the presentation of the performances achieved from an environmental, social and governance point of view. In fact, the data relating to each of the pillars of the pursued ESG strategy are reported.

The **graphics** are seen by the Company as an innovative element that allows the stakeholder to read the document more easily.

> Reading pages and pages of reports is not easy for the stakeholder, who perhaps would like a summary. The danger is that all the work done risks being an end in itself. This is why we developed the graphics part. Furthermore, it is also a necessity for us because thanks to the graphics we can be more incisive. By graphics we mean infographics relating to data, but not only that: sometimes we also refer to concepts. For example, in the years 2018–2020, we decided to make the Balance Sheet, the Income Statement and the Cash Flow Statement graphic with a visual metaphor. Making the balance sheet more appealing allows the reader of the report to understand it better and in a new way. We also did the same for some non-financial metrics, such as the packages handled by logistics.

The integrated report evolves continuously with the aim of preparing an "*integral*" report, i.e. integrated in its entirety with around a hundred pages. Furthermore, the document is also made accessible in a more concise version that is easily distributed to stakeholders.

Producing an integrated report was not an easy process, especially because being among the first there were no examples to follow. In 2011 (the first year of the report's adoption) the IIRC Framework itself was still in draft form.

Despite this, the Company decided to welcome the challenge. Certainly, there have been several improvements over time.

Since its second edition, the document has been **certified** by an auditing firm, which is the same of the financial statements. Over the years it has received some awards, confirming the quality achieved by reporting in the Italian and European panorama (in 2016, 1st place in the Financial Statement Oscar organized by FERPI, as "*Best Integrated Report*" and 1st place in the Integrated Thinking Award awarded from the MEDEF in Paris).

The Links Between Sustainability and Corporate Strategy

Aspiag Service's strategy is to all intents and purposes an ESG strategy, aligned with the sustainable development objectives of the UN 2030 Agenda. For the Company, in fact, the strategy is inextricably linked to sustainability, understood in its broadest sense (not only environmental, but also social and governance) and transversal to all Company levels. In particular, Aspiag Service has identified 7 **Sustainable Development Goals (SDGs)** most connected to its business and reference target:

- 3 Good Health and Wellbeing;
- 7 Affordable and clean energy;
- 8 Decent Work and Economic Growth;
- 10 Reduce inequalities;
- 11 Sustainable Cities and Communities;
- 12 Responsible Consumption and Production;
- 13 Climate action.

For this reason, there are many initiatives undertaken in the field of sustainability, relating, for example, to product innovation, the social sphere and environmental issues. The resulting performances are the result of a business culture built over time which allows for generating value through the creation of income, work and saving resources, to produce an increasingly stronger integration between sustainability and economic performance.

Along the entire supply chain, it seeks to develop synergies and establish a strong professional relationship, contain costs and reduce impacts, while at the same time guaranteeing its customers adequate prices and product quality. Furthermore, the Company has developed a **checklist** to monitor and promote the environmental sustainability of its private label suppliers.

One of the fundamental elements of the Company's strategy is attention to **innovation** and development, as it represents one of the greatest competitive advantages. This aspect is enhanced thanks to the contribution of collaborators and external subjects (such as entrepreneurs, Public Administration, local authorities and others) and is implemented within a **Development Plan**, which summarizes a series of parameters for the study of the reference territory and any possible expansions.

The Company conducts an analysis of its stores to identify margins for improvement and renovation, expansion or relocation interventions. Innovation also passes through the **architectural recovery** of historic premises in city centers and places of historical-cultural interest; these interventions allow for the valorization of the reference context and the redevelopment of urban areas or former industrial areas. Some examples of architectural recoveries that have taken place over the years are those relating to the restoration and enhancement of the ancient walls in the retail store of Cremona, or the certified class A retail store by CasaClima in Silandro (BZ) or the recovery of the Art Nouveau building of the Teatro Italia (VE).

Customer involvement occurs not only with means of communication, but also thanks to the promotion of online and in-person events and courses, which give space to local producers and local excellence. A specific app has been created for customers—App Despar Tribù—which through games allows users to get discounts and receive information on local products, initiatives and events related to, among other things, sustainability.

The sustainable strategy influences the product offering. Customers, in fact, increasingly base their consumption choices on sustainability and seek out products that are conscious of attaining low environmental impact, recycling, reuse and that show clarity of production methods and provenance.

A further element of attention concerns the **awareness of staff** with ad hoc information and training interventions. During 2023, the entire recruiting procedure was formalized in a manual, thus ensuring standardization of the selection methods, making it more objective. Furthermore, the Company also actively participates in Career Days at universities, establishing a preferential channel of contact with young undergraduates and graduates.

Regarding products, in 2023 the Company committed to the development of **S-Budget products** to expand the range of first-price products. This is a line intended for customers who are attentive to savings, but who do not want to sacrifice quality, guaranteed by strict controls on the supply chain. In the non-food sector, the launch of **Econvivo** and **Verde Vera** private label products (eco-sustainable lines for home cleansing and cosmetics) continued. Both lines dedicate part of their turnover to **reforestation projects in the area**. Furthermore, the Verde Vera cosmetics line features environmentally sustainable packaging (thanks to the use of 100% recycled plastic and sugar cane labels).

Furthermore, the entire sales process, in addition to providing a quality offer, aims to propose an innovative, welcoming and sustainable retail store for the customer, thanks to many endeavors:

- The introduction of **electronic labels** to replace paper ones (currently present in two stores);
- The activation of **"*anti-waste*" coupons**, thanks to which it is possible for the customer to purchase soon-to-expire products at an affordable price;
- **Lean transformation**, i.e., the extension of this methodology to some retail stores, improving their efficiency.

From an environmental point of view, in addition to the aforementioned ISO 14001 certification, a **Company Mobility Manager** was appointed in 2022 with the aim of promoting the reduction of environmental pollution caused by employees with the use of their own vehicles in daily travel.

In terms of energy consumption, the Company is committed to greener solutions for the development of the network: the retail stores are in **energy class A3 and A4** and use **Full LED light sources** and **cool roof** systems, which, thanks to solar energy, reduces the annual energy requirement necessary for cooling the shop by 33% and increases the efficiency of the solar panels on the roof by up to 20%. Furthermore, the installation of **solar panels systems** and **high-efficiency heat pumps** is planned for the new stores and renovations.

> For some years now, we have had an important focus on **products**, especially in terms of environmental issues. For example, with some suppliers we have developed private label products and a checklist which is nothing more than a questionnaire in which we try to understand how sensitive our suppliers are to environmental issues. The objective is to create synergies and promote a common strategy. Our Company is ISO 14001 certified. Maintaining this focus allows us to better address future environmental impacts. Talking about these issues with suppliers is easier for us if they also speak the same language.
>
> Another strategy is to intervene in the sales network with **renovations or the opening of new retail stores**. With these investments, we try to increase our environmental sustainability with class A3 or A4 buildings, which is no small feat for a retail store. We are also very committed to architectural recovery: we try to be present in city centers and historic places to safeguard the artistic heritage and industrial memory.
>
> Our strategy also involves the **social aspect** of sustainability, as we develop projects for our collaborators, such as welfare plans or the Company's supplementary contract.
>
> Finally, for more than ten years, we have been communicating our commitment through the drafting of an **integrated report**. For us, it is not just an exercise, but a tool to get to know and improve ourselves and improve ourselves over time. We are aligned with the UN agenda and have identified some SDGs which our Company can work on more decisively. In 2020 we also received a **positive loan**, a financing line with sustainability elements, which recognized our commitment over time, but which allowed us to follow up these contributions with new action plans.

> We have identified the priority Sustainable Development Goals (SDGs) and we have based our strategy, our capital, our Key Performance Indicators (KPIs) and our system for monitoring results and impacts on these themes.

One of the main reasons for adopting a sustainable strategy is for the **improvement of the Company's image and reputation**, but also to increase the **satisfaction of its customers**, who are the main interlocutor for the creation of value. The integrated report, in fact, allows the Company to be more transparent, thereby increasing customer satisfaction. Collaborators also demonstrate greater satisfaction, thanks to the welfare projects that concern them. In general, therefore, the sense of belonging grows, as well as the Company's competitive advantage. The **relationship with the stakeholders**, who are involved in the selection process of the material topics and the identification of corporate risks, improves. Thanks to this strategy, economic results and financial performance also improve, and this in turn generates a virtuous circle as it produces new resources that can be invested to favor the environment and society.

> Ten years ago, talking about sustainability was not easy: it was perceived of as an extra compared to the operations that each Company's management and collaborators pursued within the Company. To date, the path is clear and it is much easier to talk about these issues within the Company. Creating a culture towards sustainability is not an easy aspect and we must continue to work on it every day, since it is not a static theme, but one that is constantly evolving.

From an internal perspective, therefore, reporting improves **synergy** and **collaboration** between the different Company's functions, thanks to common objectives to work on together. This has allowed to create a culture that stimulates to move forward towards new projects and not rest on the objectives already achieved. From an external perspective, stakeholders such as banking institutions, suppliers, the end customer and the community are very attentive to the publication of the report and request it, demonstrating that they understand the value and relevance of the communication.

> We care a lot about reporting precisely because we have made a significant effort to align it with financial reporting, in structure and content. We want to give a clear and transparent vision of the value that the Company generates and the different facets that this value takes on, given that we distribute 90% of it to our stakeholders. For this reason, even if it was not an obligation, as a company we set out to demonstrate how solid and transparent we are towards the market, and above all that the report is not an end in itself and is not used to seek financial justification, since this aspect can be found in the financial statements.

To conclude, Aspiag Service's ESG strategy finds concreteness within what is defined as the **Sustainability Manifesto**, with ten promises for a just, inclusive and sustainable future, with the aims to:

1. Care for the planet;
2. Believe in people;
3. Guarantee the quality and sustainability of products;
4. Give value to the community;
5. Promote and ensure health and well-being;
6. Choose to be transparent;
7. Support local producers;
8. Have confidence in local entrepreneurship;
9. Invest in the territory;
10. Fight food waste and promote a culture of recovery.

The Involvement of Stakeholders and the Development of the Materiality Analysis

Relationships with stakeholders are a fundamental strong point for Aspiag Service as they guarantee better satisfaction. Thanks to its support from the experts and dialogue with the various stakeholders, it is possible to determine the material topics that impact how business is conducted.

The **stakeholder engagement** process is delegated to specific individual company functions. Each function manages relationships with its stakeholders because it knows them best and, therefore, has the right tools. For example, the HR Department interfaces with trade unions, while the Public Relations Department with public institutions.

Although the stakeholders are many and varied, the Company has never defined a scale of priorities, but considers them as a whole.

> We make an effort to give priority rather than just scores. What we do is continuous involvement, each functions according to its own needs, and, on the occasion of more complex projects such as the definition of the materiality matrix, we have had the support of focus groups. We don't organize complex roadshows, but we have still achieved some interesting results.

The interaction with stakeholders therefore leads to the selection of a series of material topics and the main impacts (actual or potential, positive or negative) of the Company on the economy, environment and people. This process is characterized by the following phases:

- **Understanding the context** of the organization by determining the business model, a description of the ESG context and identification of which stakeholders are influenced by the Company activity;
- **Identification of impacts** by sector, products and geographical areas;
- **Assessment of the extent of the impacts** in order to define priorities for the Company;
- **Prioritization of the most important impacts** to define a list of material topics that will be subject to reporting (Fig. 5.1).

The Value Creation Process and the ESG Performance Indicators

Following the guidelines of the <IR> Framework, Aspiag Service shows in the report its value creation process using the six different types of capital: **financial** (given by the liquidity available for its business), **material and infrastructural** (owned or leased properties, retail stores, administrative offices, logistic platforms, machinery, equipment and stocks of marketed products), **organizational** (processes, management procedures and activities aimed at guaranteeing the quality and safety

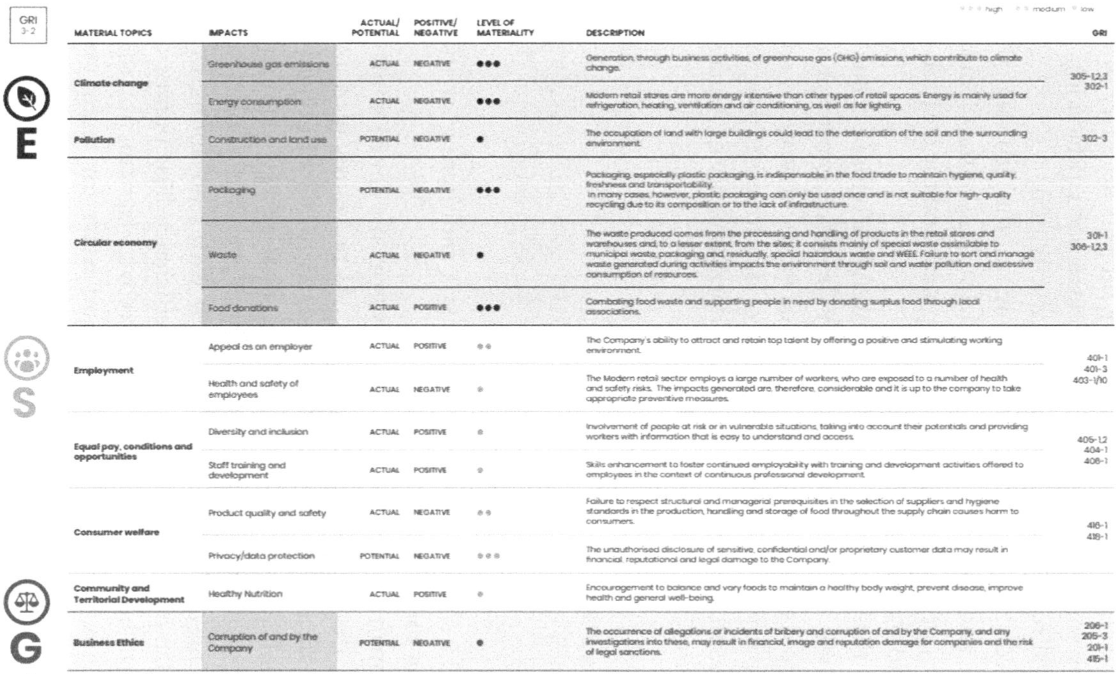

GRI 3-2

●●● high ●● medium ● low

MATERIAL TOPICS	IMPACTS	ACTUAL/ POTENTIAL	POSITIVE/ NEGATIVE	LEVEL OF MATERIALITY	DESCRIPTION	GRI
E						
Climate change	Greenhouse gas emissions	ACTUAL	NEGATIVE	●●●	Generation, through business activities, of greenhouse gas (GHG) emissions, which contribute to climate change.	305-1,2,3 302-1
	Energy consumption	ACTUAL	NEGATIVE	●●●	Modern retail stores are more energy intensive than other types of retail spaces. Energy is mainly used for refrigeration, heating, ventilation and air conditioning, as well as for lighting.	
Pollution	Construction and land use	POTENTIAL	NEGATIVE	●	The occupation of land with large buildings could lead to the deterioration of the soil and the surrounding environment.	302-3
Circular economy	Packaging	POTENTIAL	NEGATIVE	●●●	Packaging, especially plastic packaging, is indispensable in the food trade to maintain hygiene, quality, freshness and transportability. In many cases, however, plastic packaging can only be used once and is not suitable for high-quality recycling due to its composition or to the lack of infrastructure.	301-1 306-1,2,3
	Waste	ACTUAL	NEGATIVE	●	The waste produced comes from the processing and handling of products in the retail stores and warehouses and, to a lesser extent, from the sites; it consists mainly of special waste assimilable to municipal waste, packaging and, residually, special hazardous waste and WEEE. Failure to sort and manage waste generated during activities impacts the environment through soil and water pollution and excessive consumption of resources.	
	Food donations	ACTUAL	POSITIVE	●●●	Combating food waste and supporting people in need by donating surplus food through local associations.	
S						
Employment	Appeal as an employer	ACTUAL	POSITIVE	●●	The Company's ability to attract and retain top talent by offering a positive and stimulating working environment.	401-1 401-3 403-1/10
	Health and safety of employees	ACTUAL	NEGATIVE	●	The Modern retail sector employs a large number of workers, who are exposed to a number of health and safety risks. The impacts generated are, therefore, considerable and it is up to the company to take appropriate preventive measures.	
Equal pay, conditions and opportunities	Diversity and inclusion	ACTUAL	POSITIVE	●	Involvement of people at risk or in vulnerable situations, taking into account their potentials and providing workers with information that is easy to understand and access.	405-1,2 404-1 406-1
	Staff training and development	ACTUAL	POSITIVE	●	Skills enhancement to foster continued employability with training and development activities offered to employees in the context of continuous professional development.	
Consumer welfare	Product quality and safety	ACTUAL	NEGATIVE	●●	Failure to respect structural and managerial prerequisites in the selection of suppliers and hygiene standards in the production, handling and storage of food throughout the supply chain causes harm to consumers.	416-1 418-1
	Privacy/data protection	POTENTIAL	NEGATIVE	●●●	The unauthorised disclosure of sensitive, confidential and/or proprietary customer data may result in financial, reputational and legal damage to the Company.	
Community and Territorial Development	Healthy Nutrition	ACTUAL	POSITIVE	●	Encouragement to balance and vary foods to maintain a healthy body weight, prevent disease, improve health and general well-being.	
G						
Business Ethics	Corruption of and by the Company	POTENTIAL	NEGATIVE	●	The occurrence of allegations or incidents of bribery and corruption of and by the Company, and any investigations into these, may result in financial, image and reputation damage for companies and the risk of legal sanctions.	206-1 205-3 201-1 415-1

Fig. 5.1 The materiality list (*Source* 2023 integrated reporting of Aspiag Service S.r.l.)

of the products sold), **human** (intangible assets of skills and knowledge of those who work in the Company), **social and relational** (the Company's relationships with external key subjects necessary to enhance the company image, its reputation and customer satisfaction), **natural** (set of natural resources used for company activities).

Undoubtedly, the good results relating to the economic-financial performance and, therefore, the commercial success of the Company also allow for the pursuit of sustainable development and the creation of value for the territory in which it operates.

In 2023, the Company recorded an overall economic value of over 2 billion euros, with an increase in both the value generated and that distributed to its stakeholders. The retained value, however, is reinvested in the Company for the implementation of development programs.

Below is some information on the ESG performance of Aspiag Service taken from the 2023 Integrated Report.

E-Environmental

Energy

Also in 2023, Aspiag Service carried out a monitoring of its energy consumption for ISO 14001 sites.

The Company makes technological investments aimed at green solutions for the development of the network. As previously mentioned, the retail stores are in energy class A3 and A4, with Full LED light sources and cool roof systems that reduce the annual energy requirement for cooling the store and increase the performance of the solar panels on the roof. In newly opened stores and those with renovations, the installation of solar panels systems and high-efficiency heat pumps are used to replace gas boilers. If possible, heat recovery systems for the refrigeration systems for heating the rooms and water for sanitary use and closing systems for the refrigerated counters are included. Furthermore, the refrigeration units of the stores have been equipped with a floating condensation system to reduce the energy impact of food refrigeration. This is a set of devices that allow the activity of the refrigeration unit to be modulated according to climatic-environmental conditions, thus reducing consumption and maintenance costs.

Emissions

The reduction of emissions is guaranteed by various renovations made for the retail stores. For example, heating and air conditioning systems are regulated based on external temperatures, and the heat generated by the refrigeration systems is reused to heat water for sanitary use, while heating and LED lighting systems are used in over 100 points of sale. Finally, the refrigeration systems use refrigerant fluids with low environmental impact and the older systems are gradually being replaced with newer CO2 ones.

Since 2014, the Company has purchased certificates of guarantees of origin in reference to the energy used. For 2023 they will cover 95.88% of electricity consumption from the grid. Also in 2023, the Company quantified its direct and indirect greenhouse gas emissions according to the ISO 14064–1 standard.

Waste

In carrying out its business, the Company also pursues the reduction, recovery, recycling of waste and the disposal of any hazardous waste. The waste derives from the processing and management of products in retail stores and warehouses, to a lesser extent from the offices and represents special waste similar to municipal waste, packaging and, in a residual part, special hazardous waste. In addition to the Company's collaborators, suppliers and customers are also directly involved in the process of mitigating the negative impacts of waste production. For suppliers, this is done by carrying out specific audits and packaging review projects for the communication of information on the correct disposal of packaging; other awareness-raising activities are carried out for the customers. To cite some examples, the transport of fruit and vegetables and meat products takes place with reusable crates, and in 2023 76.6% of waste was sent to recycling facilities.

S-Social

Customer Satisfaction

The Company engages its customers both through traditional channels and digital tools. These include the Despar Tribù App, which provides discounts and updates on products, initiatives and events. The employees can also read the Company house organ here.

In 2023, two customer satisfaction surveys on shopping experiences were conducted: satisfaction rose from 88.1% in April to 88.9% in November.

The Food Quality Department carries out checks at suppliers and logistic platforms while those at the retail stores are carried out by Food Safety, ensuring maximum compliance with hygiene standards throughout the supply chain.

Responsibility as an Employer

For Aspiag Service, personnel management involves listening to the needs of workers and identifying a meeting point to reconcile the personal needs of employees and the organizational needs of the Company, in compliance with regulatory provisions.

The Personnel Management Department operates in this direction by carrying out prevention activities relating to organizational choices and contractual and training activities.

The Company's policies include the preference for permanent contracts, which favor the establishment of healthy, long-lasting working relationships based on mutual trust and collaboration (in 2023 the working relationships fixed-term contracts represented approximately 11% of the total workforce).

With reference to gender diversity, equality of salaries between men and women and the conciliation between work and private life are guaranteed. Furthermore, the inclusion and integration into the workplace of the disadvantaged and people with disabilities is also encouraged.

The focus of Aspiag Service was mainly the diffusion of an inclusive culture aimed at greater dialogue and listening, starting from those who hold roles of responsibility. For this reason, managers have been trained on how to conduct interviews with their collaborators.

The collaboration with the Cooperative Vite Vere Down Dadi continued and kept growing within the framework of the "iDem" project, which enables young people with disabilities to enter the world of work through the creation of colorful, handmade shopping bags in line with the fundamental values and objectives of equality and social inclusiveness.

An important signal that goes in the direction of developing and valuing people is the assignment of the "Family Audit" certification to administrative office in Mestrino (PD), which certifies the attention to the needs for a family-work balance and the development of its employees.

For the next three years, the Company aims to further develop the initiatives already in place, including those connected with smart working and flexibility, intergenerational cohesion, training on stereotypes and disabilities, parenting and family care issues, information related to the contractual health policy and specific events and actions highlighting the topic of sustainability.

Aspiag Service offers specific training courses depending on the tasks performed and emphasizes the importance of continuous updating. In 2023, two courses were promoted with the University with the aim of developing young talent. A three-year development plan is provided by the Purchasing Academy so that employees can acquire the transversal and specific skills needed to be able to perform the role of Category Manager. In addition, a vocational training course called "*Scuola di Mestiere – Macelleria*" was designed and developed, both in the classroom and on the job for employees, specialists, technicians and butcher department managers, teaching them about the meat supply chain, market trends, innovative cuisine and section-specific sales indicators.

Aspiag Service maintains a high standard of safety for its employees and third-party employees, preventing injuries from occurring and mitigating any damage. The safety of retail stores, offices, warehouses and the Meat Centre, as well as machinery and equipment, is the subject of constant evaluation and improvement, thanks also to synergies between different company functions. The in-house Prevention and Protection Service, which interfaces with the Workers' Safety Representatives, constantly works towards these objectives. Following an audit by the leading national organisation DNV in May, ISO 45001 certification was confirmed for all business units. The standard covers the Occupational Health and Safety Management System.

Responsibility Towards Communities and the Territory

ESG performances also include Aspiag's support for the territory and the community, achieved through various activities such as fundraising, donations and sponsorships.

These activities allow the Company to contribute financially to initiatives and associations in its territory, but also to spread greater knowledge about these organizations and the activities they carry out, thus creating greater awareness among its collaborators.

A further example of these activities is the free food education program "*Le Buone Abitudini*", intended for primary schools in the area to spread knowledge on healthy eating through discussions with experts and specific programs customized for different age groups.

G-Governance

The Company's Corporate Governance system is oriented towards maintaining the stability of roles over time to make long-term planning easier. In addition to regulatory compliance, it has equipped itself with voluntary control tools to guarantee greater quality and safety of internal processes. Below are some examples:

- The inclusion of areas related to food, workplace and environmental safety in **the Safety Department**;
- The **Organizational Model 231/01**, with the Supervisory Body, the Code of Ethics, the Internal Regulations and the Mapping of Powers, the Protocol Manual and the Sanctioning System. This Model allows

for better risk management and supports the pursuit of the Sustainable Development Goals (SDGs) issued by the UN.

With specific reference to the **Code of Ethics**, it reports the rights, duties and responsibilities of any Aspiag Service interlocutor and represents a contractual condition for direct workers or for those with whom external relationships are established. Its compliance is considered fundamental to prevent the presence of irregularities and conflicts of interest. All participating subjects must carry out their activities in compliance with the following general principles: legality, correctness in relationships both internal and external to the Company, transparency in terms of completeness and correctness of the information process, diligence, confidentiality, fairness, responsibility towards the Company, protection of members and creditors and professional ethics.

Furthermore, since October 2023 the Company has been equipped with the **ESG-Safety** function, which includes the environmental, food and workplace safety offices together with the food quality and ESG reporting offices. The ESG-Safety director holds the function of compliance officer. This function is able to guarantee better control of company risks.

Since 2024, to ensure correct participation of all other Company's functions, two new roles have been envisaged:

- The **sustainability ambassador**, which concerns all managers as sustainability ambassadors for their corporate function;
- The **sustainability practitioner**, which refers to the operational contacts for their function on ESG issues, appointed by the ambassador.

Both of these figures are aimed at sharing the Company's ESG strategy and providing a periodic update on the progress of the activities undertaken.

Within the ESG-Safety management, there is an **ESG team** to coordinate the management on ESG issues.

5.1.4 Conclusions

The Aspiag Service case demonstrates how dealing with sustainability means first and foremost promoting a cultural revolution along its entire supply chain, which involves a redefinition of mission, business model, strategy and corporate governance structure. The case reports an interesting example of an integrated report, emphasizing how the integration between financial and non-financial issues is important, not only at a reporting level. Furthermore, attention towards the environment is added to the care towards people, which passes through their well-being and their opportunities for training and professional growth.

> We are aware of knowing what it means to address sustainability issues. We have done it for a long time and the aim is to do it in the near future too. There is always room for improvement both in terms of reporting and planning and the Company wants to invest in this direction.

5.2 Snam S.P.A.

5.2.1 The Energy Sector, Between Rising Costs and New Supply Strategies

The past few years have been characterized by great upheavals, which began with the outbreak of the COVID-19 pandemic in China in the second half of 2019 and its diffusion in Europe at the beginning of 2020, then followed by the Russian invasion of Ukraine in February 2022 and tensions in the Middle East and the Red Sea area. This unstable situation has caused significant upheavals in all sectors, with a particular impact on the energy sector. In fact, there was an increase in the prices of energy materials, which led to high inflation, reaching levels that Italy had not reached since its entrance into the European Union.

In 2021, the Italian economy, together with the European one, witnessed a rebound in GDP, driven mainly by a recovery in consumption, following the reopening after the closures imposed by Covid-19.

The recovery in consumer demand and production has not only generated economic growth, but also a surge in the costs of raw materials, and in particular energy materials. The outbreak of the war in Ukraine occurred in this context, favoring a surge in energy prices, causing the Italian inflation rate to return to high levels, as those of the 80s. If, on the one hand, the price of oil has reached high, although not exceptional, levels, as has already happened during previous crises, on the other, gas prices and electricity prices have reached historic highs. Italy, together with the other countries of the European Union, suffered the greatest consequences, since the main source of supply of energy resources, in particular for gas, was represented by Russia: in 2021 the EU depended on 41% of Russian gas.[5] The fallout from Russia's invasion of Ukraine was perceived as a threat to the Western world, and as a result several sanctions were put in place to try to undermine the Russian economy. In response, Russia in some cases eliminated gas supplies, as with Bulgaria, Poland, Lithuania, Finland and Latvia, and in other cases only partially reduced them. In response to such actions, the EU has adopted a series of measures aimed at reducing dependence on Russia and defending itself against price increases. In particular, the RepowerEU plan was approved, which is based on a common European action aimed at freeing Europe from dependence on Russian fuels, starting with gas. Thanks to these measures, the dependence on Russian gas, coming from pipelines, fell from 41% in 2021 to 8[6]% in September 2022. The lower supplies were replaced by the search for new suppliers and the increase in supplies of liquefied natural gas (LNG), which grew by 19 billion cubic meters between January and July 2022, representing 32% of total net gas imports. Italy has also committed to preparing for the arrival of LNG, through the purchase by Snam, on government mandate, of the Golar Tundra regasifier ship, which acts as a storage point for liquefied natural gas.

[5] https://eur-lex.europa.eu/legal-content/IT/TXT/HTML/?uri=CELEX:52022DC0547.

[6] Snam 2023 Annual Report, p. 187.
https://www.snam.it/content/dam/snam/pages-attachments-search/en/documenti/bilanci-annuali/2023/annual_report_2023.pdf.

The establishment of the European Energy Platform[7] has favored the development of new agreements with new and reliable energy partners, in order to diversify and guarantee the European Union's energy supply. Energy supply protocols and partnerships have been signed with Egypt, Algeria, Azerbaijan, Israel, Algeria, Canada and other African, American and Asian nations. Furthermore, the drive for diversification was not limited to the search for new suppliers, but there was also the development of the use of renewable energy and the acceleration of the use of hydrogen and biomethane.[8]

In 2023, numerous initiatives aimed at mitigating the energy crisis have started to produce improvements. Europe has diversified its gas supply, reducing imports from Russia from 45 to 14% (in Italy they are less than 5%) and relying more on liquefied natural gas.

In this context, the development of a sustainable energy strategy, capable of also achieving the objectives of containing greenhouse gas emissions by 2030 and the achievement of the ambitious objective of zero emissions by 2050, has received a strong boost that will continue to influence future trends and will make the EU a continent resilient to any upheavals caused by changes in international geopolitical balances.

5.2.2 History, Mission and Vision of Snam[9]

The history of Snam has its roots in the first half of the last century. In particular, on 30 October 1941 the National Methane Authority, founded in 1940, together with the Regie Terme di Salsomaggiore and the Società Anonima Utilizzazione e Ricerca Gas Idrocarboni (Surgi) founded the **Società Nazionale Metanodotti (Snam)**, with the aim of building and maintain the methane pipelines and provide for the distribution and sale of gas, with a share capital of 3 million lire. During the war years, Snam played an important role in the methanization of

[7] It is based on voluntary membership and has the aim of supporting the common purchase of gas for everyone. EU countries and some European partners.

[8] http://documenti.camera.it/leg19/dossier/pdf/RI013.pdf.

[9] Snam 2023 Annual Report, pp. 22–23. https://www.snam.it/content/dam/snam/pages-attachments-search/en/documenti/bilanci-annuali/2023/annual_report_2023.pdf.

the nation, developing the first gas pipeline network for Italy, which in 1948 covered 257 kilometers, in 1950 it exceeded 700, exceeding 4600 in 1960, mainly concentrated in the plain Po Valley.

The 1960s were characterized by a strong expansion of the methane pipeline network along the Peninsula, including the construction of pipelines capable of serving the capital and Puglia, managing 8000 kilometers of network. In the 1970s Snam worked on the construction of methane pipelines capable of bringing methane from Holland and Siberia to the Bel Paese. In 1983, with the conclusion of the Transmed works, 2400 kilometers long, capable of bringing Algerian gas to Italy, Snam obtained the record for having built one of the longest methane pipelines in the world for those years. In 1997 work began on the construction of the Greenstream, the underwater gas pipeline for imports from Libya, and a new import line from Russia was also developed. In advance of the European directives on the liberalization of the gas market, Rete Gas Italia was born, which took over the technological assets and skills for the transport of natural gas from Snam. In 2001, GNL Italia was founded, 100% owned by Rete Gas Italia, to manage LNG regasification activities. In 2002 the legislator implemented the European directive for the liberalization of the gas market and proceeded with the separation of transport and dispatching activities from others, such as sales. On 6 December 2001 the shares of Rete Gas Italia, renamed Snam Rete Gas (SRG), were listed on the Italian Stock Exchange. In 2009, Snam Rete Gas, through the acquisition of Stogit and Italgas, became the leading operator in Europe in terms of the size of its invested capital.

After the first 10 years of 2000, Snam managed to control the gas market through: Snam Rete Gas, operating in transportation and dispatching; LNG, active in regasification; Italgas, focused on distribution; Stogit, focused on storage. Given the notoriety of the brand, the company name was changed from SRG to Snam, retaining the name for the new Snam Rete Gas which dealt with gas transport activities. Through the change of name, Snam assumed the status of Corporate company, which controls 100% of the Group companies. In 2012, there was the separation from ENI and the acquisition of 31.5% of Interconnector UK. Based on the first international acquisition in 2013, the

Group began a period of acquisitions to extend its presence globally. Finally, in November 2016, the split of Italgas from Snam took place and trading began on the Mercato Telematico Azionario managed by the Italian Stock Exchange of the shares of the company that left the Group.[10] Since 2017, international agreements have been developed for development and international presence and business policies that are attentive to the environment and sustainability have been implemented. Finally, Snam has played and is playing a central role in the process of diversifying gas supply sources to reduce dependence on Russia, following the invasion of Ukraine.

Snam's history is also intertwined with sustainable development; in fact, it was among the first companies to approach non-financial reporting. Already in 1995 it published the first environmental report, adopted voluntarily. This report presented data relating to impacts on the environment, such as atmospheric emissions, waste management and many other topics. In 2000, the Company received the environmental management certification according to the UNI EN ISO 14001 standard, by an independent body, for gas compression plants and LNG regasification.

In 2002 the then SRG became part of the FTSE4Good family of sustainability indices. Four years later, in 2006, Snam Rete Gas established the first corporate sustainability functions internally. The following year it published the first sustainability report. Two years later, in 2009 it joined the UN Global Compact and became a member of the Dow Jones Sustainability World Index and the ECPI Ethical Index Global. In 2016 the internal board committee on sustainability issues was established and in 2018 Snam changed its "purpose" by focusing on the issues of protecting the world and began investing in sustainable mobility, energy efficiency and biomethane.

In 2019 Snam began testing hydrogen in its network and created a business unit entirely dedicated to the development of hydrogen, playing a central role in the development of the energy transition. In 2020 Snam set itself the objective of decarbonisation by 2040 and together with CDP founded Arbolia for the development of green areas and the

[10] https://www.snam.it/it/noi-snam/chi-siamo/la-storia.html.

absorption of CO2. In 2021 Snam included ESG criteria in its statute, achieving primacy among Italian companies listed on the stock exchange. Finally, in 2022, Snam was involved at the forefront in the strategy of diversification of supply sources, in the implementation of strategies for the energy transition and the development of new alternative sources. In the same year, the "Enviromental, Social & Governance and Energy Transition Scenarios" endo-board committee was established to integrate ESG, technological innovation and climate transition themes.

Snam Today[11]

Snam is one of the world's most important **gas operators at an international level** and expands its presence through participation in foreign companies. It is a company listed on the Italian Stock Exchange, whose capital is made up of institutional investors, own shares, strategic investors, i.e. bodies controlled by the State and private investors. In particular, the reference shareholder is CDP Reti,[12] which holds 31.4% of the capital, followed by Romano Minozzi with 7.5%.[13]

As emerged in the previous paragraph, Snam has been active for over eighty years and deals with the transport, regasification, storage and dispatching of natural gas in the national, European and international contexts. In recent years, it has also focused its attention on the energy transition, developing and researching new sources of sustainable energy, such as biomethane and hydrogen. In fact, it is possible to identify two businesses in which the Group operates, the first concerns gas infrastructure and the second precisely energy transition.

The first business area is divided into the following subcategories:

1. **Transport**: Snam, through its subsidiary Snam Rete Gas, guarantees the transport of natural gas throughout the Italian territory via

---

[11] Snam 2023 Annual Report, pp. 22–23, 24–29. https://www.snam.it/content/dam/snam/pages-attachments-search/en/documenti/bilanci-annuali/2023/annual_report_2023.pdf.

[12] Cassa Depositi e Prestiti Reti, the financial institution controlled by the Ministry of Economy and Finance whose purpose is the development of the Italian economic and industrial system.

[13] Data updated to February 2024.

a widespread network of gas pipelines, guaranteeing energy security. The gas is introduced from import points, regasification plants, production and storage points to reach the final points. The network is made up of 13 compression plants which are able to guarantee the flow of gas along the entire peninsula;
2. **Storage**: in this area, Snam operates through Stogit, which manages storage plants, capable of introducing new gas into the supply network and capable of protecting itself from risks linked to fluctuations in needs and extraordinary events. The storage system has a continuous flow, i.e. it stores gas during periods of lower demand and introduces it into the network at times of greater demand but also in the event of import interruptions;
3. **Regasification**: in this business, the Group is active through Snam FSRU and GNL Italia, which deals with the regasification of liquefied natural gas that arrives in Italy by sea. Currently, the Panigalia plant (La Spezia) has been operational since 1971. Furthermore, this business was at the center of the source diversification strategy implemented by the government following the stop of Russian gas; in fact, in 2022 Snam purchased two floating regasification plants.
4. **Small Scale LNG and Sustainable mobility**: in this business, the presence is guaranteed by Greenture, which intends to support the process of decarbonization of transport and off-grid applications by encouraging the diffusion and use of natural gas biomethane and hydrogen.

The business of the ecological transition, however, is structured as follows:

1. **Biomethane**: this sector is supported by the work and technical know-how of Bioenerys. The Group focuses on promoting the development of biomethane infrastructure and its use throughout the country. This occurs with a view to the development of the national energy transition, since biomethane is a renewable and sustainable energy source, and the achievement of decarbonization targets. The push for the development of this new fuel was given by the resources

provided by the PNRR and the Biomethane Decree, which will allow Snam to create the biomethane platform;
2. **Decarbonization projects**: the Decarbonization Projects function, founded in 2022, guarantees the management of hydrogen and carbon capture and storage projects for ensuring the achievement of European and global decarbonization goals. In fact, since hydrogen does not generate emissions of carbon dioxide and other types of climate-changing gases, it represents a clean energy source. Also CCS represents an opportunity for the decarbonization process. For this reason, Snam intends to contribute with investments in the Ravenna CCS project, arising with the collaboration with Eni, and included in the European Commission's Projects of Common Interest (PCI) list;
3. **Energy efficiency**: represents an opportunity to promote sustainable development, innovation and decarbonisation. In fact, the purpose of energy efficiency operations is to rationalize the use of energy. Snam is present in this business through its subsidiary Renovit which, founded in 2021, offers innovative energy efficiency solutions, leveraging government incentives and promoting self-consumption.

In 2023, many of Snam's projects have recorded important progress. For example, the Adriatic Line was declared strategic and approved at the European level, so as to be able to receive REPowerEU funds. Furthermore, the Company recorded a 57% drop in methane emissions and achieved its 80% sustainable finance target three years earlier than expected.

Mission, Vision and Purpose of Snam[14]

Snam represents the number one continental company in gas infrastructure and is the only operator active on the entire value chain. Drawing on this functional integration, the Company has defined its first mission as that of **being suppliers of energy infrastructure for a sustainable future in compliance with the great challenge of the**

[14] Snam 2023 Annual Report, p. 39. https://www.snam.it/content/dam/snam/pages-attachments-search/en/documenti/bilanci-annuali/2023/annual_report_2023.pdf.

energy trilemma (guaranteeing reliable, competitive and environmentally friendly supplies).

The goal is to become a multi-molecule European operator capable of managing a modular, flexible and future-proof infrastructure that supplies energy to Italy and Europe. Snam's purpose is therefore "***energy to inspire the world***", qualifying itself as an enabler committed to transporting what the world needs most to improve itself.

The vision intends to guide the evolution of the sector thanks to an increasingly innovative network of sustainable energy.

These elements together guide the Company in facing the challenges of the future.

5.2.3 Snam's Financial and Non-financial Reporting Structure[15]

As already described in the presentation of the stages that have marked the history of Snam, reporting on sustainability issues dates back to the second half of the 1990s. In 1995 the first **Environmental Report** was published, giving rise to a path that in 2006 led to the first publication of the **Sustainability Reporting**.

Currently, consistently with a "*Core & More*" approach of Accounting Europe, Snam has structured the reporting system in an **integrated** way, with the aim of providing stakeholders with all the economic, social, environmental and governance information requested in a detailed and transparent way. Furthermore, the activities carried out, the performances achieved and future objectives are reported. According to this approach, the most relevant information for a wide range of stakeholders is contained in the "*Core*" reports, while additional details for a more limited number of stakeholders are found in the "*More*" reports.[16]

The "***Core***" reporting includes the Annual Financial Report, which includes within it the **Non-Financial Statement** (NFS) drawn up in compliance with the legislative decree of 30 December 2016, n. 254

[15] https://www.snam.it/en/esg/our-commitment-to-sustainability/reporting.html.

[16] These are the Report on corporate governance and ownership structures and the Report on the remuneration policy and fees paid.

of Implementation of Directive 2014/95/EU of the European Parliament. The Integrated Report follows the framework promoted by the Value Reporting Foundation (VRF). In addition to the NFS, it contains the Directors' Report, the Consolidated Financial Statements and the Financial Statements.

Within the NFS there are relevant data and information from an environmental, health and safety, social perspective, relating to personnel and prevention of active and passive corruption, as emerged from the materiality analysis carried out during the year. The Integrated Report represents the link between strategy, governance, economic-financial, social and environmental performance. In essence, it describes to stakeholders the Company's value creation process in the short, medium and long term, as well as the risks, opportunities and challenges to be faced. The NFS, therefore, represents the main tool for communicating non-financial information. In addition to this document, the information is also reported in summary form within the Sustainability Profile.

With the aim of anticipating the requests of the Corporate Sustainability Reporting Directive (CSRD), in force since 2024, the Company has restructured its sustainability reporting since 2023, integrating into the NFS information on governance, sustainability strategy, management of impacts, risks and opportunities and materiality analysis. In addition, Snam has begun a process of adapting the reporting to the requirements of the European Sustainability Reporting Standards (ESRS). This information up to 2022 was presented within the Directors' Report.[17] Starting in 2023, Snam has begun to implement an internal control framework to monitor the main quantitative information reported in the Sustainability Declaration. The control model is defined in synergy with that relating to financial reporting.

The 2023 Integrated Report

The structure of the **Integrated Report** is characterized by the letter to the stakeholders from the President and the CEO, the description of the

[17] Snam 2023 Annual Report, p. 7. https://www.snam.it/content/dam/snam/pages-attachments-search/en/documenti/bilanci-annuali/2023/annual_report_2023.pdf.

main historical moments that characterized Snam's path during the year, the history of the Company, the business model and the strategic plan, the description of the economic-financial performances, the management performance in the business sectors and the main risk and uncertainty factors; following, in a separate section, is the Non-financial Statement, which reports the main social, environmental and governance information. In conclusion, there is a report from the auditing firm.

The NFS is drawn up in accordance with the "***GRI Sustainability Reporting Standards***" of the Global Reporting Initiative, according to the updates released in 2021 and the sector standard GRI 11 (Oil and Gas Sector 2021).

Snam and the Development of a Sustainable Strategy[18]

> Integrating sustainability into business strategy is the basis of our long-term vision.[19]

For Snam, **sustainability** is at the center of its business strategies. It has always been attentive to the definition of a sustainability strategy based on decarbonization and ecological transition, on the commitment to guarantee safety at work and constant professional growth, in a sustainability governance environment that guarantees adequate skills in all Group companies.

> Having sustainable strategies and communicating them increases the positive image of Snam at all levels, of local units, institutions, the financial community and investors.[20]

The elements that characterize its **business model** are sustainable growth, transparency, valorization of talents and diversity, protection and social development of the territories. To do this, the industrial plan and

[18] Snam 2023 Annual Report, pp. 38–57. https://www.snam.it/content/dam/snam/pages-attachments-search/en/documenti/bilanci-annuali/2023/annual_report_2023.pdf.

[19] https://www.snam.it/it/esg/la-sostenibilita-nei-processi/reporting.html.

[20] Re-elaboration taken from the interview.

the ESG objectives are interconnected in order to concretely achieve the Sustainable Development Goals defined by the United Nations (Fig. 5.2).

The sustainable commitment is also confirmed within the new **2023–2027 Strategic Plan**. In particular, the Company intends to develop a pan-European multi-molecule energy infrastructure for a sustainable future, through the readjustment and continuous modernization of the network, to prospectively accommodate growing volumes of decarbonized molecules, also thanks to innovation and technology. Furthermore, investments in the energy transition platform and in sustainability and transformative innovation will continue, which are fundamental for achieving the objectives of the Strategic Plan and the Decarbonization Strategy.

To do this, Snam plans to invest 11.5 billion euros over the time horizon envisaged by the Plan (+15% compared to the previous 2022–2026 Plan) destined for the gas infrastructure businesses and the energy transition platform. A role of fundamental importance, then, will be played by sustainability and innovation, in which Snam will invest 400 million euros. It is also important to point out that 37% of net investments will be aligned with the EU Taxonomy, while 58% with the SDGs.

Snam's sustainability strategy is fully integrated into the Group's operations and corporate strategy and is focused on **seven directions**, each with seven ambitions for 2027. The first two (**Green Transition and Multi-molecule Infrastructure**) have the aim of developing the energy transition platform to enable the decarbonization of the system and the development of an inclusive path. The third direction is **Carbon Neutrality**, which involves a continuous process of reducing emissions and decarbonizing activities. Due to the instability of the external context, the Company has carried out a revision of its intermediate objectives for 2027, 2030 and 2032 (equal to −25%, −40% and −50%, respectively), confirming carbon neutrality at 2040. Furthermore, zero net emissions are expected across all emission categories (Scope 1, 2 and 3) by 2050. As regards methane emissions, Snam recorded a 55% reduction compared to 2015 which guaranteed it A Gold Standard by the United Nations Environment Program (UNEP). Consequently, it

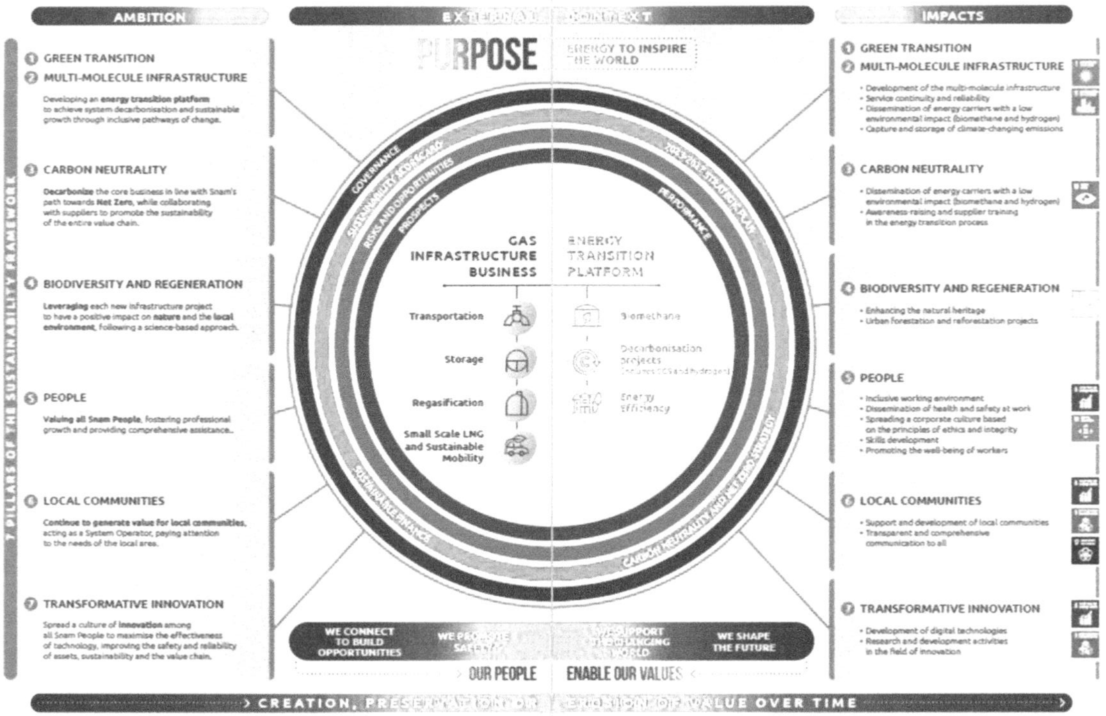

Fig. 5.2 Snam business model (*Source* 2023 NFS of Snam)

decided to define a new, more challenging target of -64% by 2027. Snam believes in the important role of green gases in reducing emissions and for this reason works to promote the recognition of their strategic role through various European Union initiatives. The fourth concerns **Biodiversity and Regeneration**, with the aim of generating a neutral to positive impact on nature by 2027, according to the guidelines of the Science Based Target for Nature (SBTN) framework.[21] The fifth direction concerns **People**, who for Snam are one of the main enabling factors for the energy transition. For this reason, investments are planned in training and motivation, so as to encourage professional growth and offer an inclusive working environment that takes care of employees also in terms of health and safety. Next, we have the local communities, for which it is a priority to generate value and invest in listening and dialogue initiatives. The goal is to distribute A value of more than 1 billion euros per year at a local level. Finally, the seventh and final direction is that relating to **Transformative Innovation**, since to achieve energy efficiency it is necessary to maximize innovation. For this reason, at least 3% of annual revenues will be dedicated to applied industrial innovation and research and development projects.

Based on the sustainability strategy, the **Sustainability Scorecard**, a tool introduced in 2020 to monitor Snam's progress in various areas, was updated. Key performance indicators relevant to the seven pillars mentioned above have been introduced with a target of 2027. The Sustainability Scorecard integrates business and strategic objectives with those relating to sustainability, incorporating the seven pillars mentioned above. It is also aimed at improving transparency in the communication phase.

[21] This framework aims to increase positive impacts on nature and people along the entire value chain.

The Stakeholder Engagement and the Materiality Analysis[22]

Since 2016, Snam has adopted a policy aimed at involving **stakeholders** based on four fundamental phases:

1. Identify the different categories of stakeholders through a mapping process;
2. Analyze and understand the profile of stakeholders and their perception of the Company's activities;
3. Investigate the interests and issues relevant to each category of stakeholder, including through periodic meetings;
4. Communicate management results to stakeholders in relation to relevant issues.

The stakeholder engagement policy was updated in 2023 and has the aim of establishing a continuous dialogue with the Company's main stakeholders, defining material issues, maintaining the company's reputation and identifying the main risks and opportunities.

Snam carries out the materiality analysis required by the sustainability reporting standards, in accordance with Legislative Decree 254/2016—which transposes the Community Directive 2014/95/EU called "*Non Financial Reporting Directive*", the GRI Universal Standards 2021 and the peculiarities of the sector.

Following the introduction of the Corporate Sustainability Reporting Directive (CSRD), the concept of **double materiality** was applied, which is made up of two dimensions:

- **Impact materiality** (a sustainability issue is relevant when it concerns the significant impacts of the company, negative or positive, actual or potential, on people or the environment in the short, medium or long term);
- **Financial materiality** (a sustainability issue is relevant from a financial perspective if it involves or can reasonably be expected to have

[22] Snam 2023 Annual Report, pp. 64–66, 229–249. https://www.snam.it/content/dam/snam/pages-attachments-search/en/documenti/bilanci-annuali/2023/annual_report_2023.pdf.

significant financial effects on the company or generates risks or opportunities that have or can reasonably be expected to have a significant influence on the development of the company, the financial situation, the economic result, the financial flows, the access to financing or the cost of capital in the short, medium or long term).

In both cases, the analysis considers not only the impacts of the Company's operations, but also the entire upstream and downstream value chain.

The process for defining the relevant themes follows the following steps:

1. Understanding the context in which Snam operates;
2. Identification of sustainability issues and related impacts, risks and opportunities;
3. Assessment of impacts, risks and opportunities by top management and stakeholders belonging to the main categories;
4. Aggregation of results and definition of relevant themes and related impacts, risks and opportunities.

Also in 2023 the theme "*Climate change*" is confirmed in the first place, demonstrating Snam's efforts towards this topic. Next is "*Energy security and accessibility to energy*", also in light of the events that characterized the external context in 2022–2023. Subsequently, the theme "*Health and safety*" reflects the Company's attention towards its workers. The theme "*Business conduct*" has grown in relevance compared to 2022, as has the theme "*Equal treatment and opportunities for all and skills development*". "*Innovation, digitalisation and cyber security*" and "*Economic performance and value creation*" were considered less significant compared to last year. Other important topics (even if not material) are "*Waste*", "*Air Pollution*" and "*Water*".

The Value Creation Process[23]

E-Environmental

Snam and the Environment

Climate change, as emerged from the materiality analysis, appears to be central for Snam, which has developed a **Carbon Neutrality and Net Zero strategy** to achieve carbon neutrality by 2040 for Scope 1 and 2 emissions, and net zero emissions by 2050 for all direct and indirect Group emissions.

Snam's Scope 1[24] and 2[25] emissions amounted to approximately 1,413,122 tons of CO2eq (-7% vs. 2022); to these are added Scope 3[26] emissions equal to 1,589,833 tons of CO2eq (+18% vs. 2022) including 777,513 tons of CO2eq linked to the Supply Chain and 639,326 tons of CO2eq linked to Associates: the total of Scope 1, Scope GHG emissions 2 Market based and Scope 3 of the Group is therefore equal to 3,002,955 tons of CO2eq (+5% compared to 2022).

In 2023, Snam's total energy consumption was equal to 17,885 TJ (+1.4% vs. 2022), almost entirely attributable to natural gas (95.9%) used mainly for the operation of the gas turbines used in compression plants that provide the pressure necessary for the transport of gas (pushing consumption) and in storage concessions (storage consumption) which, globally, represent 79% of total consumption, a value which is slightly reduced compared to previous years. The residual part of the energy mix includes electricity (3.4%) and other fuels (diesel, petrol, LPG and heat), which together are equivalent to 0.7% of energy consumption.

---

[23] Snam 2023 Annual Report, pp. 250–418. https://www.snam.it/content/dam/snam/pages-attachments-search/en/documenti/bilanci-annuali/2023/annual_report_2023.pdf.

[24] They correspond to emissions directly produced by assets owned and/or operationally controlled by the company.

[25] They represent indirect emissions for which the company is responsible only for the use of energy but not for the emissions generated by the energy supplier.

[26] It consists of all indirect emissions linked to a company but which do not depend on its control.

During 2023 Snam confirmed its commitment also thanks to the use of energy from **renewable energy sources**. The Group purchased electricity from renewable sources, reaching a share of 94,545 MWh (+27 vs. 2022). Furthermore, the share of Snam green electricity on the total went from 52% in 2022 to 54% in 2023.

The Group's energy efficiency results are in line with the targets, while, concerning the Sustainability Scorecard, with regard to the annual production of electricity from photovoltaic systems in the regulated sector, Snam has largely exceeded the target of 860 MWh by 2023, reaching 980 MWh. In 2023, the energy efficiency works of the Group's buildings led to gas savings of 50,000 m^3 compared to 40,000 m^3 in 2022 and 190 MWh of electricity, an increase compared to the 145 MWh of the previous year, resulting consistent with the achievement of the 2025 target (savings of 75,000 m^3 per year of gas and 250 MWh per year of electricity).

In addition to its commitment to reducing emissions linked to the operation of its business, Snam can play a role as an enabler of the **energy transition**. This allows to avoid emissions that would otherwise have been generated by other actors belonging to the country system.

Since 2018, the Snam Group has started a process of aligning its financial strategy with sustainable development objectives, starting to increase its commitment to the field of **sustainable finance**. In this context, the objective of increasing the weight of sustainable finance instruments on total funding to 80% by 2026 and the issuing of bonds to finance investments in the field of environmental sustainability and energy transition was identified. Snam, as a member of the United Nations Global Compact, has also joined the CFO Coalition for the SDGs, which aims to promote sustainable finance and investments to achieve the Sustainable Development Goals.

Snam is also committed to the field of **biodiversity protection**. The Company adopted a series of policies for managing the impacts, risks and opportunities related to this area. Concerning the biodiversity strategy, Snam defined targets aligned with the guidelines of the Science Based Target for Nature (SBTN) framework. The Group has developed an approach for infrastructure management, which controls all phases from design to decommissioning of the work, focused on minimizing impacts, through a strategy composed of four aspects:

1. Minimize the temporary impacts linked to the construction and decommissioning phases of the work, through measures to avoid causing damage and guarantee the conservation of the environment, biodiversity, landscape and the health of the population of the territory in which the work is realized;
2. Avoid building new infrastructures in areas of particular archaeological, natural or cultural interest and in geologically unstable contexts. Furthermore, try to exploit the areas already occupied by the systems to avoid contamination of other environments;
3. Restore the morphological and vegetal conditions pre-existing in the territory before the construction of the work, with naturalistic engineering projects and recovery of native fauna and flora;
4. Compensate for the impacts generated by the construction of infrastructures through a five-year plan for reforestation, care and maintenance of flora and the implementation of environmental monitoring projects (PMA).[27]

A further space in the environmental protection strategy is occupied by **waste management** which, although not among the significant issues that emerged from the materiality analysis, sees the Group committed to containing the impacts generated by them. In relation to the activity carried out, waste is generated which mainly refers to two macro-categories, plant maintenance and well drilling, and is composed of ferrous material entirely reused within the circular economy model proposed by the company. In 2023, waste production grew by 58% compared to the previous year, going from 143,516 to 227,524 tons, of which 96% was non-hazardous. However, this data is consistent with the growth of the businesses of Bionerys and Renovit. Furthermore, approximately 70% is recovered, while almost all of the remaining part is destined for disposal. The fight to reduce waste is demonstrated by

[27] The PMAs consist of actions aimed at monitoring and analyzing the environment in which the work is developed. They have the objective of verifying the renaturalization process of the area by comparing the pre- and post-operam conditions.

the project launched by Snam for the dematerialization of incoming and outgoing mail. Suppliers and partners were involved in this initiative and were asked to send their communications through the supplier portal, with the aim of reducing paper management. On top of that, all newspaper and magazine subscriptions have been changed to 100% digital.

The last aspect of the environmental strategy focuses on the **management of water resources**. Although the use of water is marginal, by virtue of the operational activities carried out, the Group pays close attention to its correct use. In 2023, 57,317,540 cubic meters of water were withdrawn, of which 99% was seawater and the remainder was freshwater. Sea water is used to cool the systems, while freshwater is mainly used for offices, fire prevention systems and irrigation of green areas. The increase in water supplies with respect to 2022 (5,565,104 m^3) is due to the commissioning of the Golar Tundra FSRU. However in regasification activities, seawater is withdrawn for the cooling of the auxiliary plants both in the GNL Italia plant and in the FSRU, after which it is completely discharged into the sea in the same volume, but at a slightly higher temperature (within legal limits).

Approximately 87% of other wastewater is conveyed into sewer networks, where this is not possible, constructed wetlands have been built which allow wastewater waste to be eliminated, while the remaining 13% is discharged into the soil and surface water bodies.

With respect to 2022 (5,565,104 m^3) is due to the commissioning of the Golar Tundra FSRU. However, in regasification activities, seawater is withdrawn for the cooling of the auxiliary plants both in the GNL Italia plant and in the FSRU, after which it is completely discharged into the sea in the same volume, but at a slightly higher temperature (within legal limits).

Approximately 87% of other wastewater is conveyed into sewer networks, where this is not possible, constructed wetlands have been built which allow wastewater waste to be eliminated, while the remaining 13% is discharged into the soil and surface water bodies.

S-Social

Relationships with Communities

Snam's infrastructural network is spread throughout the Italian territory and this allows it to have a widespread presence along the entire peninsula and to establish relationships of dialogue with local realities with the aim of promoting their socio-economic progress and care of their heritage environment and landscape.

Relations with communities are mainly managed by the Group's Foundation, which focuses on the issues of food, educational and energy poverty by developing initiatives aimed at the territories, in collaboration with training institutions, students, local bodies and associations. The activities implemented include the energy requalification of public buildings, the reduction of school dropouts and support for young people's access to future craftsmanship.

One of the main actions implemented to support the territories concerns **corporate volunteering**, which represents the Foundation's true strength. In 2023, 5970 hours were dedicated to volunteering activities, exceeding the annual target of 4800 set by the Sustainability Scorecard.

The main volunteering activities focused on support courses for the business planning of five cooperative companies, after-school initiatives for students from fragile conditions and programs to combat food waste.

A main focus is placed on relations with the world of training, in particular Snam carries out two projects linked to the world of schools:

1. Young energy, which supports students in entering the world of work by introducing them to corporate business;
2. Tirreno Scuola@2030, a communication, training and information project aimed at high schools.

Snam and People

People represent the fundamental element for achieving the objectives and the success of Snam, which is why growth and training paths are developed to encourage the growth of the skills of its workers and collaborators.

In recent years, in line with the development of the business, the company population has grown significantly: as of 31 December 2023, 3798 people were employed in Snam, recording a growth of 5.2% compared to 2022. The number of exits has increased compared to 2022 (+54), half of which linked to voluntary negative turnover and consensual terminations of the employment relationship. 52% of employees have a technical diploma and 36% have a degree. Furthermore, the working relationship offered is stable and continuous: this is demonstrated by the length of service of approximately 14.5 years and the signing of a permanent employment contract by 93% of workers.

Relations with the company population also involve corporate welfare policies, to which Snam is very attentive as demonstrated by the achievement of the objectives set by the Sustainability Scorecard. Starting from 2018, the **Welfare Plan** was developed with the aim of guaranteeing services capable of meeting the needs of employees. Furthermore, the Snammy platform was developed which includes all the initiatives envisaged by the Plan and allows workers to access more than 30 welfare services offered by the company. Employee assistance and support initiatives can be grouped into five areas of intervention: health, family and education, well-being and work-life balance, finance and savings and social commitment.

As already mentioned, one of the success factors in relationships with the company population concerns the **possibility of professional growth**. In 2023, 139,614 hours of training were provided (up 15% compared to 2022).

The commitment to caring for the people who work in and for Snam is also demonstrated by the plans aimed at protecting **health and safety** in the workplace. For this reason, Snam has equipped itself with a management system certified according to the UNI ISO 45001 standard "*Management systems for health and safety at work*" and procedures and systems to prevent accidents and illnesses at work and promote protection and workers' health. Although 21 workplace accidents occurred in 2023, the severity index for employees plus contractors decreases compared to the previous year, standing at 0.05 compared to 0.48 in 2022. The prevention and creation action of a corporate culture attentive to safety is confirmed by two initiatives implemented by the Group:

- Snam4Safety, which intends to strengthen awareness in the field of safety of workers, both employees and contractors;
- Zero Accident Award, pays a premium, in the form of welfare credits, to employees who have not suffered injuries during the year.

The health of employees, like their safety, is subjected to constant monitoring through periodic health surveillance actions linked to the specific risks to which the worker is exposed. Furthermore, the working environment is periodically analyzed to monitor the biological, physical and microclimatic aspects with the aim of ensuring a workplace that complies with hygiene and health standards. In the three-year period 2021–2023, no situations of occupational diseases emerged from the analyses.

The last point of the people strategy concerns the creation of an **inclusive, free and open working environment**, where the uniqueness and diversity of the individual represents added value for the entire community. Due to the nature of the business, characterized by a high male presence, gender diversity has always been a point on which Snam focuses. Starting from 2020, the female presence increased by 18%, resulting in 670 women in 2023, equal to 18% of all workers, also thanks to the new 132 female hires that took place in 2023. To increase inclusion, from 2021, Snam organizes Inclusion Week—Stronger Together, a week-long program of events dedicated to the development and valoriation of the uniqueness of people. The importance of the issue of diversity for Snam was confirmed by obtaining, in April 2023, the gender equality certification formalized by the DNV accreditation body.

Relationships with Suppliers

Regarding its suppliers, Snam applies the principles of the so-called **Just Transition**, aimed at implementing a path to decarbonization of the economy that is inclusive and fair towards all the actors involved and creates decent job opportunities.

The Group maintains that suppliers are to be considered fundamental allies for the development of its business and the achievement of sustainable objectives. For these reasons, it is essential to strengthen relationships and promote sustainable practices along the entire value chain. The Company promotes the spread of a culture of legality among them, taking an active role in the fight against corruption. For this reason, it has adopted a **Human Rights Policy** and a **Supply Chain Policy**, through which it manages relationships along the supply chain.

Furthermore, Snam promotes the adoption of the **Code of Ethics**, which guarantees the protection of human rights, and makes use of suppliers and collaborators who share the principles and values contained in the Code. Suppliers are also asked to sign the Ethics and Integrity Pact, aimed at encouraging the creation of a relationship of trust with the Company.

Also for 2023, relationships with suppliers were based on four pillars:

- Application of innovation in procurement processes;
- Valorization of supplier skills to develop new know-how along the entire supply chain;
- Have a vision open to change to prevent future needs;
- Be flexible, so as to be able to respond to market needs and guarantee speed in the provision of the services offered.

The paper dematerialization process has significantly involved all suppliers with the creation of the **Supplier One Platform** which offers new technological solutions throughout the entire supply process. Technological innovation has made it possible to improve relationships with suppliers optimizing and reducing interaction times and has made the exchange of information more frequent, as well as making the flow of materials faster and safer. In 2023, the process of dematerialization of transport documents, started in 2022, in the warehouse and logistics sector, was consolidated, which led to the digitalization of transport documents (DDT) and the identification tag of delivery packages.

The collaborative relationship with suppliers is also based on the **training courses** organized by Snam to support awareness of sustainability issues and in particular to reduce Scope 3 emissions. In 2023, two cycles of meetings were organized with the main suppliers belonging to the DT&T category, focusing on the discussion of possible ESG strategies to be developed. These involvement initiatives aim to provide each actor in the value chain with the appropriate skills to implement sustainable behaviors. In particular for each product class, reward criteria have been constructed based on the ESG targets to be considered when evaluating supply offers.

Furthermore, the Group intends to create a collaborative and long-lasting relationship with its suppliers and for this reason provides parameters for their selection, based on the evaluation of quality, price and reliability of performance and the sharing of commitment towards the use of innovations in its management process and the implementation of ESG policies. These criteria are evaluated by Snam according to objectivity, transparency and traceability, evaluating the current and future potential of each new protective supplier.

Particular attention is paid to respect for human rights in all phases of supply. Furthermore, the **General Tender Specifications** contain specific references to respect for health and safety in the workplace and the economic treatment of its employees. Once you have passed the preliminary checks you can be included in the list of Snam suppliers, from this moment you are constantly subjected to a performance monitoring process to guarantee compliance with the sustainability parameters and compliance with the efficiency and quality standards. A supplier who fails to meet the agreed targets may have his qualification suspended, limited or in the worst case revoked.

Finally, starting from 2024, Snam has started a process to define a **Supplier Code of Conduct**, in order to create a specific document for the adequate management of relationships with suppliers.

G-Governance

The Corporate Governance Structure and the Code of Ethics

In its organizational model, Snam provides a **sustainability governance system**. In fact, one of the Company's prerogatives is to introduce governance to support and encourage correct interaction between it and the context in which it operates.

The Board of Directors plays a role of central importance in achieving the pursuit of sustainable development, as prescribed by the Corporate Governance Code, defining strategies and monitoring sustainability objectives. It makes use of the contribution of all management and three Committees, the ESG and Energy Transition Scenarios Committee, the Control and Risk and Related-Party Transactions Committee and the Appointments and Remuneration Committee. The latter, in particular, proposes ESG performance objectives to which the variable remuneration component of management and executives is indexed.

The governance system is a traditional model and complies with current and sector regulations and follows the principles contained in the Code of Ethics, which is an integral part of the organizational model pursuant to Legislative Decree no. 231/2001. The Snam Board of Directors also has the aim of ensuring the diffusion and integration of a corporate culture aimed at combating climate change. It supervises the risks and opportunities associated with climate change and the activities for ensuring the management of these issues by management. The CEO is also responsible for the control and management of risks related to climate change and management plans periodic meetings to identify new initiatives related to climate change and implement and monitor the strategies identified previously.

Finally, there is an **ESG and Energy Transition Scenarios Committee** (ESGSTE), which receives periodic induction sessions to integrate ESG issues within the Board of Directors. Among the tasks carried out by the Committee are, for example, the examination of long-term energy transition scenarios and issues, technological innovation and circular economy issues, sustainable finance initiatives, integration policies into the business model environmental, social and governance issues, sustainability guidelines, objectives and processes and sustainability reporting with the related correct use of reporting standards. The Committee is also responsible for monitoring and ensuring Snam's participation in international initiatives on the environment, social and governance.

5.2.4 Conclusions

The analysis of the Snam NFS confirms the high importance of sustainable development issues within the Group's strategy. In fact, in the Italian context it was one of the first to report the non-financial impacts of its economic activities. In analyzing the Report, it emerged that all the topics foreseen by the ESG criteria are treated and each of them is given the same importance, creating a complete and exhaustive Sustainability Report.

One of the added values of this case is the exemplification of a complete re-adaptation of its business model, its corporate governance structure and the strategy to include issues related to sustainability, both from an environmental and social point of view. Furthermore, the Sustainability Scorecard, based on objectives to be achieved in the long term, highlights how the Snam Group companies are oriented towards the future and do not focus on a mere narration of objectives already achieved but on what needs to be done in future years.

Finally, from the overall analysis of the Sustainability Report, it emerges that the energy sector and the companies operating in it in the coming years will play a central role in pursuing the energy transition and security objectives, also envisaged by the 2030 Agenda. In this context, Snam places the country as a driver of sustainable development at the center of the country system.

5.3 The OVS Group

5.3.1 The Trend of the Fashion Sector

The fashion industry is known for its high economic relevance. In 2022, the 80 largest fashion multinationals had a total turnover of 566 billion euros.[28]

If we make specific reference solely to the Italian context, the country's fashion sector recorded revenues of 98 billion in 2022, with a growth of 18% compared to 2021, reaching the highest value it had held in 20 years.[29] The turnover growth trend slowed down in 2023, with a result of 111.7 billion euros (+3.2%). The slowdown was mainly due to the increase in prices, which caused a reduction in sales volumes.

Unfortunately, however, associated with the revenues of the sector, the problem relating to the impacts on our ecosystem that the world of fashion produces is often mentioned. In particular, it is responsible for approximately 20% of global drinking water pollution and 10% of carbon dioxide emissions.[30] Furthermore, it has been estimated that the textile industry is the main cause of plastic pollution in the seas: more than half a million tons of plastic microfibres end up in the sea during the washing process of plastic-based fabrics, such as polyester and nylon.[31]

The main cause of these negative externalities lies in the so-called *fast fashion* phenomenon, which consists of the production of low-quality clothing in a short time at a very low price. This mechanism allows collections to be launched in a very short time and educates the end customer on excessive consumption of products, which, in a short time, become waste and are replaced with as many low-quality items. Furthermore, in the past, this phenomenon has often been associated with the

[28] Report on fashion from the Mediobanca Research Area.

[29] https://www.ilsole24ore.com/art/la-moda-italiana-I-102-miliardi-ma-corsa-ricavi-rallentera-4percento-AEkHaqjC.

[30] https://www.europarl.europa.eu/topics/it/article/20201208STO93327/l-impatto-della-produzione-E-dei-rifiuti-tessili-sull-ambiente-infografica.

[31] https://unece.org/forests/events/sdg-9-fashion-industry-innovation-and-infrastructure.

violation of human rights due to the presence of child exploitation and poor working conditions.[32]

All these elements have led to the need for the sector to introduce a change of direction in order to stem the negative impacts produced and restore a good relationship with its customers, who are increasingly sensitive to issues related to sustainability and workers' rights. Recent European regulations have increased this awareness, pushing companies to review their business models. This new approach has also gradually extended to the management of the supply chains of the materials used, requiring the implementation of rigorous due diligence practices to guarantee the traceability of the products and respect for workers' rights along the entire supply chain.

Also fueling this new direction of the sector are the scarcity of the raw materials used and the onset of some events on the global scene, such as the COVID-19 pandemic and the Russian-Ukrainian conflict.

In contrast, therefore, to the phenomenon of fast fashion, "*green fashion*" emerged, dedicated to a conversion of the fashion world from a sustainable perspective, implemented also and not only thanks to the diffusion of strategies aimed at a better selection of the raw materials used (if possible, recycled and/or recyclable), the reduction of waste and the production of quality and durable clothing, so as to promote more conscious consumption. Furthermore, in recent years the phenomenon of "*resale*" has come into vogue, i.e. the sale intended to give new life to already used clothes.

The commitment of companies in the sector towards sustainability is the subject of study thanks to various indicators, such as the Global Organic Textile Standards (GOTS), which certifies the presence of a series of environmental and social criteria in the production of organic fibers, and the Business of Fashion (BoF) Sustainability Index, which focuses on the fight against climate change and the level of well-being of workers in the sector, and is the subject of specific certifications.[33]

---

[32] Think of the scandals involving Nike and Shein or other brands active in the sector. An article is given as an example: https://www.repubblica.it/moda-e-beauty/2022/10/24/news/shein_moda_low_cost_inchiesta_channel4_sfruttamento_lavoratori_fabbrica_cina-371040825/88.

[33] You can find some examples at the following link: https://limitlex.it/blogs/notizie/le-certificazioni-tessili-della-moda-nel-2022.

5.3.2 History, Mission and Vision of the OVS Group

The history of OVS begins in the second half of the twentieth century, more precisely in 1972 with the birth of "***Magazzini Oviesse***", a division of the Coin S.p.A. company, active in the management of department stores. Between the '70s and '80s, the department store model for clothing products was developed, expanding to the sale of sporting goods, leather goods, toys, perfumery and housewares. To expand its presence on the national territory, in 1999 the Coin Group acquired the non-food business branch La Standa, made up of more than 160 points of sale, which were subsequently converted into OVS stores. The 2000s represented the moment of true expansion for OVS, in 2005 the Coin Group transferred the business branch consisting of today's activities, which the brand manages, to the newly established company Oviesse S.r.l., entirely controlled by the Coin Group, and subsequently transformed into Oviesse S.p.A. In the meantime, the expansion policy also continued, in 2008 it acquired 100% of Tre.bi S.p.A., owner of the clothing stores of the Melablu chain, present in the North-West of Italy with over 60 points of sale, which following the operation became OVS stores. The strengthening of the Group continued with the acquisition in 2010 by Coin of 100% of the share capital of Upim S.r.l., one of the leaders in clothing, present in Italy with 135 stores with the UPIM brand and 15 with the BluKids brand, as well as a franchising network made up of over 200 stores. In 2011, following the change of control of the Coin Group, OVS began a business consolidation strategy by entering fully into the children's clothing segment through the acquisition of the IANA brand, operating in clothing and for children. The operation concluded in the first months of 2012 with the entry of the new brand into the OVS Kids and BluKids product lines. In the same year, the Coin Group continued its path of affirmation of leadership and acquired over one hundred points of sale of the Bernardi chain, an important clothing retailer. Part of these stores were converted into OVS stores and others were incorporated into the UPIM division. From a financial point of view, in 2014 the Coin Group started the process of spinning off the business branch consisting of the "*OVS-UPIM*" division, subsequently transferred to the company OVS S.p.A. At the culmination of this operation, in 2015 OVS S.p.A. was listed on the Milan Stock Exchange. In 2019 Tamburi Investment Parteners S.p.A. (TIP) took over the stake held by Gruppo Coin in OVS, becoming the reference shareholder, with a stake of 22.747%, made up of 4.912% of the shares owned before the operation and 17.835% of those acquired. The last stage of this historical journey is represented by the acquisition of Stefanel, a brand active in the clothing sector, which took place in 2021.[34]

The Group Today

The OVS S.p.A. Group operates in the clothing market and is the leader in Italy as a manufacturer and retailer of men's, women's and children's clothing with a market share of 9.6%.[35] The Group operates according to the typical vertically integrated retail model and also includes product development, designer and merchandiser activities. The presence on the national and international territory, however, is guaranteed by over 2050 stores through the various brands of the Group, employing over 8200 people around the world. Furthermore, in 2021 brand awareness in the Italian market was approximately 94%, achieved thanks to great customer trust.

The Group presents the following composition of **brands**, which allow it to operate (see Table 5.1).

In 2023 the Company continued its growth process, also thanks to the improvement of product quality and the reduction of negative impacts on the business.

> We pay ever greater attention to the various lifestyles that characterize the plurality of our customers, to each of which we combine a **dedicated type of product**, and often a **brand** capable of representing it.[36]

---

[34] https://www.ovscorporate.it/it/chi-siamo/storia.

[35] https://www.ovscorporate.it/it/azienda.

[36] Taken from the Letter to Stakeholders from CEO Stefano Beraldo contained in the 2023 Sustainability Report.

Table 5.1 The brands of OVS

Brand	Description
OVS	Leader in Italy in the clothing market of all kinds. It has over 1300 stores spread across Italy and abroad. Its offer is based on the characteristics of the Italian style, with an excellent quality-price ratio and strong attention to sustainability in the choice of raw materials and production processes. Furthermore, the brand is undergoing a diversification process by introducing brands to satisfy the different needs linked to different lifestyles
OVS KIDS	It boasts a high market share for children's clothing, branches out across the territories with over 450 stand-alone stores. It serves an audience of people in age groups from 0 to 15 years old, with a high quality and competitive offer based on the careful selection of raw materials and the comfort and practicality of the clothes
UPIM	It represents the most historic brand of the group, whose origins date back to 1926. It is a family store, which offers convenient shopping aimed at satisfying the needs of families. The commercial network is structured around over 300 shops, which aim to provide a local proximity service, capable of satisfying clothing and home needs
BLUKIDS	It is the UPIM clothing brand dedicated to children. It includes over 350 stand-alone stores around the world and is also present in UPIM stores. The brand follows children during their growth journey from 0 to 15 years old and is characterized by being convenient, accessible and aimed at the daily needs of mothers and children
CROFF	It is a brand that deals with home decoration, based on the dictates of contemporary and everyday design
LES COPAINS	Iconic Italian brand acquired by OVS in 2022, aimed at contemporary and elegant women
STEFANEL	Italian brand that stands out for its collections that offer a contemporary and urban clothing style. With over 100 stores in Italy and abroad, it has been part of the OVS group since 2021
PIOMBO	Brand dedicated to men and women, present in over 500 OVS stores. It offers collections created by designer Massimo Piombo. In 2023, it was launched on the international market, with stores in New York, Madrid and Paris

Mission and Vision of the OVS Group

One of the values underlying the Group's philosophy is **transparency** and it lies in the belief that sustainability requires authentic commitment, made up of mistakes and ambitious objectives.

The company's **mission** is the following: "*making beauty accessible to all*". It concerns the values that guide the behavior of all the people who participate in company processes and includes respect for the environment and the communities in which they operate. Working at OVS must be a source of growth, value and well-being for everyone.

These are the **principles** underlying the Group's philosophy:

- **Imagination** (the Company encourages the sharing of ideas by everyone);
- **Innovation** (the Company intends to lead the market and, therefore, encourages change);
- **Teamwork** (based on the sum of the value of the individuals);
- **Value creation** (for customers, stakeholders and shareholders);
- **Openness** (the Company wants to be a meeting point for the exchange of ideas and actions, respecting everyone's needs);
- **Italianity** (enhancing the virtuous aspects of our country);
- **Respect** (recognizing the value of the individual and listening to everybody).

> One of the founding values of OVS has always been transparency, which distinguishes our way of thinking, acting and telling.[37]

5.3.3 The 2023 Sustainability Report

The first Sustainability Report was published by OVS in 2016 to demonstrate what the Company has done to ensure sustainable development and reduce waste and other environmental impacts.

In 2023, in line with the directives at the national and European level, this report highlighted the commitment to pursuing sustainable development objectives.

As regards the structure, the OVS sustainability report can be divided into **six different sections**, each of which focuses on the development of different themes. In particular, the initial part, "***Vision***", contains

[37] Taken from the 2023 Sustainability Report.

the letter to the stakeholders, in which the CEO explains the main results and sustainability commitments of the Group, the exposure of the brands under the control of OVS, the main management results, the path for the implementation of sustainability strategies and the presentation of actions to contain greenhouse gas emissions. The second block presents the "***Design for circularity***" strategy, which focuses on commitments to create a concept of fashion that reuses waste and reduces the use of raw materials. The third part, "***Being fair and transparent***", focuses on the need to improve the impact of the fashion sector on living conditions and here the indicators regarding the diversity gap and policies for reducing the effects on local communities are given. The fourth section of the Sustainability Report, "***Design a better work***", shows relationships with employees both in a descriptive manner and with the presentation of indicators, such as the turnover rate; remuneration policies are also presented. The fifth paragraph, "***Making fashion a better choice***", illustrates the actions implemented to make the Group a leader in the field of sustainable fashion, and the certificates and results obtained are presented. The last chapter, "***Details***", highlights the sustainability results, with particular attention to the materiality analysis, the profile of the OVS Group, the composition of the Board of Directors, the tables regarding the various sustainability indicators and, finally, the external certification.

The report is finally subjected to a conformity assessment by an auditing firm.

The Company Strategy: Towards Greater Sustainability

OVS considers sustainable commitment as a characterizing factor of its corporate activities, implementing a business model in which each function considers the environmental and social impacts of its work. It is no coincidence that in 2023 the Company came first in the **Fashion Transparency Index** drawn up by Fashion Revolution for the third consecutive time.

Starting from 2016, there has been a strengthening of sustainable strategies based on the principles of The Natural Step framework.[38] These dictates offer a clear definition of sustainability and are universal, necessary and sufficient to describe a sustainable future.

In 2022, **OVS Innovazione e Sostenibilità** Srl was established, dedicated to digital research and innovation and sustainable development projects.

In 2023, the Company continued its **decarbonization plan** to achieve a 46.2% emissions reduction by 2030. Furthermore, it favored investment in new renewable energy sources over the purchase of certified renewable energy produced by third parties. To date, there are more than 50 photovoltaic systems, with the aim of covering 40% of electricity needs.

2023 is also the year of work for the Group on a structured definition of a **strategic sustainability plan** with the time horizon 2024-2026, which is focused on spreading the concept of circularity at a production and operational level. The four key pillars of OVS sustainability are as follows:

1. **Design for Circularity**;
2. **Being Fair and Transparent**;
3. **Design a Better Work**;
4. **Making Fashion a Better Choice**.

For each pillar, macro-objectives are then defined with targets to be achieved.

The **Sustainability Plan** is integrated into the company business plan, also in terms of budget definition.

The commitment to implementing strategies attentive to social and environmental impacts is confirmed in the use of two innovative tools attentive to the integration of an analysis model:

[38] Non-governmental organization founded in Sweden in 1989, whose aim is to spread the sustainable development framework.

1. **B Impact Assessment** makes it possible to identify the areas for improvement and future targets of the sustainability plan consistent with those proposed by organizations seeking to redefine new business models, aligning their strategy with that of Benefit Corporations;
2. **SDG Action Manager** represents the implementation of a management system for the Sustainable Development Goals by identifying those most relevant to one's business model. They are SDG 5 (Gender Equality), 6 (Clean Water and Sanitation), 8 (Decent Work and Economic Growth), 11 (Sustainable Cities and Communities), 12 (Responsible Consumption and Production).

5.3.4 Design for Circularity

Of the many objectives of the OVS production process, one is to minimize the consumption of natural resources and reduce the impact on the environment and people as much as possible. It materializes with the more sustainable creation of 90% of the collections, with the choice of virtuous materials and processes and maintaining a circular perspective. The pursuit of the ambitious objective of ecosystem conservation is implemented through a **circular business model**, focused on the correct choice of fibers, increasing the percentage of sustainable materials. Associated with this concept is the definition of the "***Better Products Criteria***", i.e. the requirements that the clothing must meet (production using sustainable fibers, low-impact production process, social or environmental certification, deriving from a special project with social impact or upcycling).

To date, over 72% of the materials used in production processes come from renewable sources.

Most of the interventions in the selection of raw materials concern the most used fibers, such as cotton, polyester and materials of cellulosic origin. This approach is also extended to wool, using only the type that carries certification that guarantees animal welfare, and to linen, purchasing only what comes from European nations. The Group has decided to remain consistent with its strategy of using recycled raw materials, which are more expensive than traditional ones, increasing the selling price of the clothing to guarantee a sustainable product.

Cotton represents the most used fiber in the Group's collections with a weight of around 70%, in contrast with the international trend which favors the use of synthetic fibers derived from petroleum and which pollute more. As of 2021, OVS has used 100% of its cotton from sustainable sources, organic, recycled or grown according to the Better Cotton Standard.

In this direction, it has launched a production line of organic and Italian fiber, called **OVS Cotone Italiano**, made in collaboration with the Cotone Organico agricultural company. This is a project aimed at reconstructing the production of Sicilian cotton that allows for control of the entire raw material supply chain, thereby managing impacts on both a social and environmental level, as well as producing a high quality and entirely Made in Italy line. One of the advantages linked to the project is the reduction of emissions for the transport of cotton, thanks to the reduction in the distance taken by the cotton to get from the field to the shop. On average, sourcing cotton from other locations requires around 15,000 kilometers of transport, while with Italian production the distance is reduced to 1700. Furthermore, direct access to production allows the Company to trace the effects that the production process generates on the ecosystem during every phase of processing.

Polyester is the second most used material in clothing collections. In 2019, OVS started making some clothing only with recycled polyester, with the aim of using 100% recycled synthetic material by 2030. In 2023, the percentage of recycled polyester present in the collections is equal to 23%.

The choice of environmentally friendly materials cannot exclude the protection of forests. In fact, cellulose fibers are used in fashion to make various fabrics, which for OVS represents 4% of the fibers used. For this reason, the Group has decided to favor the purchase of materials coming from forests managed according to the FSC (Forest Stewardship Council) or PEFC (Programme for the Endorsement of Forest Certification) standard and from suppliers who adopt controlled processes capable of guaranteeing the origin of the material and the reduced impacts along the entire production process.

5.3.5 Being Fair and Transparent

This section of the report focuses on the analysis of relationships with suppliers and the protection of workers along the entire value chain. OVS has always been attentive to the protection of people and the selection of suppliers. For this reason, it has drawn up a **Code of Conduct** which all members of the supply chain must sign and imposes the assumption of a shared responsibility, aimed at improving conditions of workers and the local communities in which they operate. The Code contains binding guidelines on social and environmental performance. This allows for the creation of long-lasting and stable supply relationships that last for an average of 9 years, initiating collaborations for the definition of supply programs capable of reducing the negative impacts on workers and the entire ecosystem. Suppliers are periodically subjected to evaluation to verify compliance with the Code of Conduct, giving equal weight to sustainability and traditional criteria (such as price, cost and service). In 2022, 325 supplier audits were conducted. This monitoring takes place through the use of the Higg platform, which allows for having an overall picture of actions in the entire fashion sector. To accelerate commitments in the selection of sustainable suppliers, OVS has issued the **Sustainability-Linked Bond**, which provides reward systems for actors in the supply chain who are attentive to sustainability issues.

In 2023, 92% of the production volume came from clothing suppliers participating in the Higg platform. The platform is made up of 104 two-evaluation modules, the environmental one (FEM) and the social one (FSLM).

Despite being aware of the difficulties in implementing actions aimed at guaranteeing salaries at least equal to the living wage, OVS management is confident in thinking that by 2040 all workers can be guaranteed a salary at least equal to the average cost of living. OVS strongly believes that the transition towards sustainable fashion requires the involvement and contribution at an international level of all the players active in the sector. For this reason, it was the first Italian clothing company to have joined the **Sustainable Apparel Coalition** (SAC). It represents a global multi-stakeholder alliance designed to spread sustainable and transparent actions in the world of fashion. Furthermore, the Group is part of the **Circular Fashion Partnership**, a project led by the Global Fashion Agenda to develop the circular economy in Bangladesh, as well as having joined the Accord on Fire and Building Safety program, to improve working conditions in the same country.

5.3.6 Design a Better Work

The third piece of OVS's sustainable strategies focuses on the Group's people (over 8000).

The chapter "*Design a better work*" of the Sustainability Report analyzes the work policies implemented during 2023, based on the principles of **equality and inclusion**. The attention paid to the development of its company population is evident from the possibility of refining and increasing the skills of each person, thanks to the multiple job positions. The growth potential within the company is cultivated right from the personnel selection phase, through various **collaborations with universities** to offer young people a complete vision of the working world and develop specific professional growth paths. In this context, there is space for the internship program, which aims to offer a 6-month training experience, and the new concept of introducing new hires into the corporate world, structured as follows:

- A program of meetings with the staff already present in the company;
- Presentation of training courses for improving skills;
- Presentation and knowledge of the products, encouraging visits to the showrooms.

During the six-month period, all people take part in a program to share personal characteristics.

The **training course** offered within the company is added to the selection of the new workforce, which OVS focuses on and considers it to be a critical success factor. Training focuses on the entire production process, encouraging the development of so-called *transversal skills*, team working ability and the propensity to change. The training activities are structured based on classroom training, group work and social learning.

During 2023, 217,341 hours of training were provided.

The **remuneration policy**, in line with the choices to support workers' professional growth, is based on meritocracy and performance, regardless of gender; in fact, the gender pay gap is below the national average. This salary difference is the result of a previous situation that OVS had inherited in 1972. Despite this, the internal strategies for improving the lives of company collaborators have allowed for the gradual reduction of salary differences. In fact, male and female sales personnel with less than 5 years of seniority have a zero difference in pay. Furthermore, compensation plans have been defined which consider various variables such as individual results and comparison with other realities. For managers and executives, variable remuneration is provided based on individual and Group results, where sustainability objectives have a weight of 20%.

Finally, in the field of welfare policies, OVS offers the possibility to access a **supplementary pension fund**, an **assistance program** guaranteed to all workers and various agreements with gyms, fitness centers and shopping opportunities at advantageous prices. In 2023, the "***Share your thoughts***" bar and a space equipped for physical activity were inaugurated. Yoga, pilates and breathing techniques courses have started in the company gym to spread a culture of psychophysical well-being.

5.3.7 Making Fashion a Better Choice

The final part of the sustainability strategy focuses on relationships with customers and in particular on communication and knowledge of products and their impacts. In line with these assumptions, OVS is committed to collecting as much information as possible on a daily basis, to have greater knowledge of the effects generated by its actions and to identify areas of change and improvement.

In 2023, for the third consecutive year the OVS Group received first place in the **Fashion Transparency Index**, an initiative that was developed by Fashion Revolution, a global movement that presses the fashion industry to implement a system that respects human rights and the environment throughout all production phases. In particular, 250 of the main fashion brands and retailers on a global scale are analyzed on the basis of turnover and notoriety and the degree of transparency in the disclosure of actions undertaken along the production chain is assessed. In the ranking, OVS achieved a much higher result (83%) compared to the other brands in the sector. This figure was achieved thanks to the efforts made in improving the areas of traceability, governance and transparency. Transparent communication aims to offer the customer a customer experience that is aware of all aspects regarding the purchased product, from the supplier of the raw material to suggestions for extending its life or giving it a new existence.

Since 2019, the **Eco Valore** project has made it possible to know for each item sold by the Group information regarding the composition, the supplier who produced it and the impact relating to three key indicators (water consumption, CO2 emissions and index of circularity). Since 2022, this information has also provided on the digital receipt for those who purchase online. Furthermore, customer perception of OVS's commitment to sustainability is also monitored thanks to a series of customer surveys and focus groups. For example, in May 2023, 1400 interviews were carried out with customers exiting selected OVS stores, with a specific focus on mothers' purchasing choices.

In the same year, the collaboration with **Humana People to People Italia**, which had begun in 2013, was resumed to encourage the recovery of used clothes. In particular, thanks to this partnership people can deliver used clothes to stores, entrusting them to the international organization. The collaboration aims to create a new way of understanding clothes, that is, clothing that can be reused and that do not end their life when they are no longer used by the original buyer. Compared to 2022, approximately 96 tons of clothes were collected (compared to 85 the previous year), of which 87% were destined for reuse, 10% for recycling and 3% for disposal.

In addition to all these awareness-raising actions geared towards the correct use of clothing, OVS selects two events annually to launch clothing in support of social issues:

- **Earth Day** represents an opportunity to create small collections with which to raise awareness on the topic of climate change;

- since 2016, OVS has joined the **Christmas Jumper Day**, an event launched by Save the Children with which Christmas jumpers are launched to raise funds for the health and education of minors. In 2023, the Christmas Jumper was sold in 580 stores and online, raising €202,000 for Save the Children.

The Materiality Analysis

The materiality analysis represents the starting point for the drafting of the OVS Sustainability Report, as it identifies the topics to be reported.

It begins with the identification of the different classes of **stakeholders**[39] relevant to the Group. OVS shows in the Sustainability Report a table that lists the main stakeholders, the stakeholder's interest in OVS and vice versa and the methods of involvement and frequency.

Based on the 2021 GRI Standards, an analysis is carried out to identify the material topics that present the most significant impacts (positive and/or negative and current and/or potential) generated (or could be generated) by OVS on the economy, on the environment and people.

In detail, the phases of the materiality analysis are the following:

1. **Analysis of the value chain and identification of impacts**, distinguishing between activities carried out directly (Direct), carried out upstream (Upstream) or downstream (Downstream);
2. **Internal assessment of impacts**, based on severity, persistence, possibility of occurrence and restoration of any general effects and presence along the value chain;
3. **Discussion with stakeholders** (which involved over 3000 stakeholders) via survey. From this activity, a substantial alignment emerged between the issues identified by the management with those reported by the stakeholders, in particular regarding climate change, protection of health and safety at work, respect for human rights,

[39] Customers, collaborators at headquarters and in stores, local communities both in the countries of production and in the locations of the stores, suppliers, competitors, institutions, pressure groups, opinion leaders, franchisees, investors, industry coalitions and new generations.

protection of employees, use of water resources and reduction of emissions;
4. **Evaluation of the material topics**, which will be included in the Sustainability Report.

OVS offers a graphic representation of the material issues, highlighting the impacts and their description, the main stakeholders they affect and the sustainable development objectives to which they contribute.

For the 2023 financial year, the results that emerged from the analysis carried out in the 2022 financial year are confirmed. The material issues that emerged from the analysis concern the well-being of employees, the circular economy and eco-design, the protection of biodiversity and animal welfare, worker training, relationships with communities and the enhancement of diversity and inclusion.

A more complete analysis of impacts, risks and opportunities for the Group is expected to be conducted for the year 2024. This need arises from the launch of the Corporate Sustainability Reporting Directive (CSRD) and the adoption of the European Sustainability Reporting Standards (ESRS). Furthermore, the analysis will be based on the principle of **double relevance**, taking into consideration the sustainability issues that influence the strategy and performance of OVS and the activities of OVS that impact society and the environment.

The Value Creation Process

Within the Sustainability Report, OVS reports the consolidated economic value generated (equal to 1,628,712 thousand euros, an increase of 0.47% compared to 2022). The report expresses the ability of a company to generate wealth for the benefit of its stakeholders. Of this amount, 83% is redistributed to the various stakeholders, while the remaining part is retained within the Group.

E-Environment

Environment

The overall energy consumption of the OVS Group is equal to 651,733 GJ, of which 86% comes from renewable sources (especially certified electricity). At the moment renewable energy is purchased only in Italy, but the extension abroad is also being evaluated. As regards electricity consumption, most shops are equipped with automatic systems for monitoring consumption related to lighting and air conditioning systems. In 2023, OVS produced 5667 GJ of electricity from photovoltaic panels, up from the 4475 produced in 2022.

Furthermore, within the Sustainability Report, the values related to Scope 1, 2 and 3 emissions are promptly reported. OVS intends to reduce emissions by increasing the use of low-emission materials, supporting the supply chain in decarbonization and eliminating the use of coal boilers.

In terms of water consumption, it is rather low, since OVS does not directly manage the production activity. In 2023, the OVS Group's water consumption was 539,253 mc, down 10% compared to 2022. Despite this, programs have been promoted to raise awareness among staff and to reduce the impacts associated with the products, through research into materials and virtuous production processes with less use of natural resources. A plan has been established to use water-efficient processes for 100% of denim by 2025. In 2023, more than 52% of the denim assortment was made with water-efficient systems that use technologies such as reverse osmosis systems for wastewater recycling, jet dyeing with reduced liquor ratio and/or ozone bleaching.

Finally, OVS also pays attention to the issue of containing waste produced in the production cycle. To do this, the following actions were undertaken:

- Since 2013, the collection of used clothes in the shop;
- Optimization of the life cycle of packaging with recycled plastic poly bags and more efficient management of hangers;

- The reuse of secondary packaging used in the logistics of production processes;
- The adoption of "green purchasing" policies, with the prevalent use of recycled or FSC-certified paper.

As regards the methods of waste disposal generated by the Group, 93% of the waste produced was sent for recycling, and approximately 3% was destined for incineration with energy recovery. Approximately 4% is destined for thermal disposal and the remaining 0.03% ends up in landfill.

S-Social

Human Resources

The OVS Group includes over 8000 people worldwide, of which 78% are women. In fact, the incidence of the female component is confirmed to be prevalent: in Italy, it is equal to 67% at the headquarters and over 80% in stores, while in foreign sales points it is 90%. Again, in Italy, over 52% of Store Managers are female.

The Group's turnover rate for permanent staff is 13.6% (compared to 8% the previous year). The increase can be explained by the phenomenon of "large resignations" which characterizes recent years and will be countered with a process of improvement of welfare and induction policies.

Another fundamental element regarding personnel management concerns training, understood by OVS as a strategic resource for professional and personal growth. The proposed activities include classroom lessons, on-the-job training, project work and social learning, and concern skills that are transversal to the company (e.g., health and safety, code of ethics, soft skills and language courses) and specific to the role held. In 2023, over 400,000 euros were invested in training and 26.4 hours of training were provided per employee (compared to 24.9 in 2022).

G-Governance

The Corporate Governance Structure and the Code of Ethics

From a corporate governance point of view, the **Control, Risk and Sustainability Committee** was established in 2014, with the aim of supervising sustainability issues connected with company activities and evaluating the NFS. Furthermore, it supervises the materiality analysis process and its results. In terms of internal organization, sustainability issues are managed by the **Corporate Sustainability Department**, which reports to the CEO, the Committee and the Board of Directors.

Furthermore, OVS has adopted a **Code of Ethics** which contains the ethical principles and behavioral guidelines for all Group companies. It reports the rights, duties and responsibilities of all the subjects who in various capacities operate within the Group or collaborate with it. Furthermore, within it, the value of people is promoted thanks to the offer of equal job opportunities without distinctions based on nationality, ethnicity, religion or personal beliefs, sex, age, sexual orientation, physical or mental disability. The Group, in fact, recognizes the value of diversity within its workforce.

5.3.8 Conclusions

OVS's sustainability strategy represents one of the excellences of the fashion sector. This is demonstrated by the various awards obtained by the Group for the actions implemented to achieve sustainable development. The Sustainability Report presents a transversal structure that touches on all the points envisaged by the GRI standard, attributing the same importance to each of them. Particular centrality in the reporting of sustainable activities is placed on the information and awareness-raising role that a fashion brand can play in developing a culture of protection of our planet. Furthermore, the policy of reducing the gender gap places OVS among the best Italian companies in terms of gender equality. Finally, the above analysis highlights how the living conditions of the populations of the so-called "*Third World*" also depend on the production choices of fashion, a concept that is very clear to OVS on which it bases many of its production choices. All this allows us to maintain that the Group implements sustainable strategies and reports them in a manner consistent with the principles of sustainable development, as defined by the UN.

Index

V. Minutiello, *The Fusion of Accounting and Accountability*,
https://doi.org/10.1007/978-3-031-81385-6

The manufacturer's authorised representative in the EU is Springer Nature Customer Service Centre GmbH, Europaplatz 3, 69115 Heidelberg, Germany. If you have any concerns regarding our products, please contact ProductSafety@springernature.com

Printed and bound by CPI Group (UK) Ltd, Croydon, CR0 4YY
01/10/2026
02225912-0002